DIBS ON CLUBS!

An **In the Bleachers** Golf Collection

by STEVE MOORE

**Andrews McMeel
Publishing**

Kansas City

For information, write Andrews McMeel Publishing, an Andrews McMeel Universal company, 4520 Main Street, Kansas City, Missouri 64111.

04 05 06 07 08 BID 10 9 8 7 6 5 4 3 2 1

ISBN 0-7407-4709-6

Library of Congress Control Number: 2004106231

To John Hayes

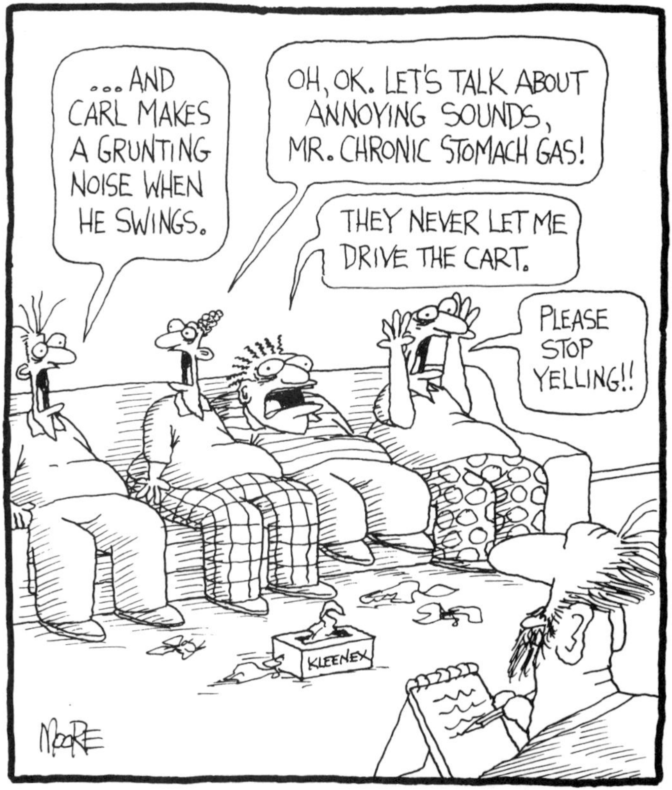
...AND CARL MAKES A GRUNTING NOISE WHEN HE SWINGS.
OH, OK. LET'S TALK ABOUT ANNOYING SOUNDS, MR. CHRONIC STOMACH GAS!
THEY NEVER LET ME DRIVE THE CART.
PLEASE STOP YELLING!!
KLEENEX
MOORE

Golf foursome in counseling

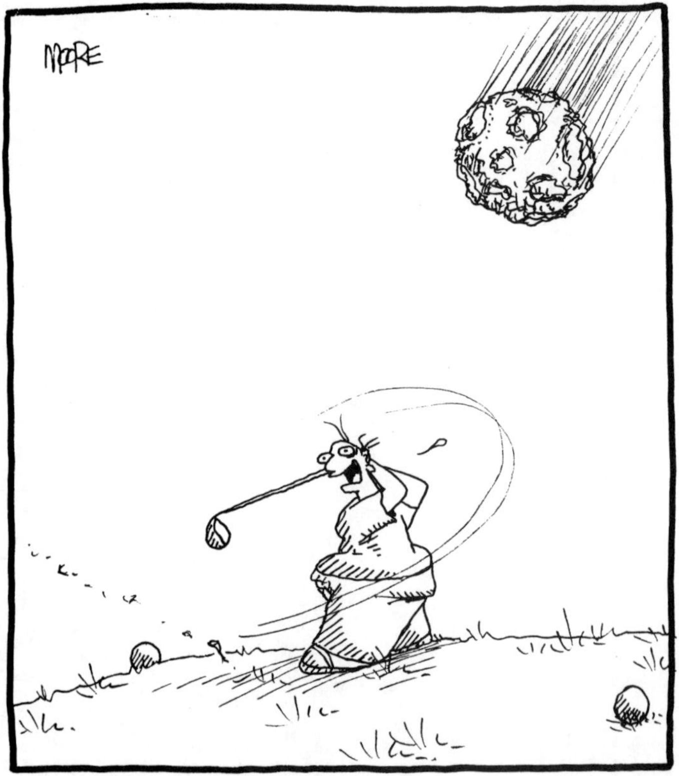
MOORE

"That's it! I did it! I finally figured out how to hit the perfect golf shot every single time!!"

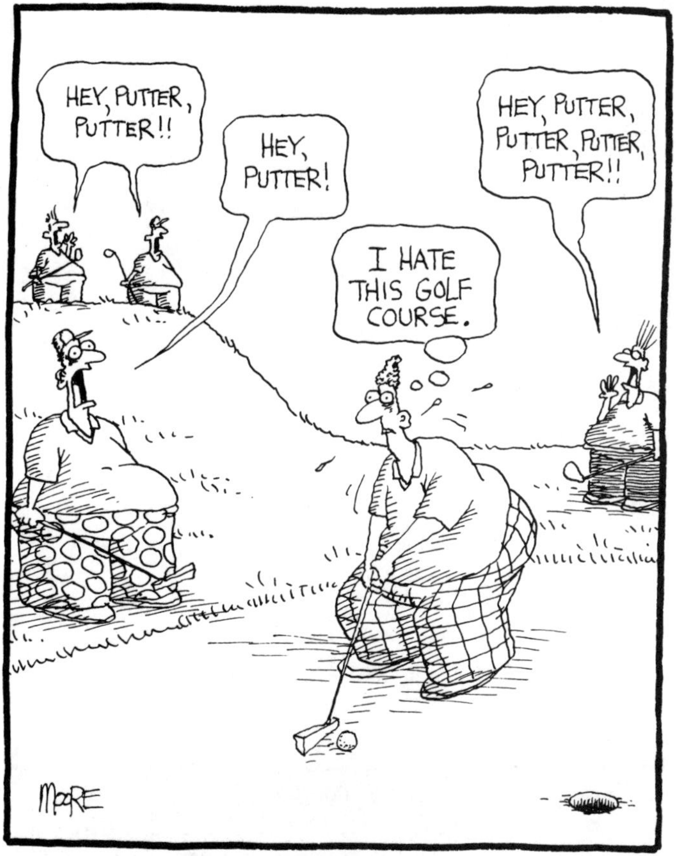
HEY, PUTTER, PUTTER!!
HEY, PUTTER!
HEY, PUTTER, PUTTER, PUTTER, PUTTER!!
I HATE THIS GOLF COURSE.
MOORE

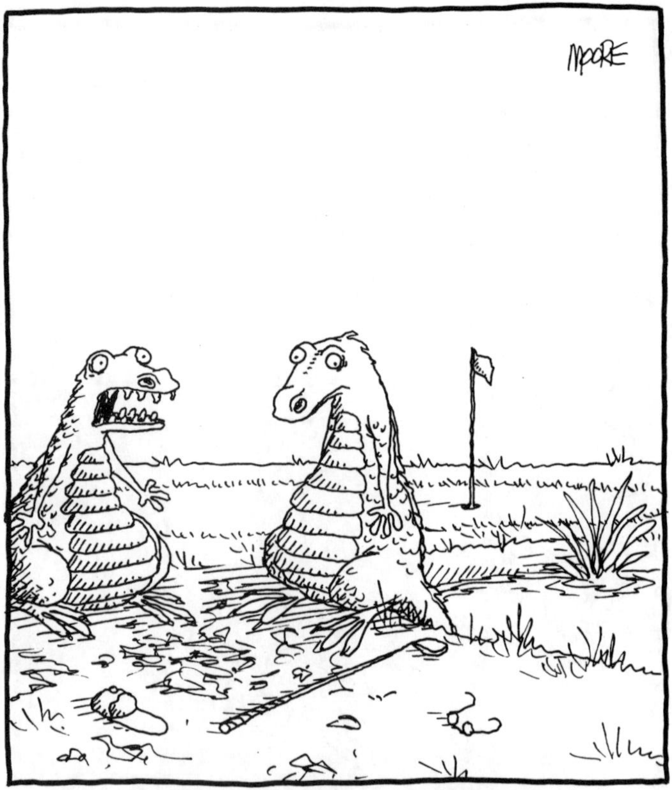
MOORE

"Stop feeling guilty, Arnold. It's our role in nature to weed out the weak, the sick, and the 20-handicapper."

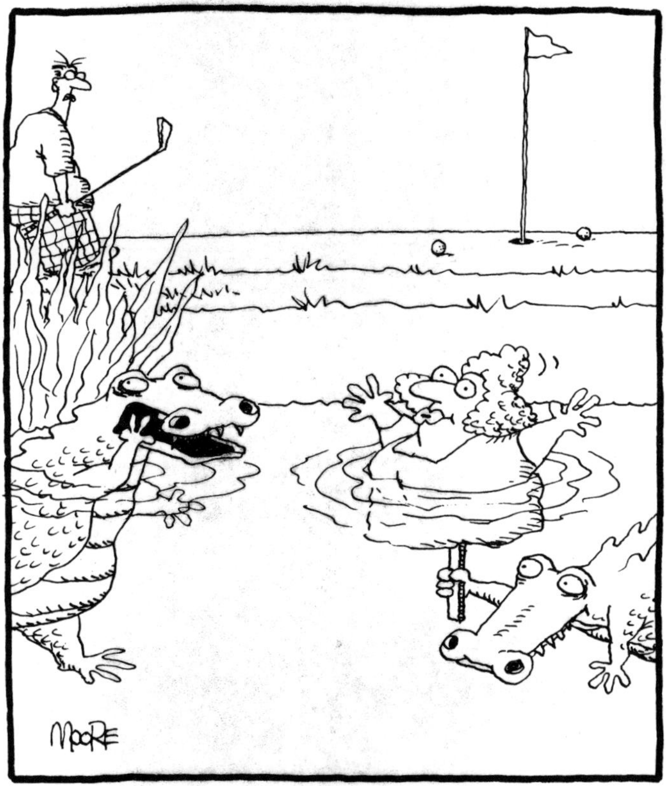
MOORE

**"Help me, Meester Golfer!
Help me, help me, help me!!"**

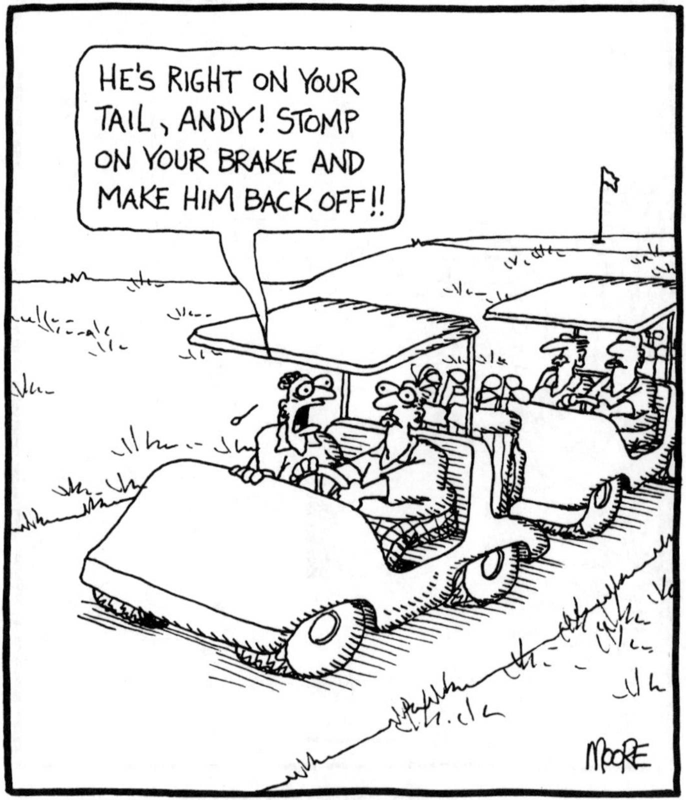
HE'S RIGHT ON YOUR TAIL, ANDY! STOMP ON YOUR BRAKE AND MAKE HIM BACK OFF!!
MOORE

Cart path rage

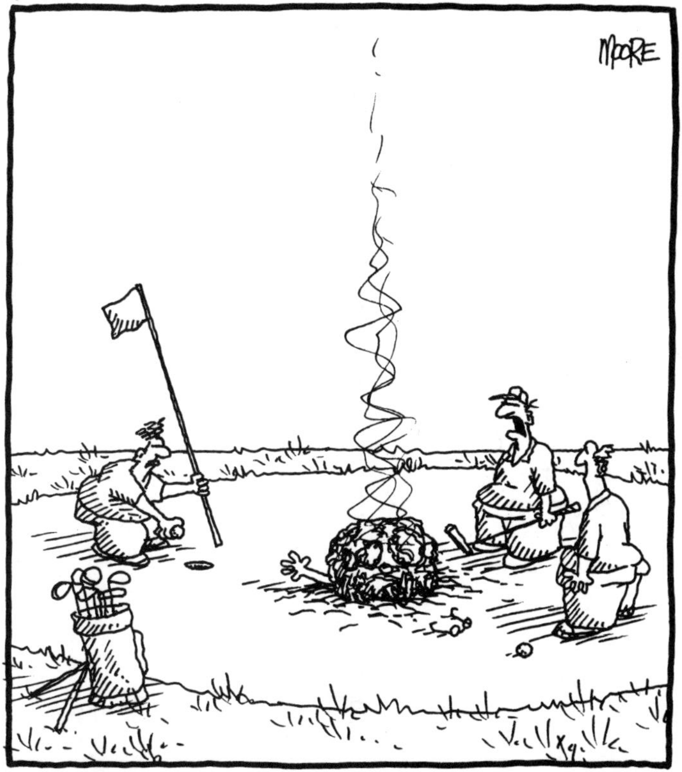
MOORE

"What are the chances? I mean, Dewey makes a hole-in-one, gets struck by lightning, *and* is crushed by a meteor all on the same hole?"

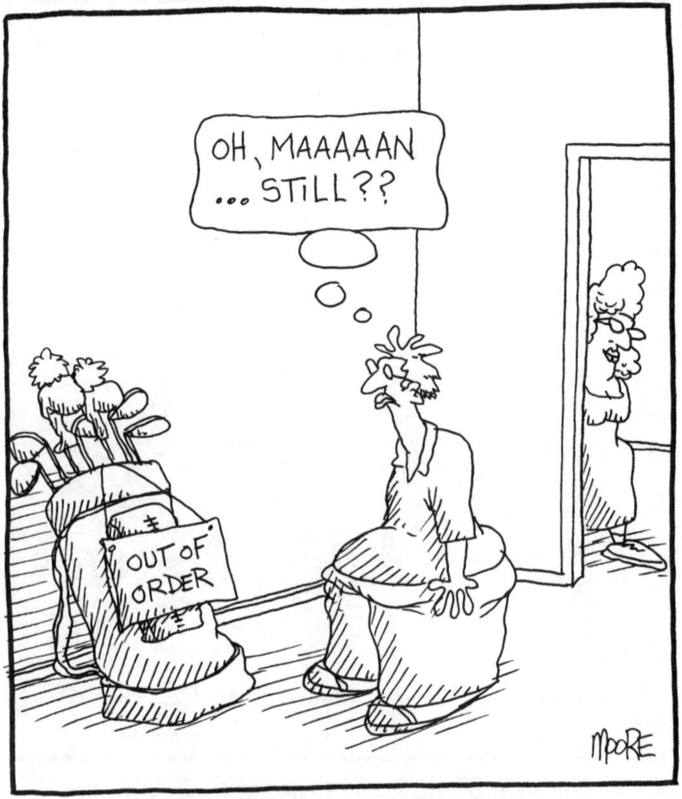
OH, MAAAAAN
... STILL??
OUT OF
ORDER
MOORE

Andrew is fooled for a second weekend in a row.

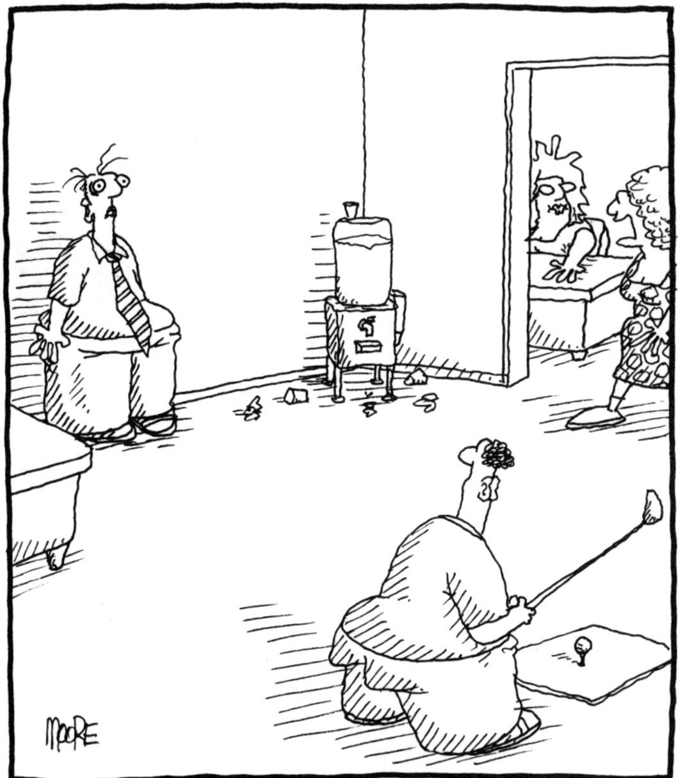
MOORE

"Jocelyn, you'd better get out here quick! The boss is about to tee off on Sullivan again!"

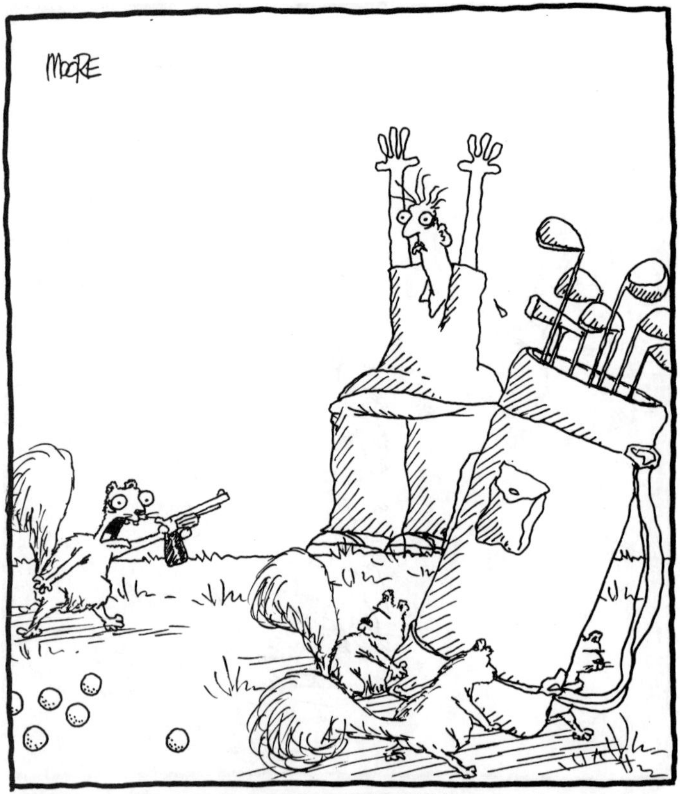
MOORE

"What, hey, whatta ya doin'? We can't just let him go. He knows too much."

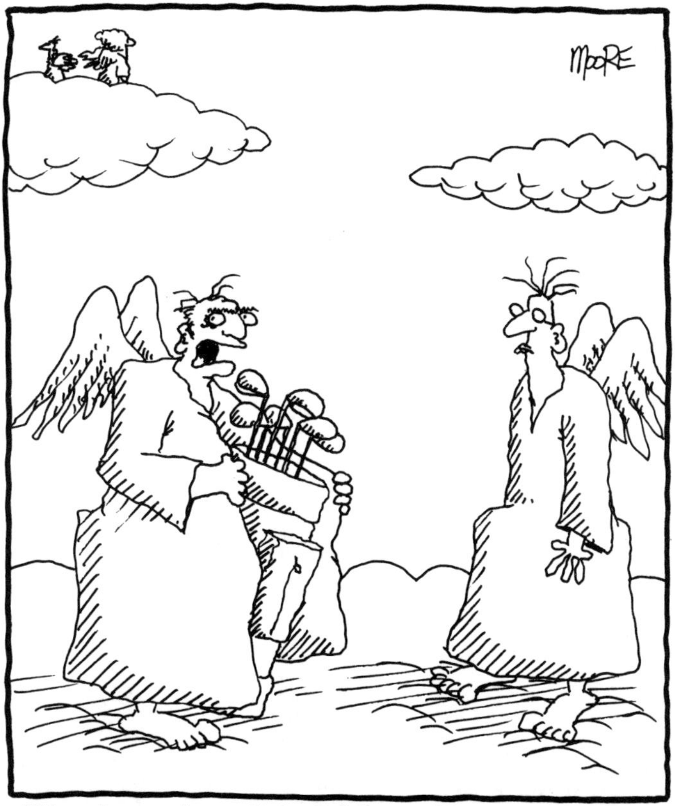
MOORE

"You know how they told us, 'You can't take it with you'? . . . Well, look what I smuggled in."

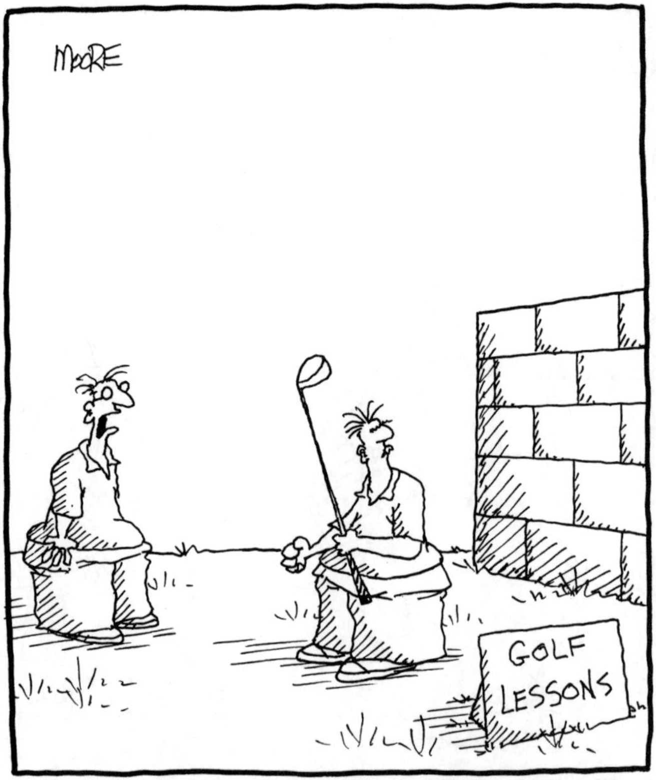
MOORE
GOLF
LESSONS
"Set the ball on the ground, hit the ball with the club, bang your head against the concrete wall. . . . Any questions?"

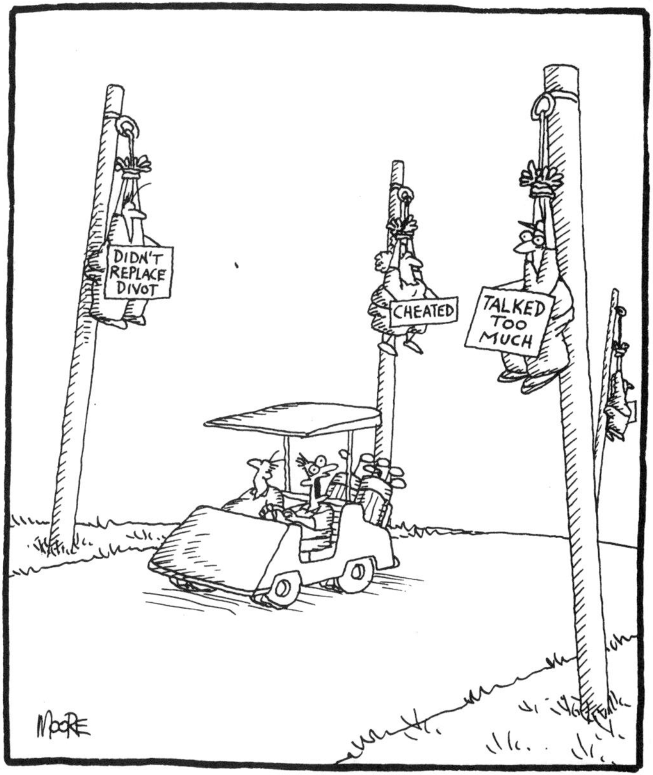
DIDN'T
REPLACE
DIVOT
CHEATED
TALKED
TOO
MUCH
MOORE

"This is a tough course."

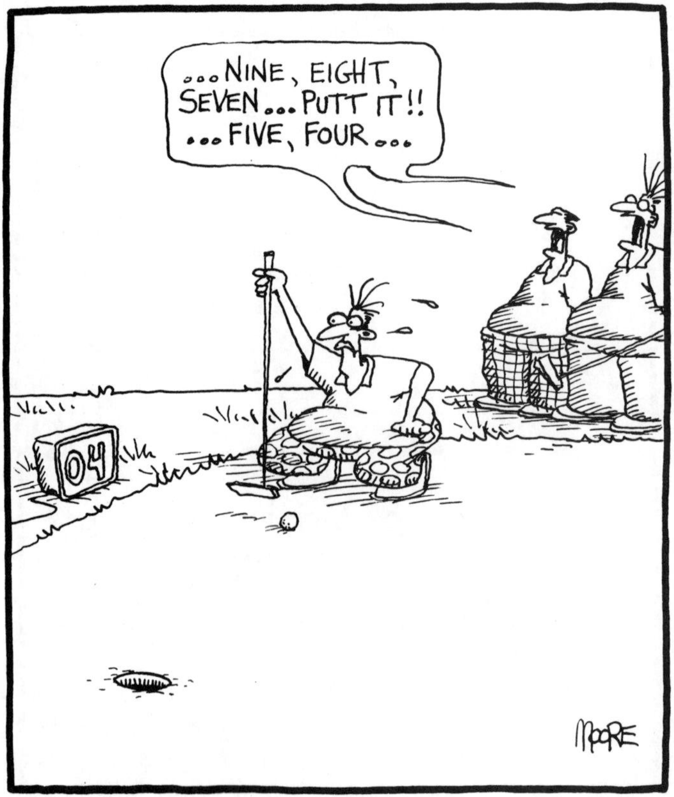
...NINE, EIGHT, SEVEN...PUTT IT!! ...FIVE, FOUR...
04
MOORE

The 20-second putt clock

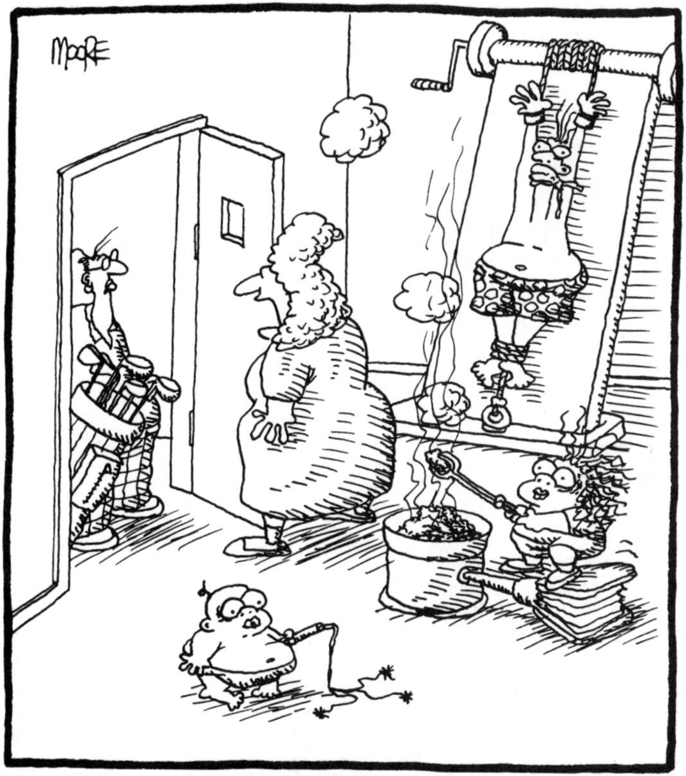
MOORE

"I'm sorry, but our kids can be very persuasive. Andy has agreed that from now on, Sunday is family day."

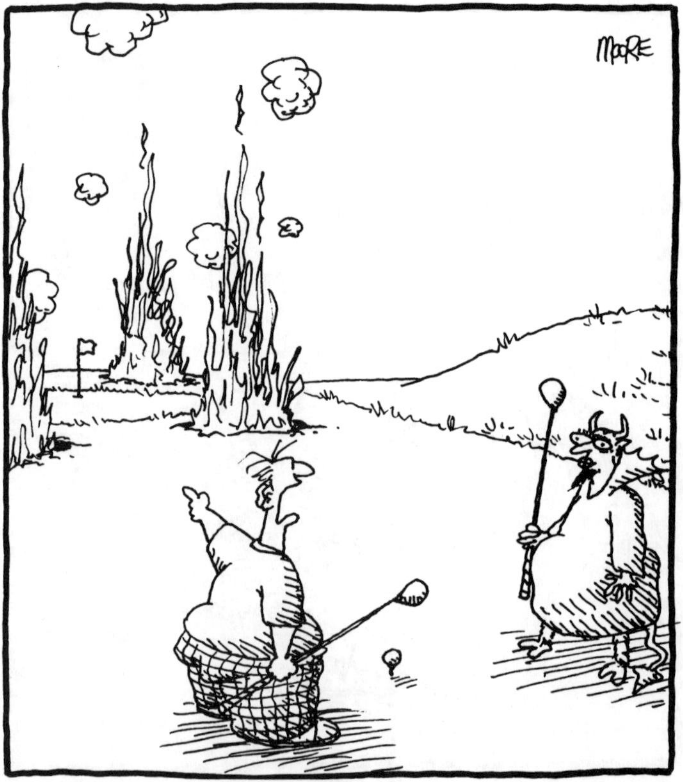
MOORE

"Hey, you're cheating! Those fire hazards weren't there two minutes ago when *you* teed off!!"

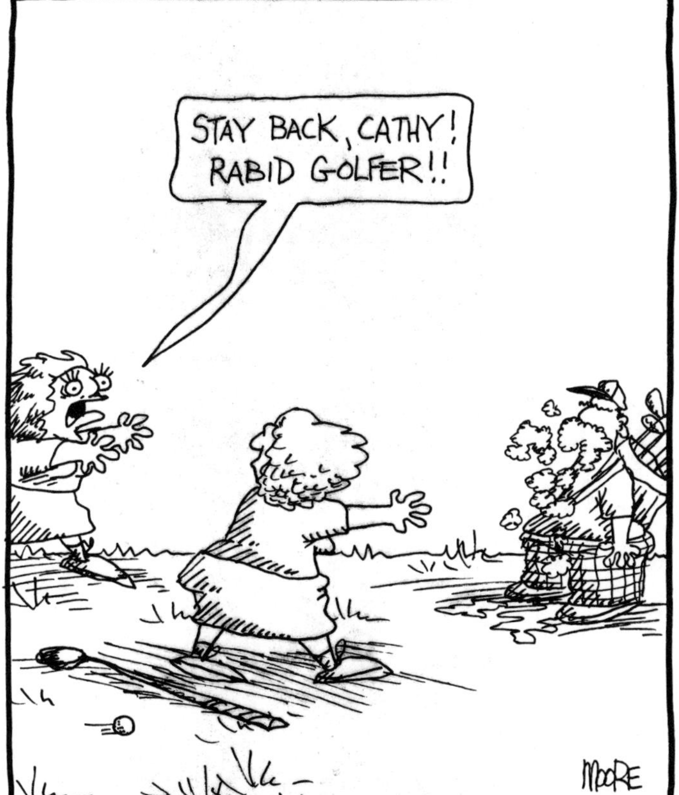
STAY BACK, CATHY! RABID GOLFER!!
MOORE

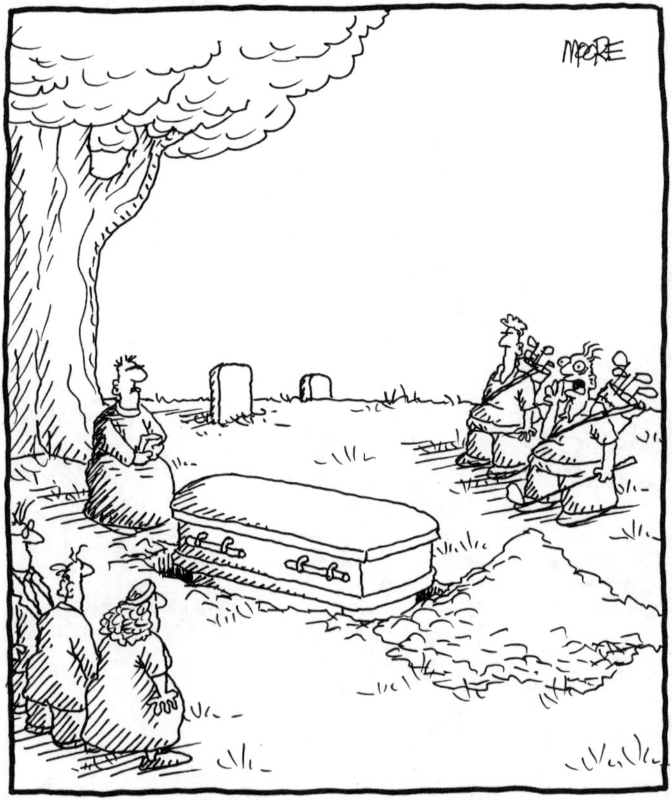
MOORE

"Mind if we play through?"

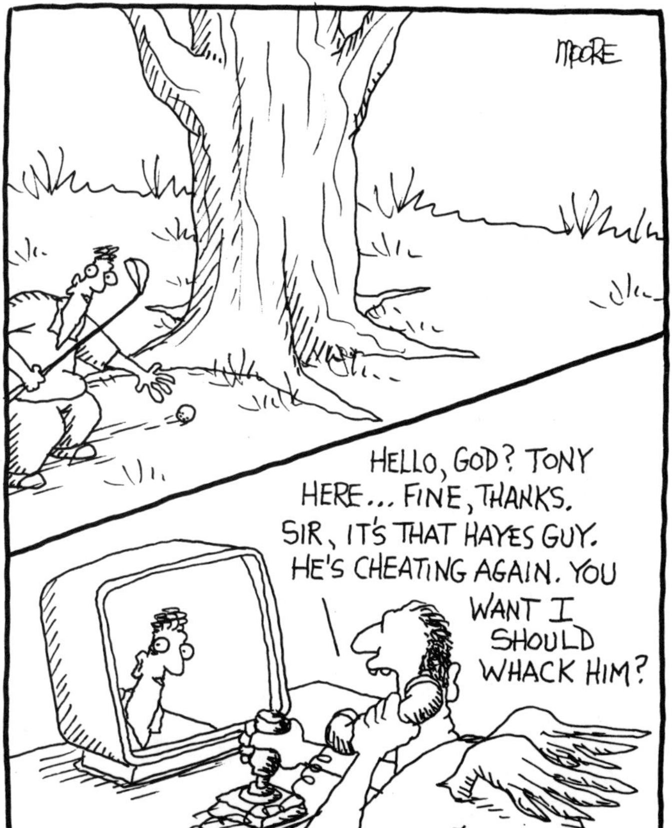
MOORE
HELLO, GOD? TONY HERE... FINE, THANKS. SIR, IT'S THAT HAYES GUY. HE'S CHEATING AGAIN. YOU WANT I SHOULD WHACK HIM?

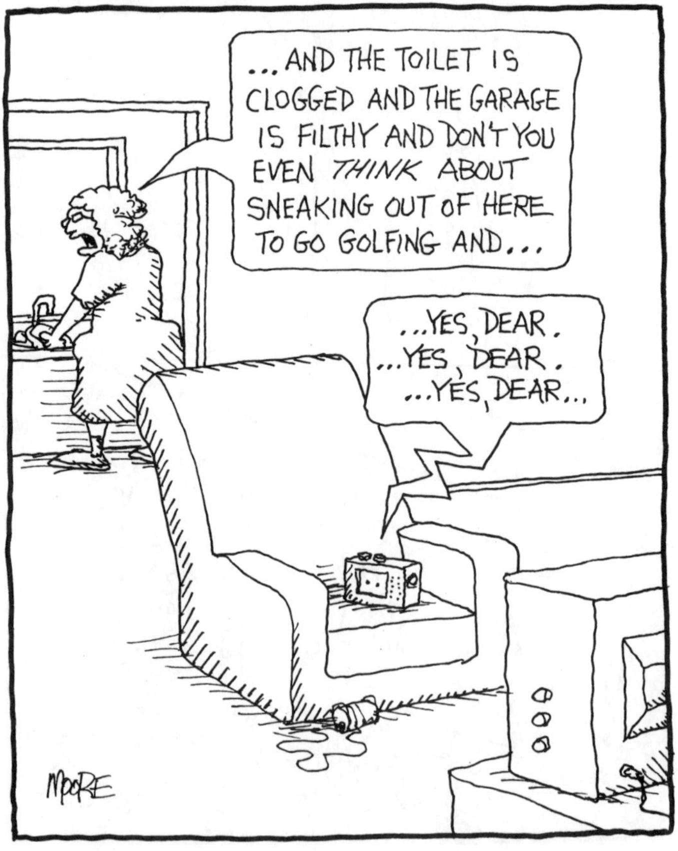
...AND THE TOILET IS CLOGGED AND THE GARAGE IS FILTHY AND DON'T YOU EVEN *THINK* ABOUT SNEAKING OUT OF HERE TO GO GOLFING AND...
...YES, DEAR. ...YES, DEAR. ...YES, DEAR...
MOORE

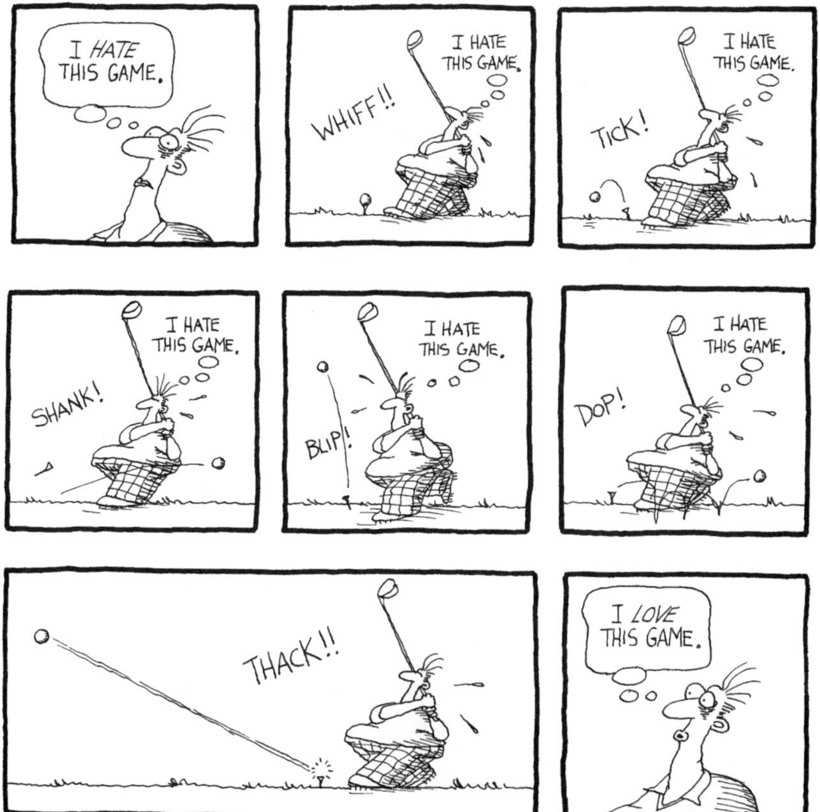
I HATE THIS GAME.
WHIFF!!
I HATE THIS GAME.
TICK!
I HATE THIS GAME.
SHANK!
I HATE THIS GAME.
BLIP!
I HATE THIS GAME.
DOP!
I HATE THIS GAME.
THACK!!
I LOVE THIS GAME.

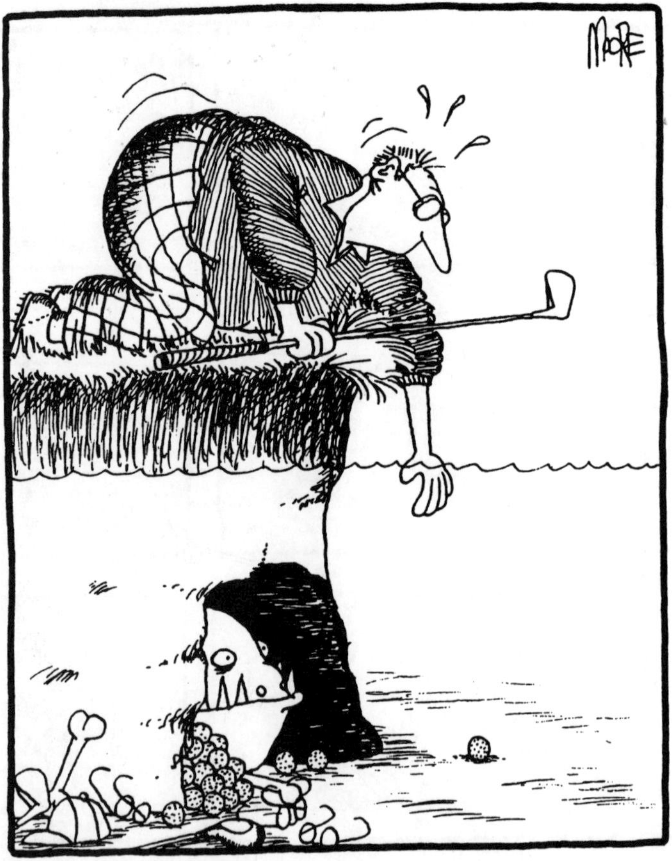
MOORE

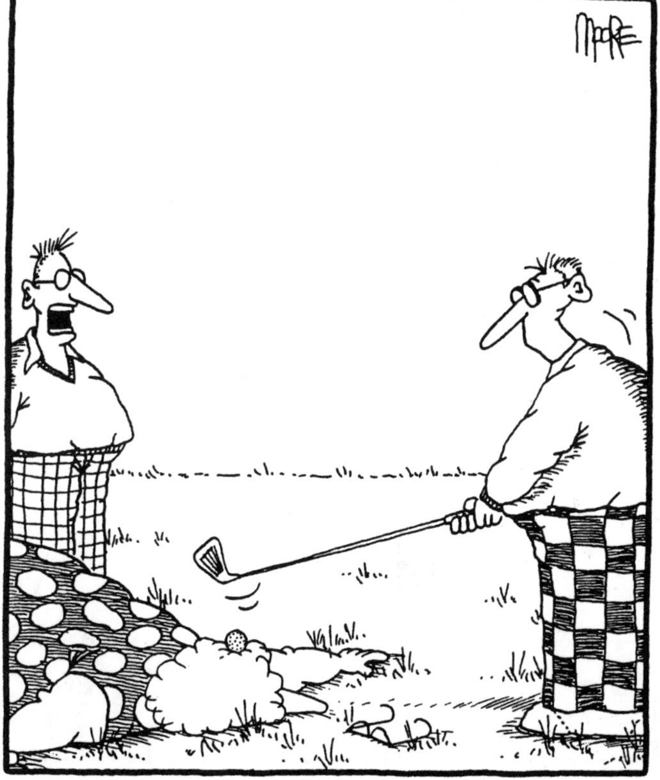
MOORE

"Hurry. She's starting to come to."

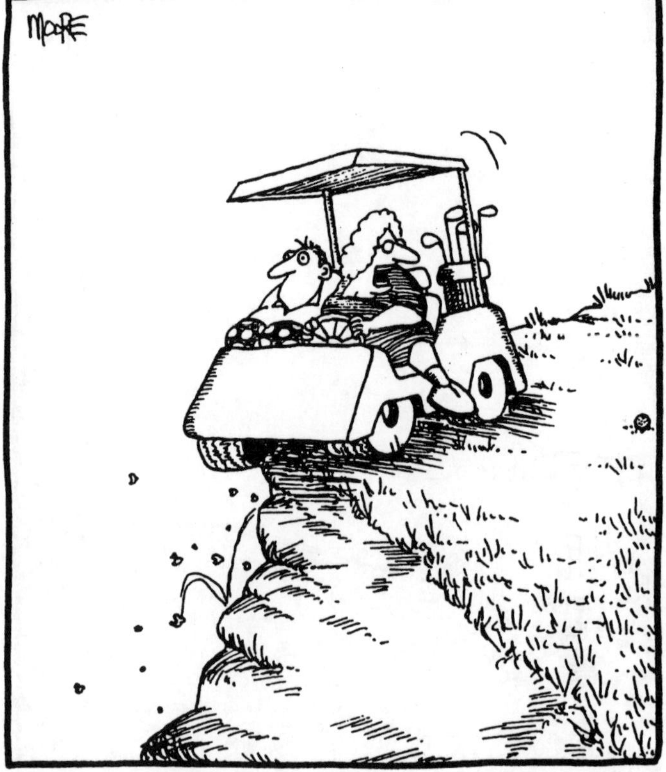
MOORE

"There's my ball. Stay in the cart, Floyd."

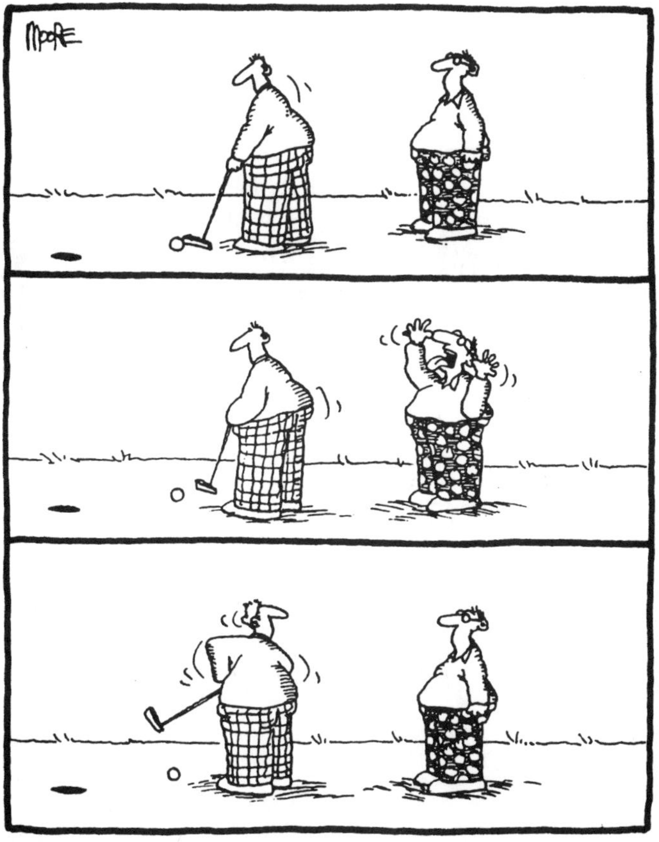
MOORE

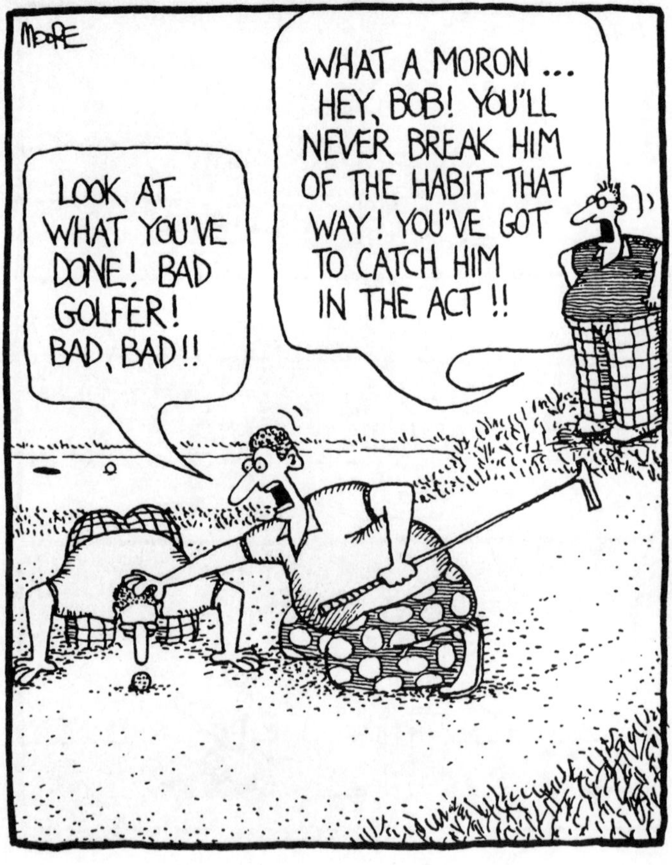
MOORE
LOOK AT WHAT YOU'VE DONE! BAD GOLFER! BAD, BAD!!
WHAT A MORON ... HEY, BOB! YOU'LL NEVER BREAK HIM OF THE HABIT THAT WAY! YOU'VE GOT TO CATCH HIM IN THE ACT!!

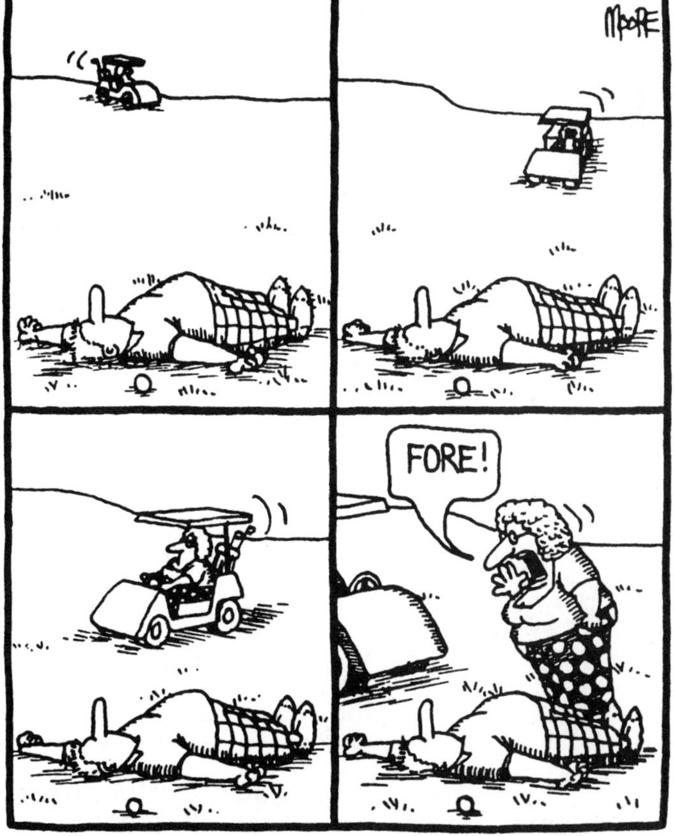
MOORE
FORE!

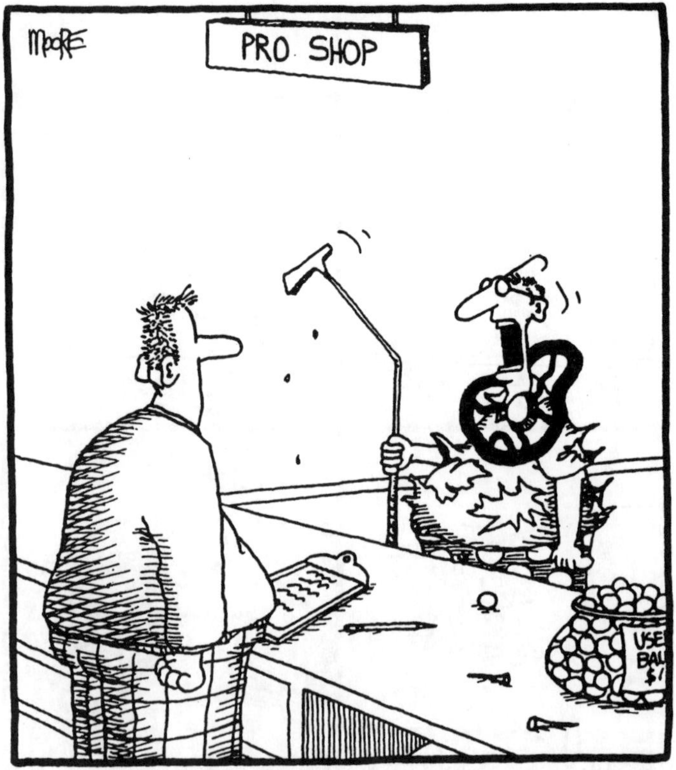
MOORE
PRO SHOP

"I need a new golf cart. . . . And you might want to send a doctor out to the 9th green."

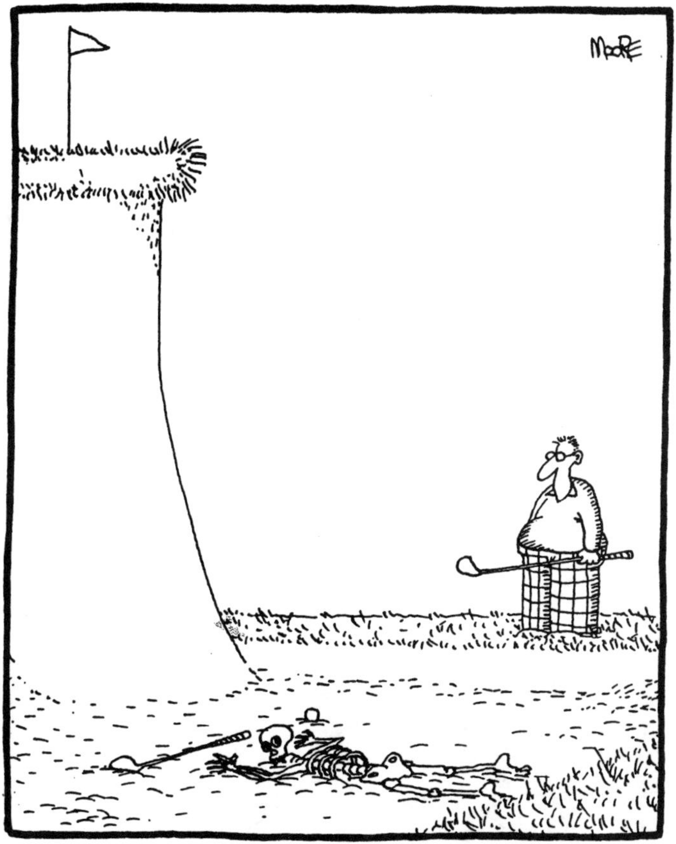
MOORE

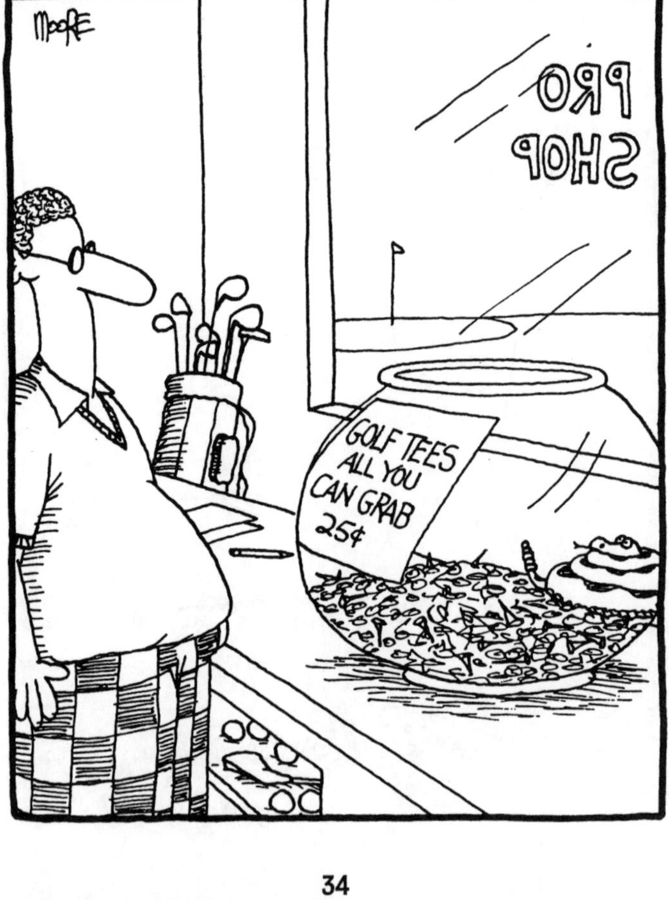
MOORE
PRO SHOP
GOLF TEES ALL YOU CAN GRAB 25¢

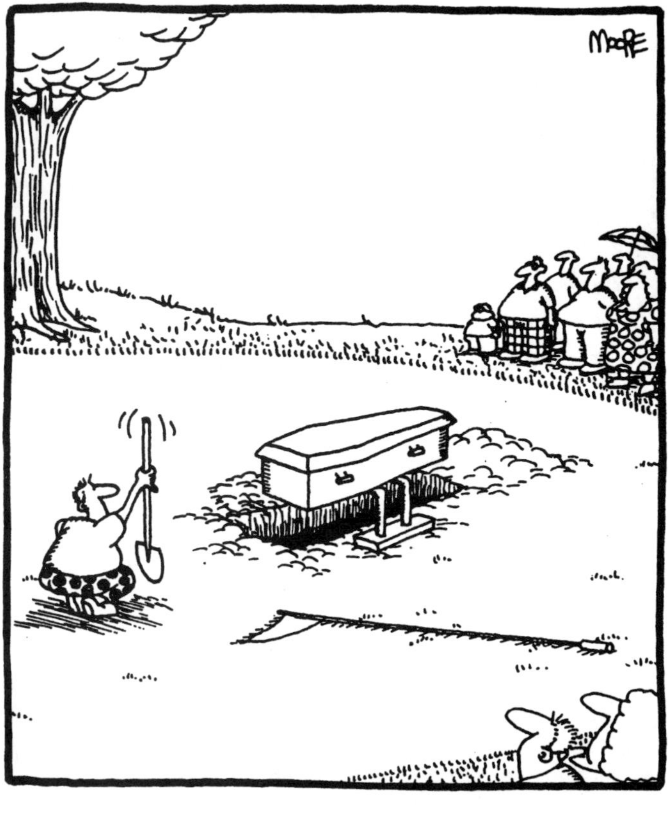
MOORE

Funeral for a golfer

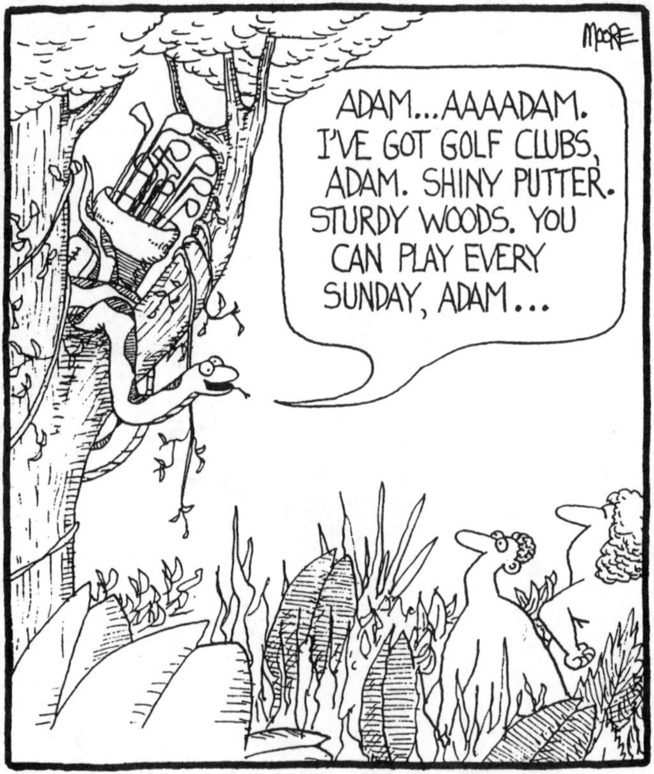
MOORE
ADAM...AAAADAM. I'VE GOT GOLF CLUBS, ADAM. SHINY PUTTER. STURDY WOODS. YOU CAN PLAY EVERY SUNDAY, ADAM...

Fall from Eden: the untold story

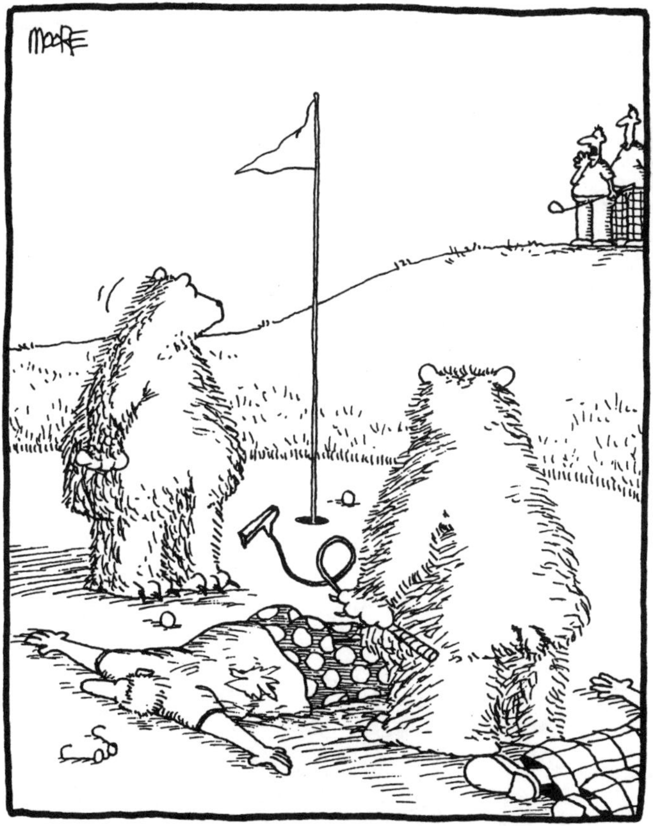
MOORE

"Yo!! Mind if we play through?"

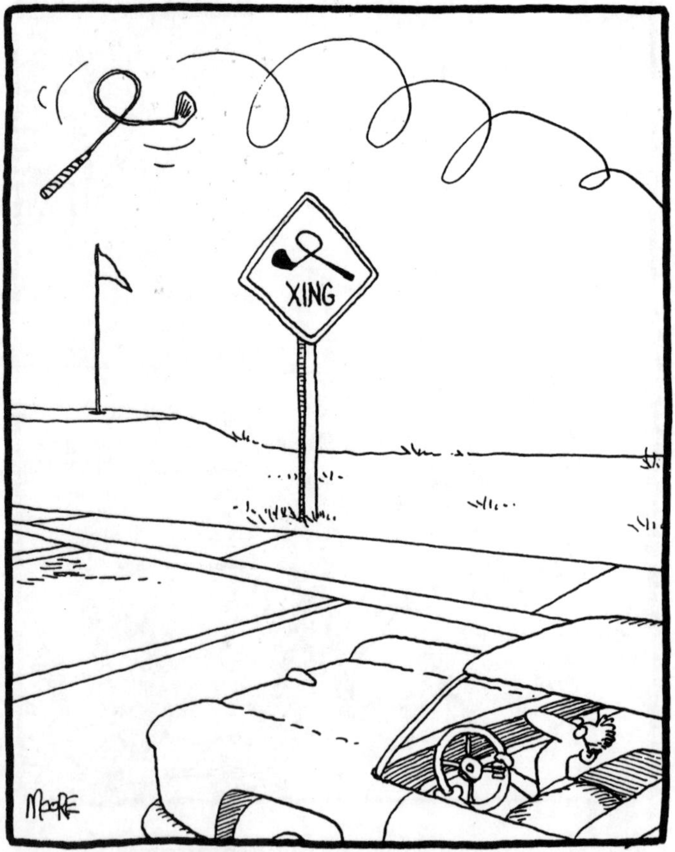
XING
MOORE

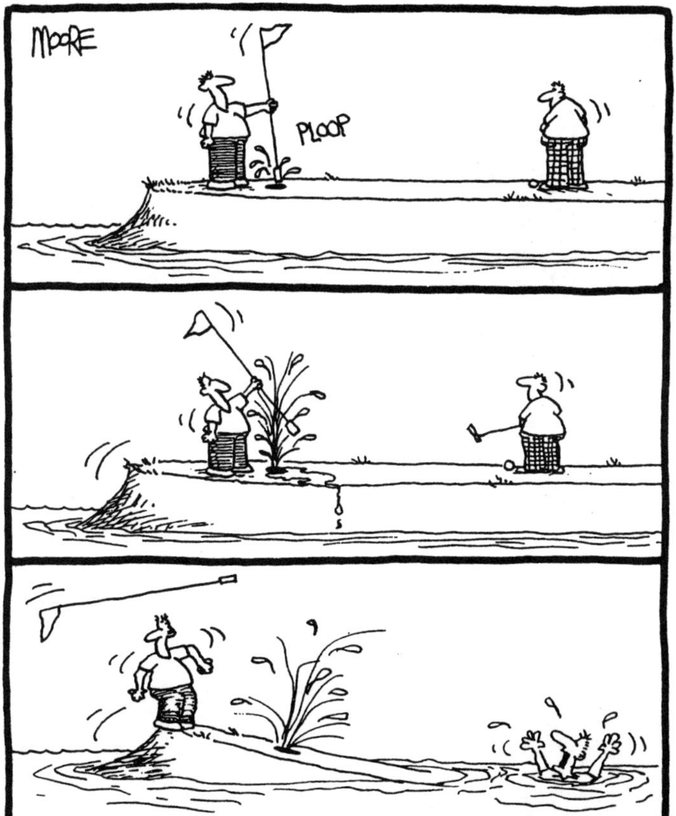
MOORE
PLOOP

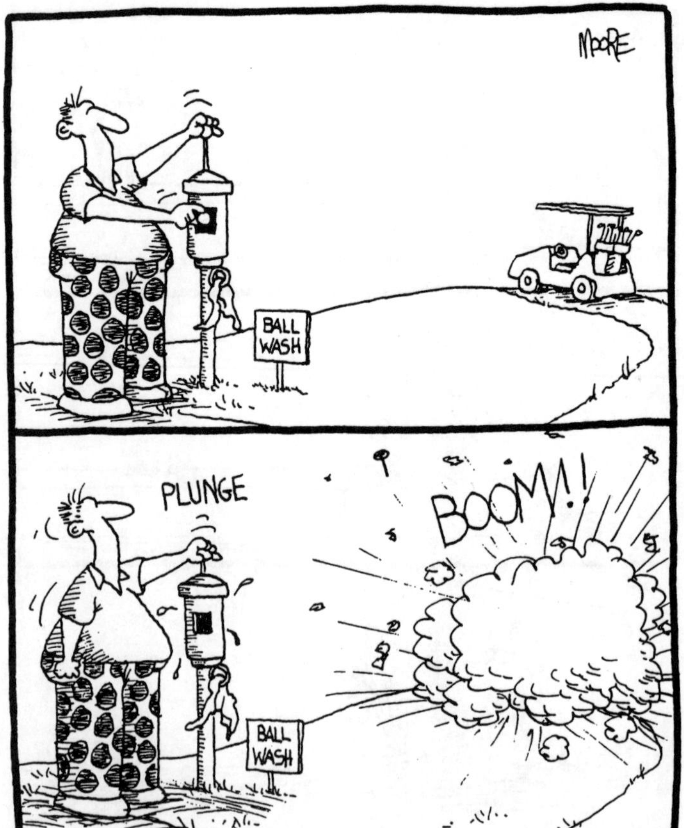
MOORE
BALL
WASH
PLUNGE
BOOM!!
BALL
WASH

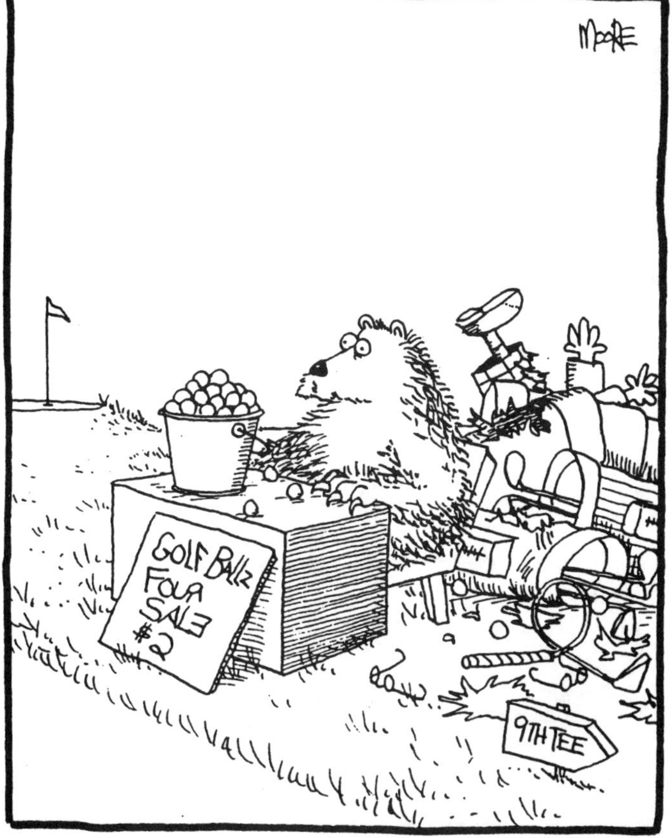
MOORE
GOLF BALLZ
FOUR
SALE
$2
9TH TEE

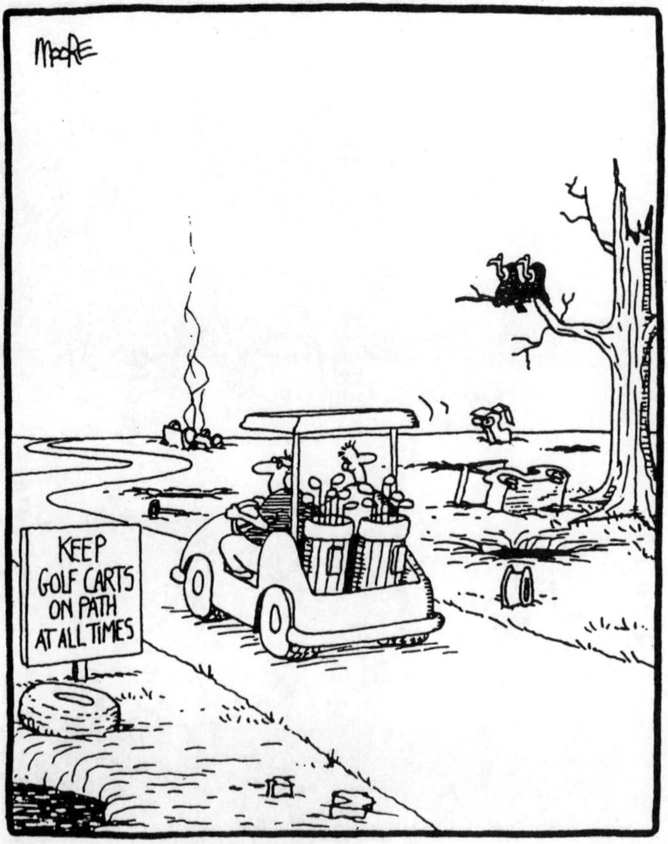
MOORE
KEEP
GOLF CARTS
ON PATH
AT ALL TIMES

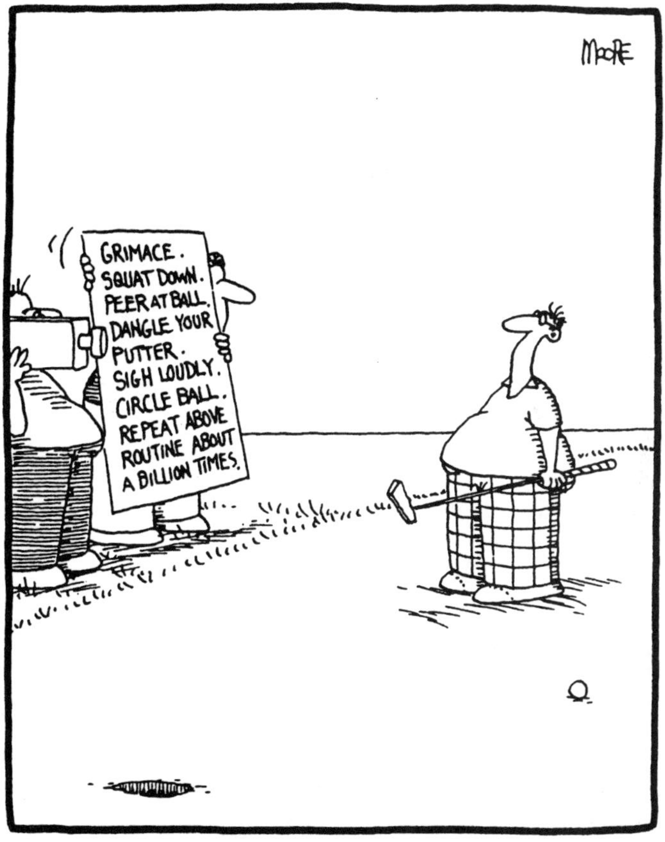
MOORE
GRIMACE.
SQUAT DOWN.
PEER AT BALL.
DANGLE YOUR PUTTER.
SIGH LOUDLY.
CIRCLE BALL.
REPEAT ABOVE ROUTINE ABOUT A BILLION TIMES.

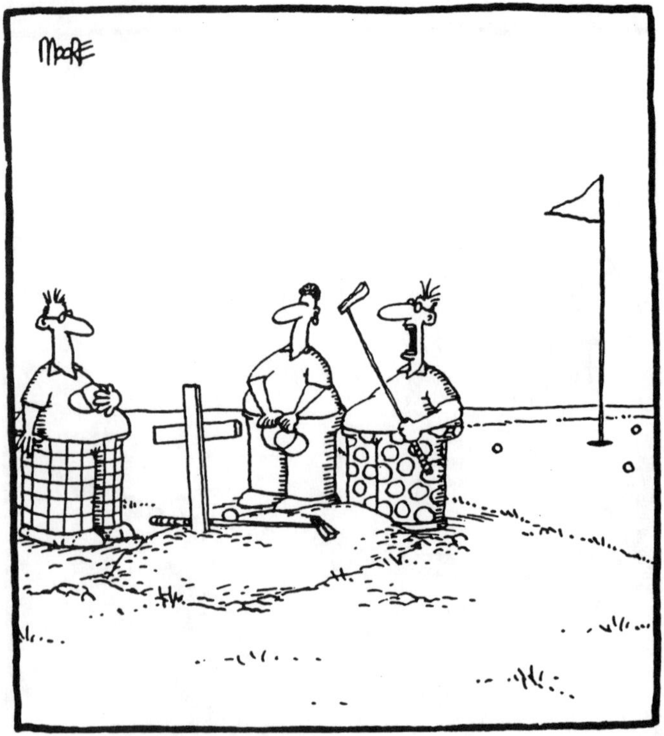
MOORE

"... A great guy, a loving husband and, uh, we're-really-going-to-miss-him-amen ... OK, let's putt out. The foursome behind us is waiting to tee off."

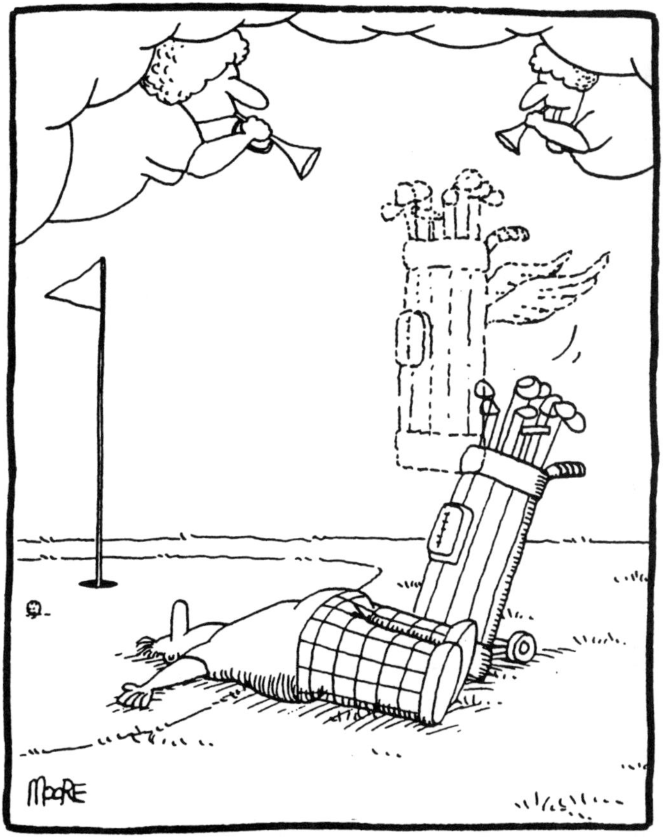
MOORE

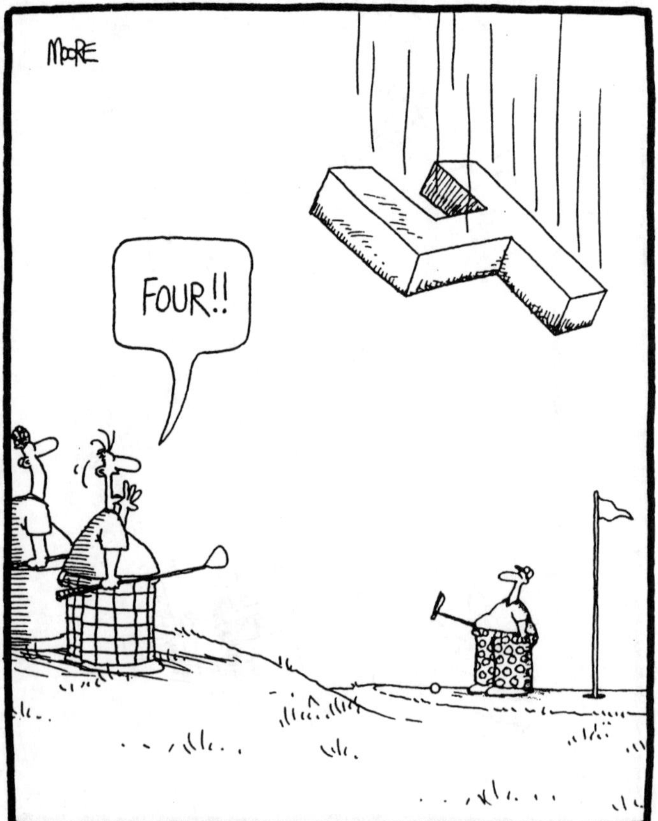
MOORE
FOUR!!

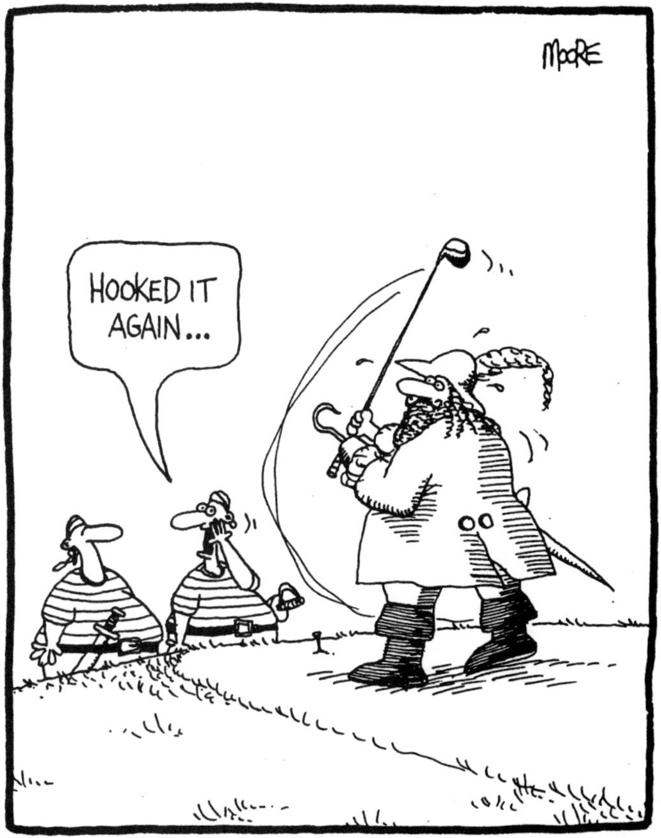
MOORE
HOOKED IT AGAIN...

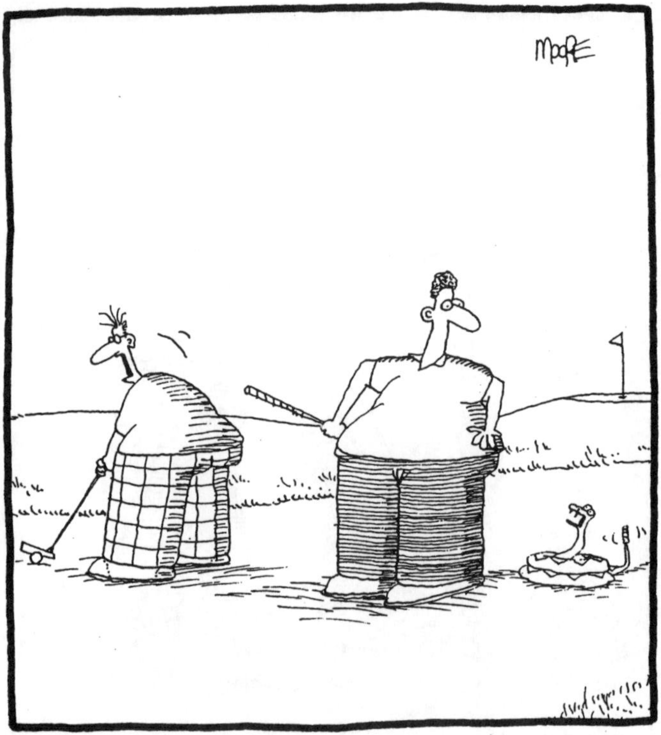
MOORE

"Don't move, Andy. Don't even breathe. If you so much as bat an eye, you're a dead man . . . now just let me putt out and I'll be right over to help you."

"Whoa, whoa, whoa!! What are you forgetting, Larry? I can't believe you were going to just walk away without replacing your divot."

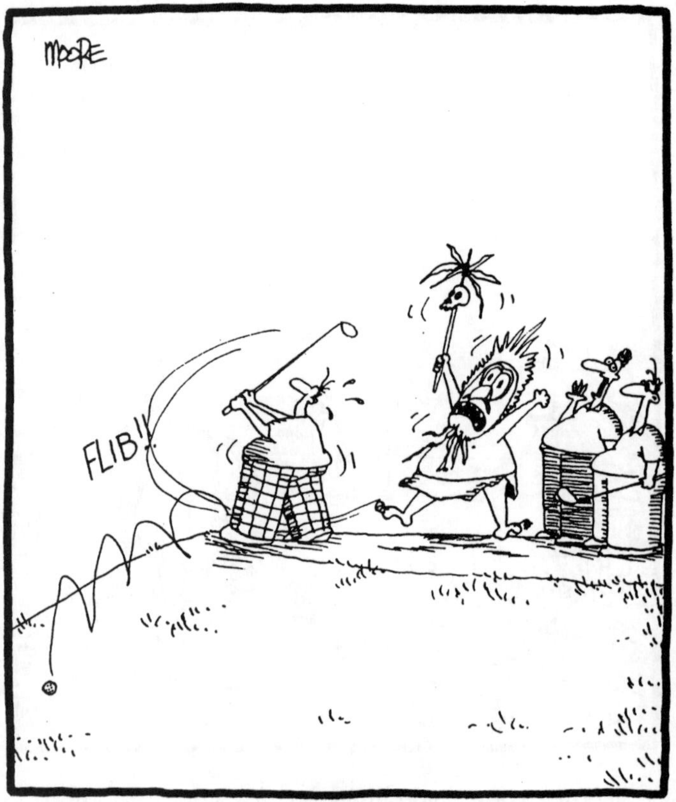
MOORE
FLIB!!

"It's working..."

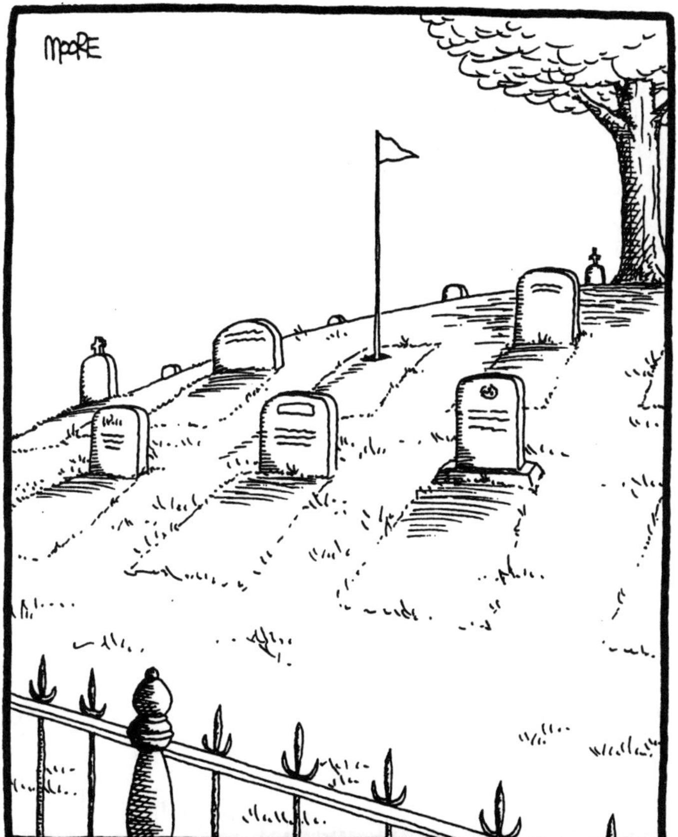
MOORE

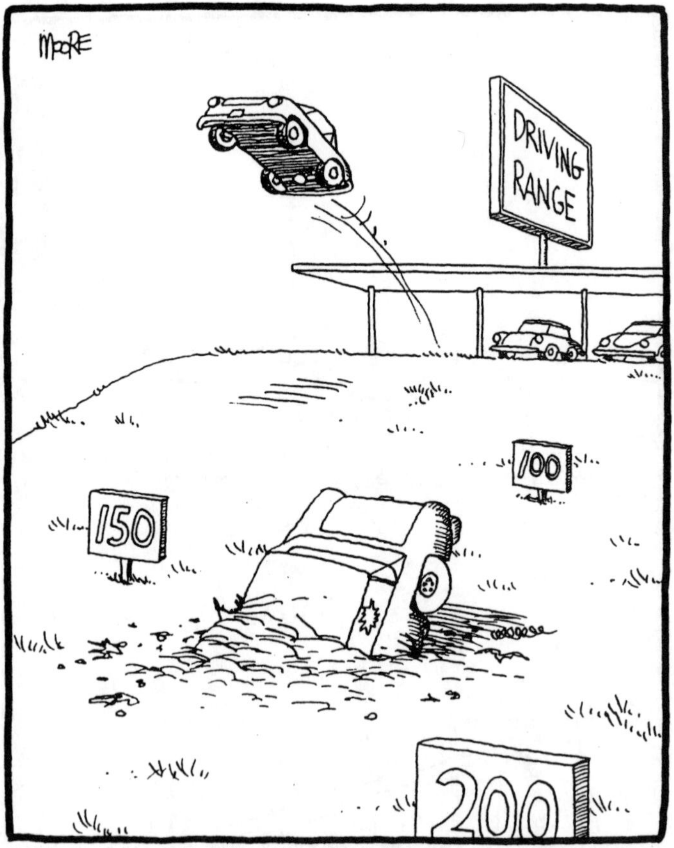
MOORE
DRIVING RANGE
100
150
200

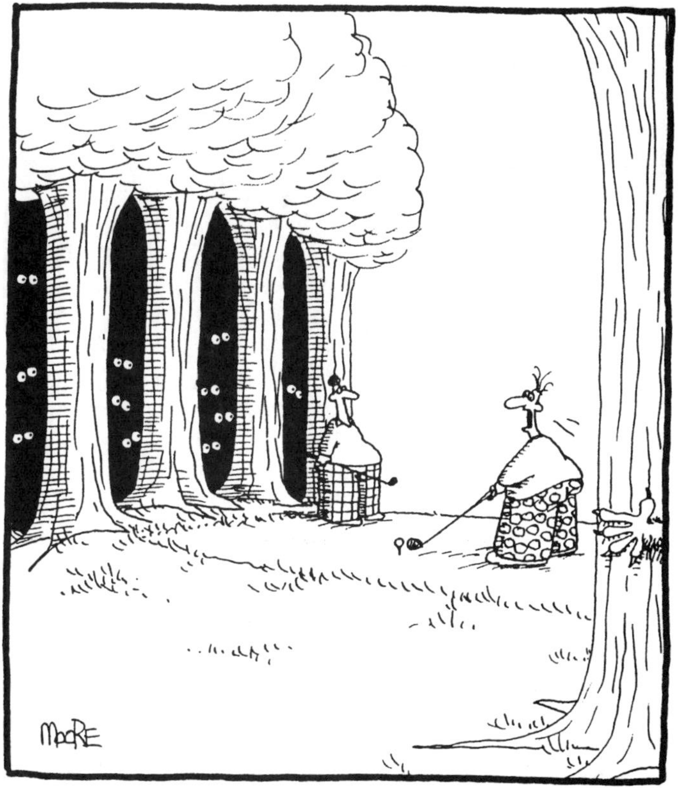
MOORE

"I hate the first tee. I always feel so self-conscious, like my every move is being watched."

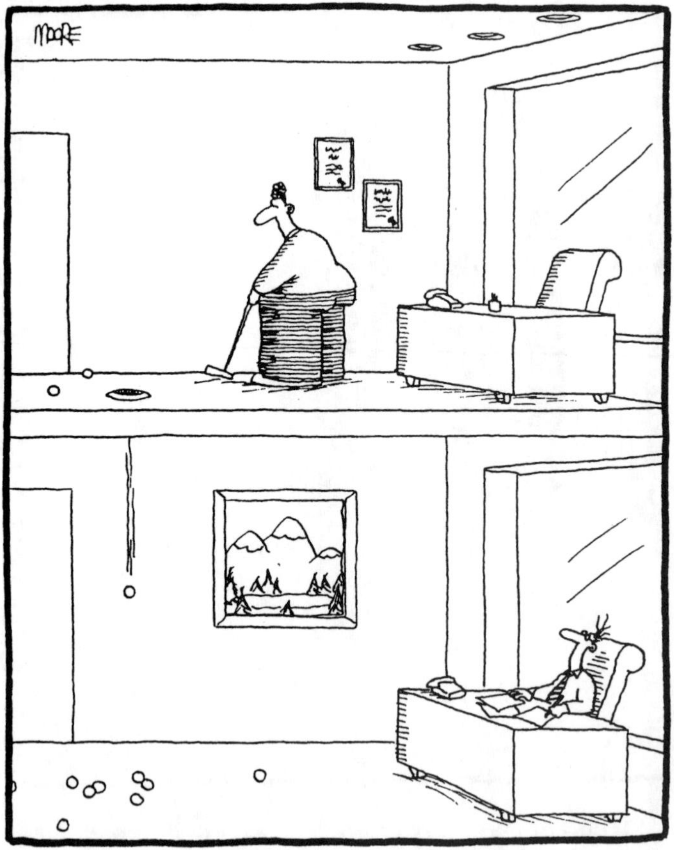
MOORE

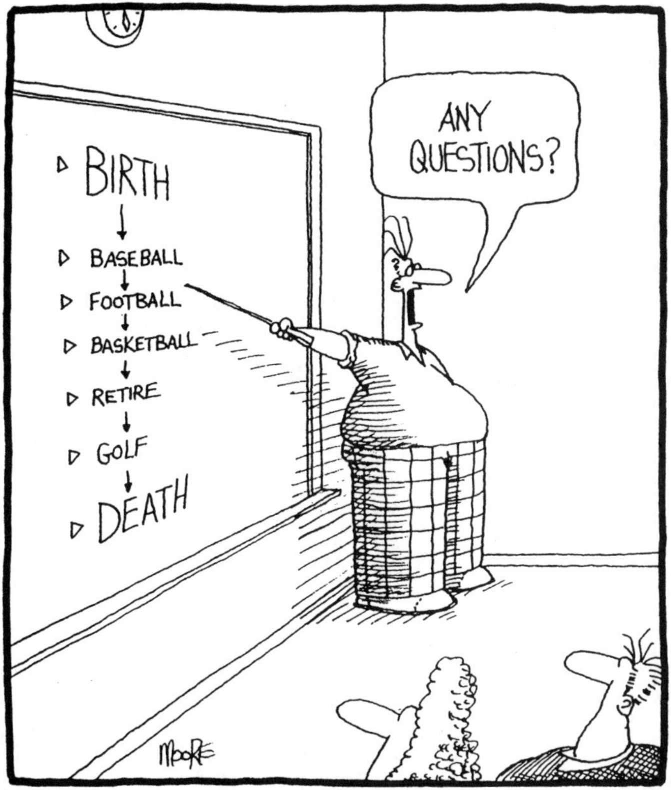
BIRTH
BASEBALL
FOOTBALL
BASKETBALL
RETIRE
GOLF
DEATH
ANY QUESTIONS?
MOORE

Life 101

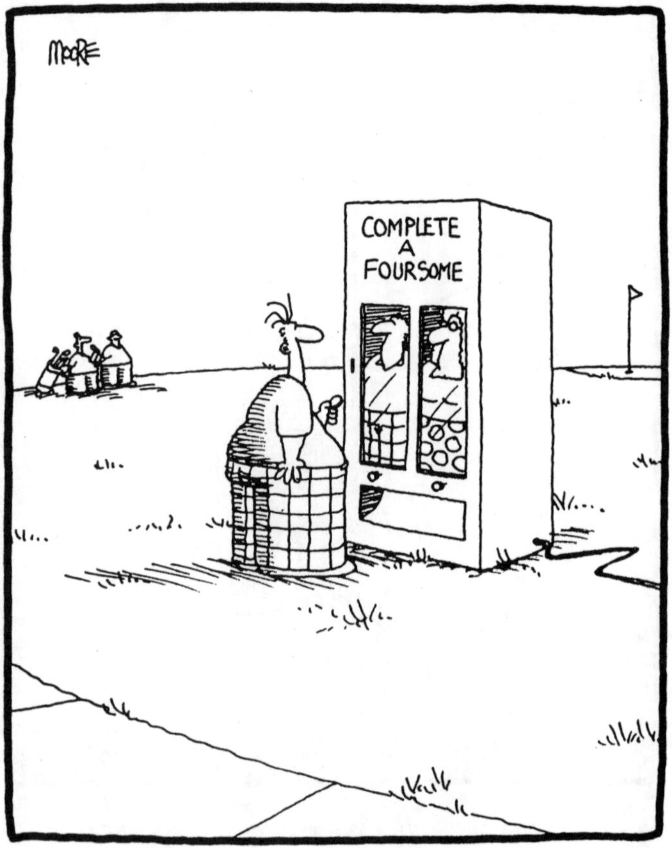
MOORE
COMPLETE
A
FOURSOME

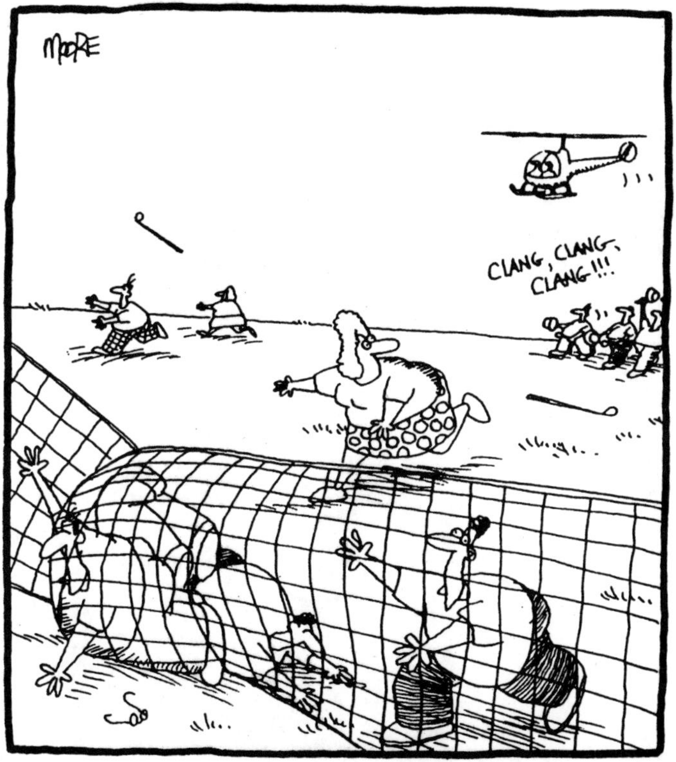
MOORE
CLANG, CLANG,
CLANG!!!

Every spring the golfers are flushed from the fairways and into nets where they are tagged and released relatively unharmed.

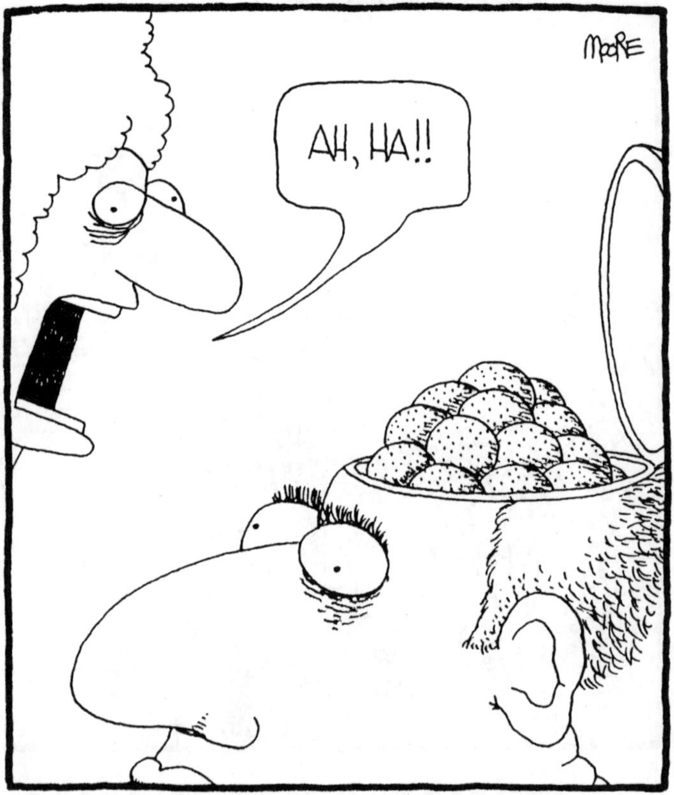
MOORE
AH, HA!!

Golf balls for brains

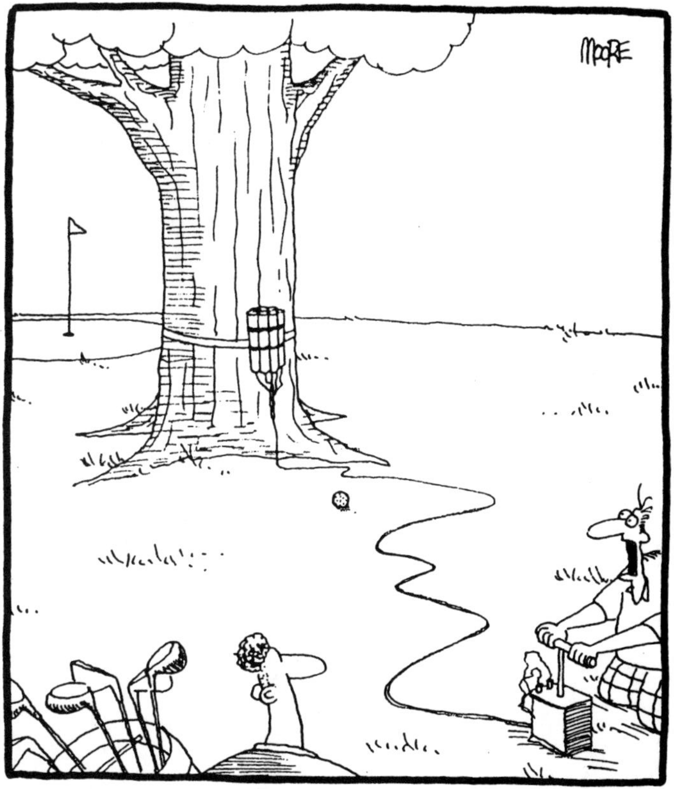

“Take cover…”

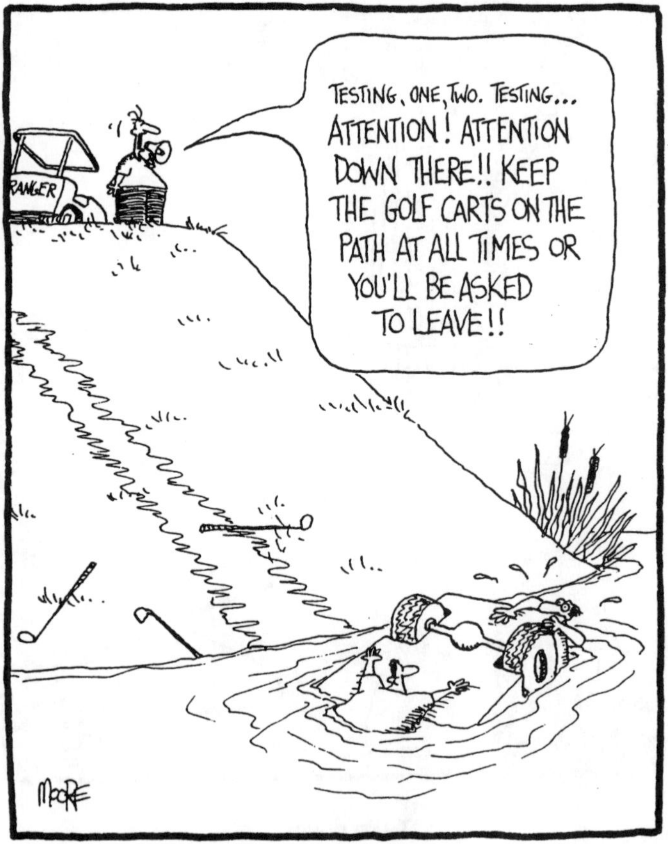
TESTING, ONE, TWO. TESTING... ATTENTION! ATTENTION DOWN THERE!! KEEP THE GOLF CARTS ON THE PATH AT ALL TIMES OR YOU'LL BE ASKED TO LEAVE!!
RANGER
MOORE

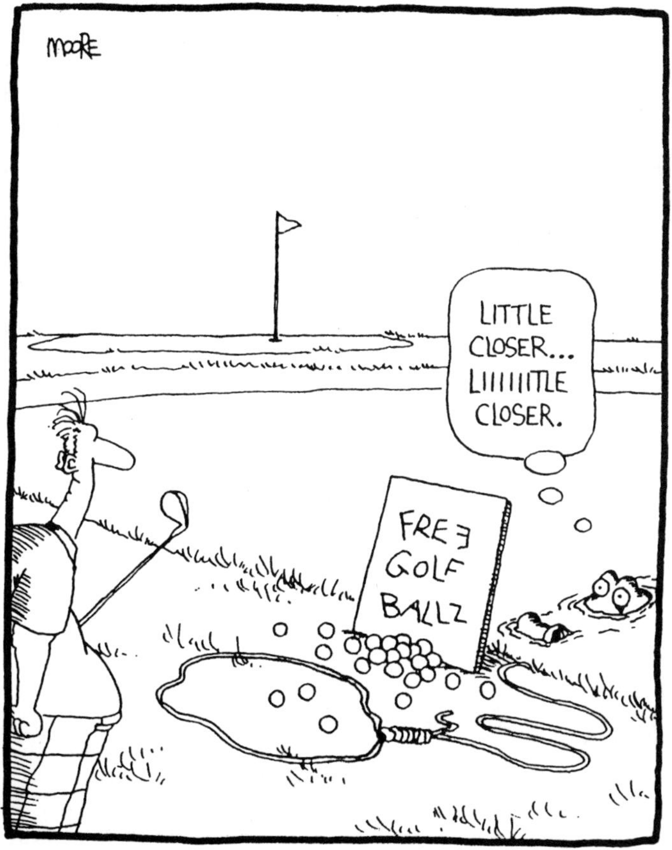
MOORE
LITTLE CLOSER... LIIIIIITTLE CLOSER.
FREƎ GOLF BALLZ

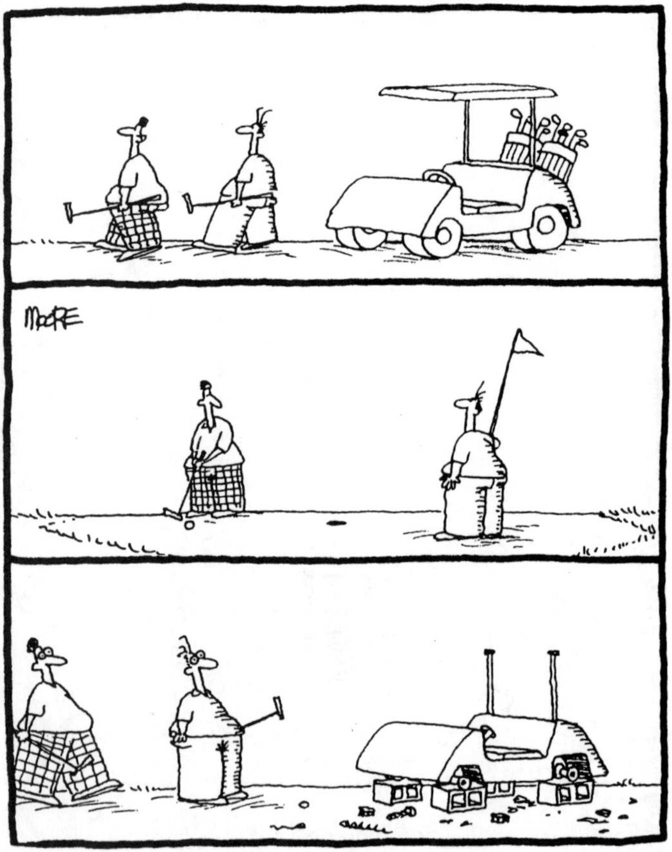
MOORE

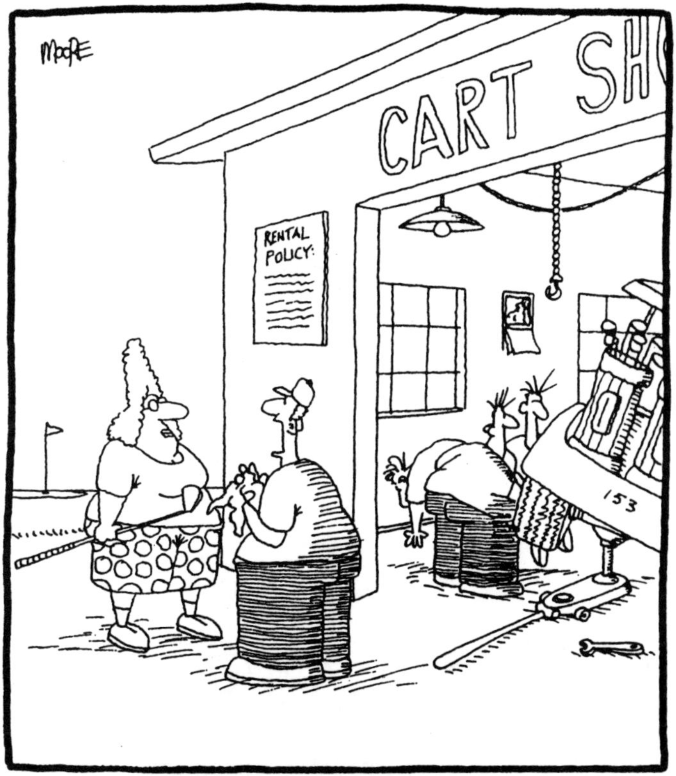
MOORE
CART SH
RENTAL
POLICY:
153

"We found the groaning noise, Mrs. Lieberman. Your husband was lodged under the axle."

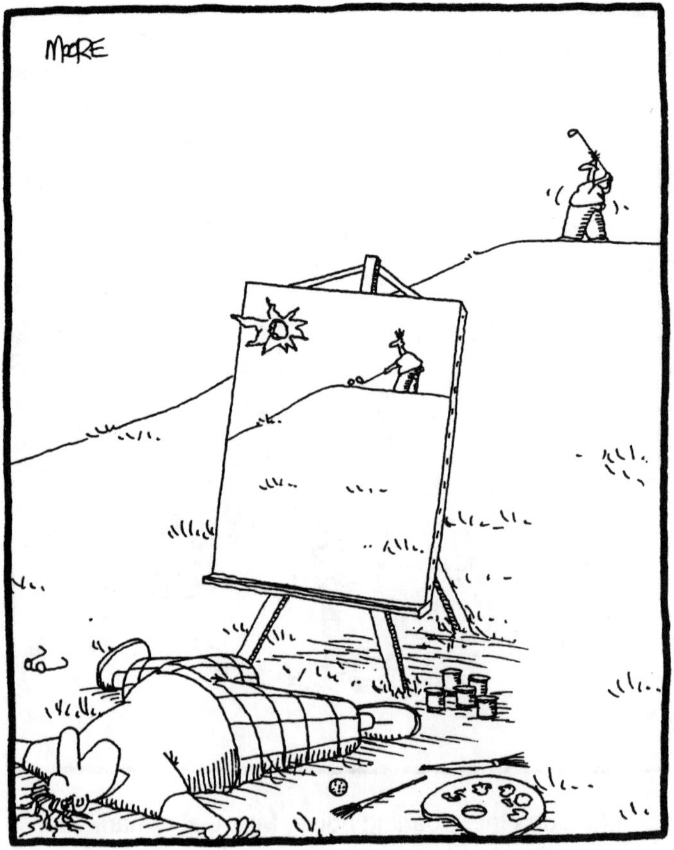

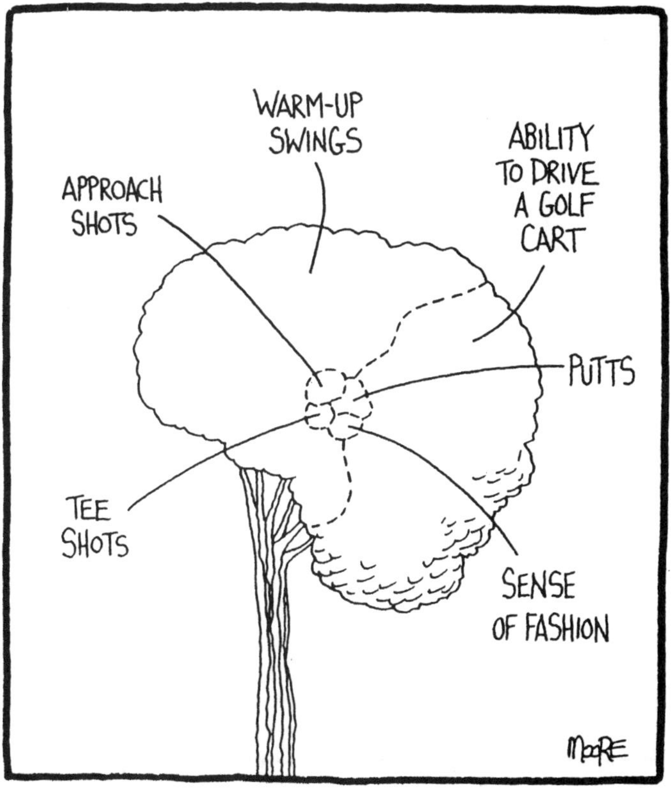
WARM-UP SWINGS
APPROACH SHOTS
ABILITY TO DRIVE A GOLF CART
PUTTS
TEE SHOTS
SENSE OF FASHION
MOORE

Control centers of a golfer's brain

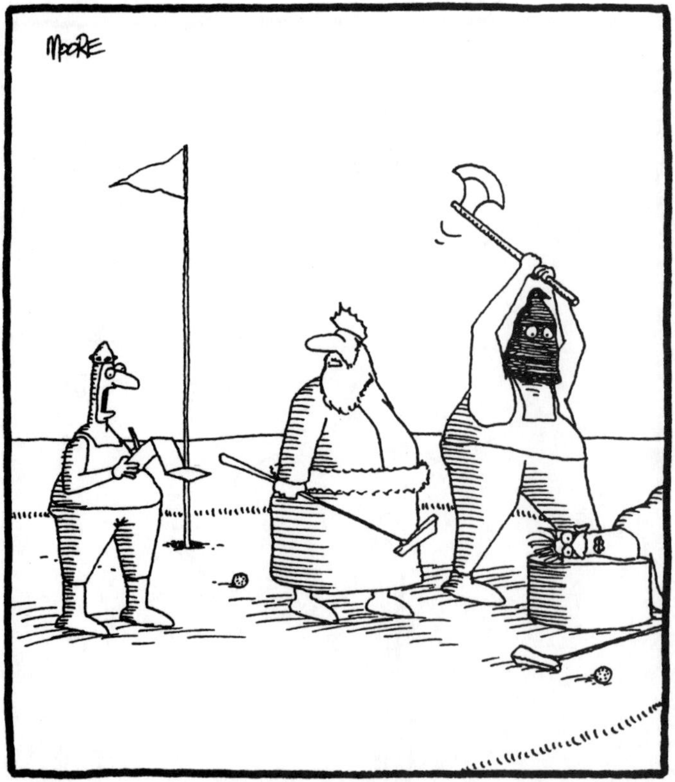
MOORE

"Wait! He didn't win, majesty. I added wrong. You actually won by a stroke."

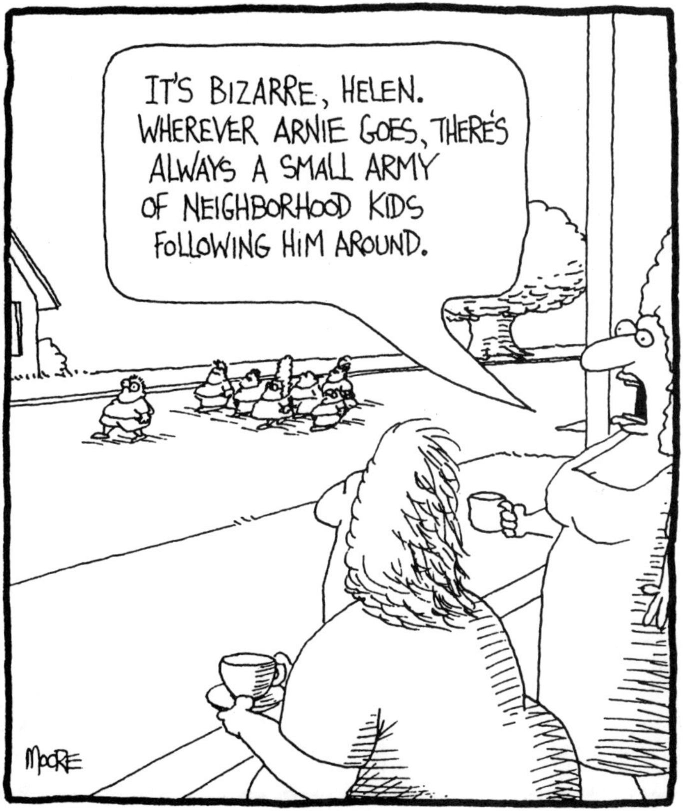
IT'S BIZARRE, HELEN. WHEREVER ARNIE GOES, THERE'S ALWAYS A SMALL ARMY OF NEIGHBORHOOD KIDS FOLLOWING HIM AROUND.
MOORE

Arnold Palmer as a kid

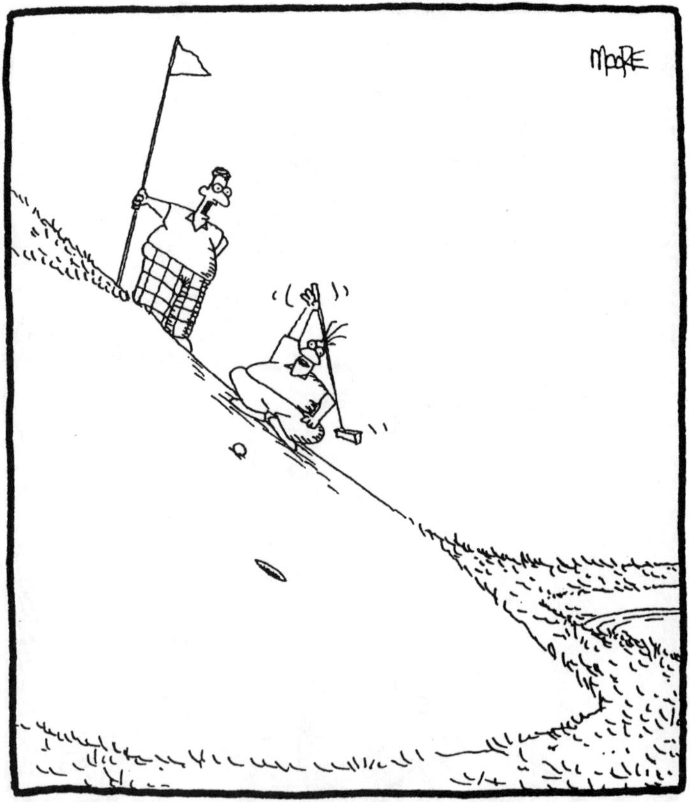
MOORE

“It'll probably break toward the water.”

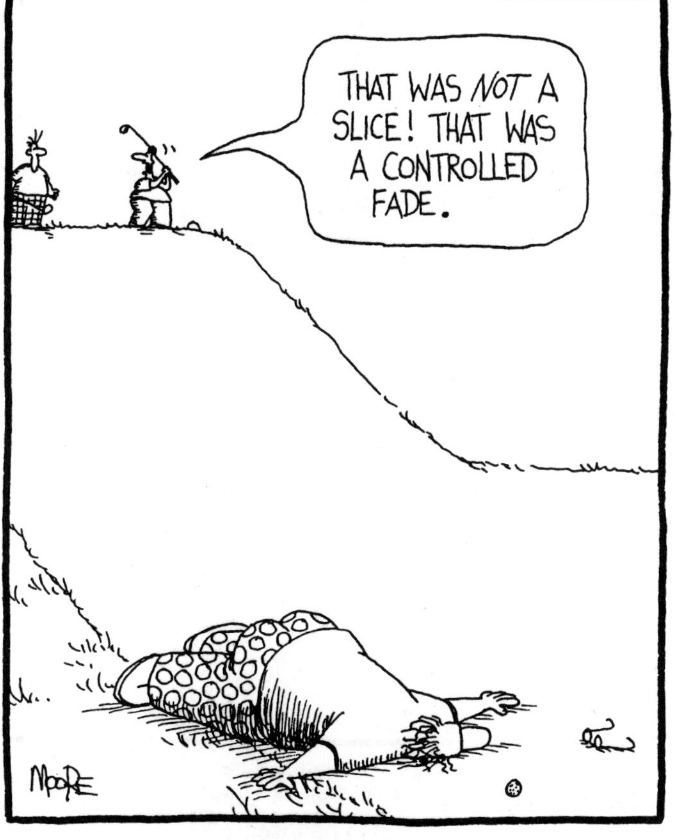
THAT WAS *NOT* A SLICE! THAT WAS A CONTROLLED FADE.
MOORE

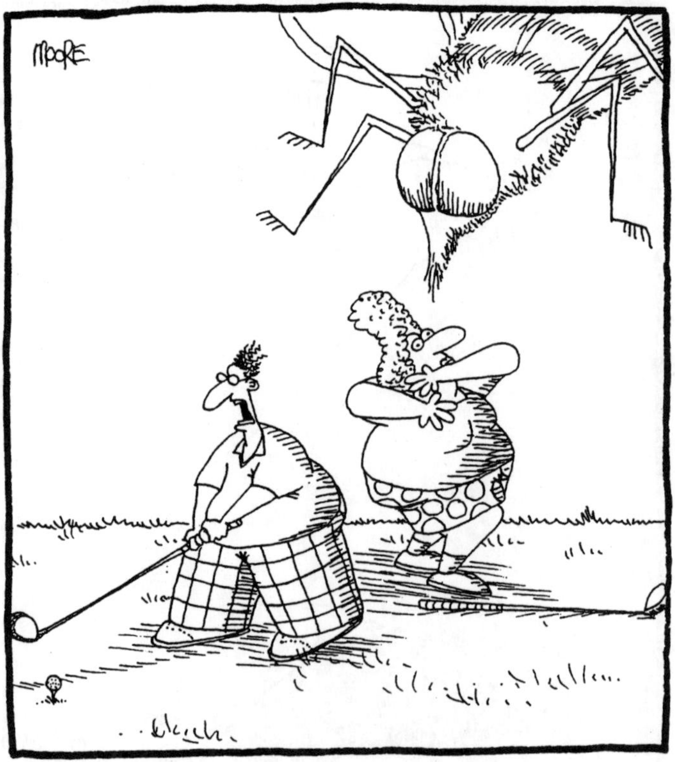
MOORE

"Just swat it away, Alice. This is a golf course. There's bound to be insects."

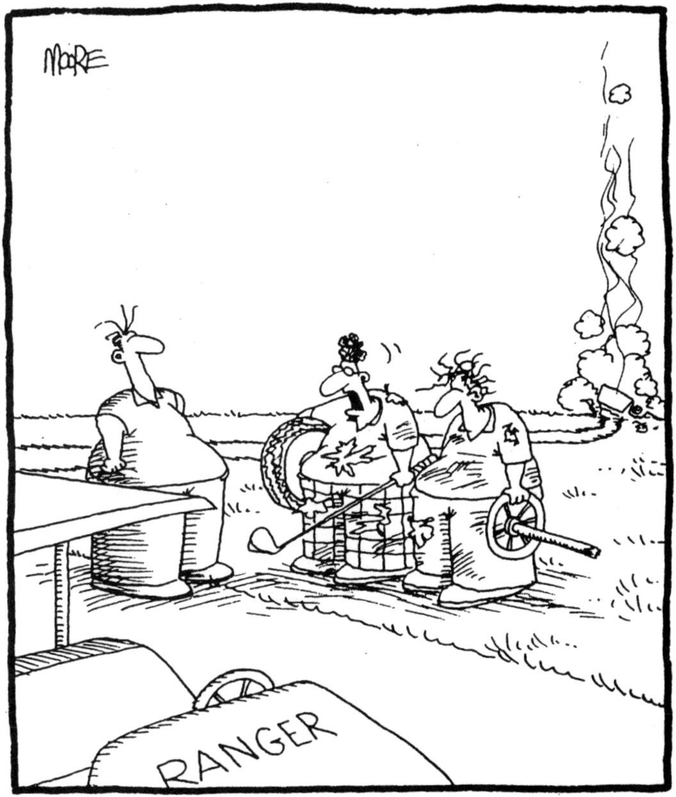
MOORE
RANGER

"We ventured off the designated cart path."

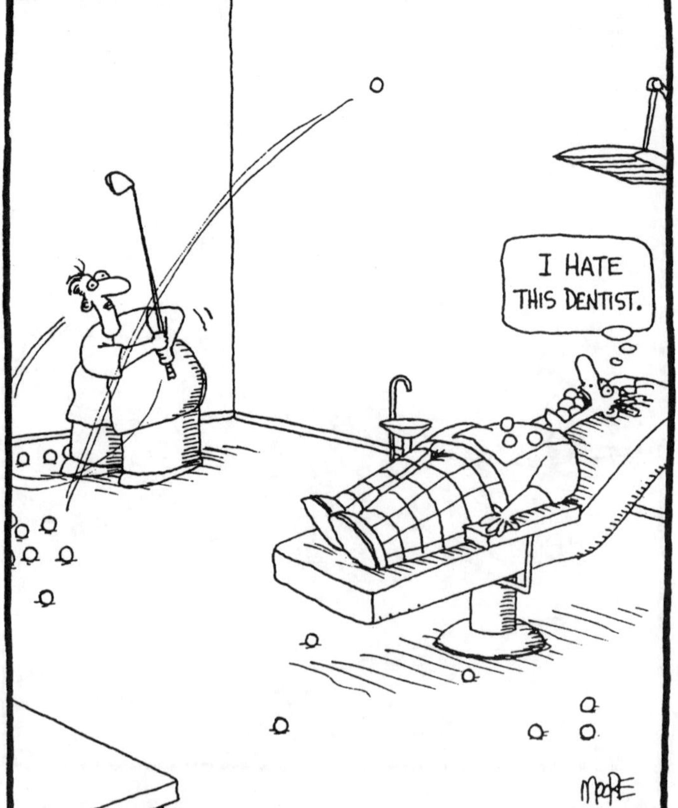
I HATE THIS DENTIST.
MOORE

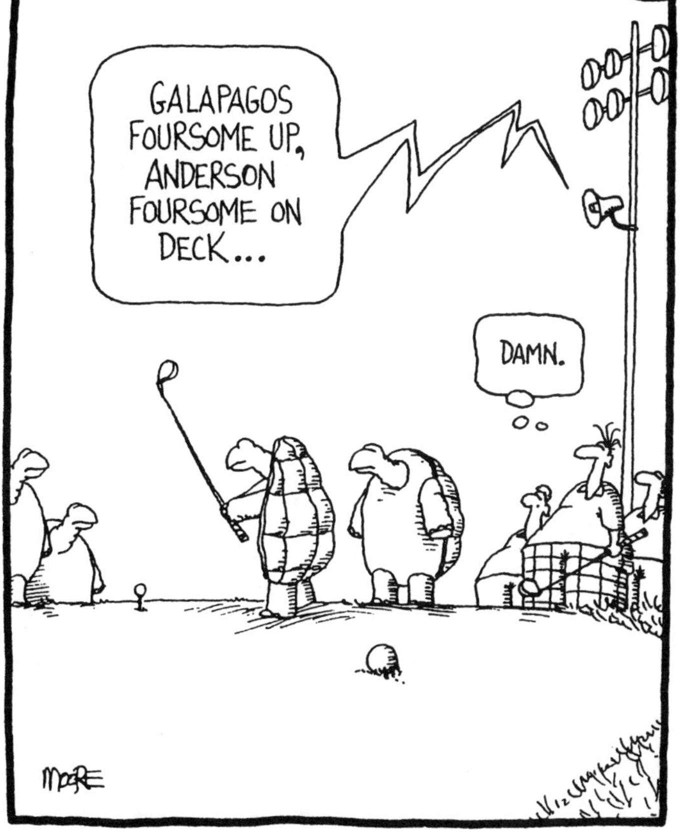
GALAPAGOS FOURSOME UP, ANDERSON FOURSOME ON DECK...
DAMN.
MOORE

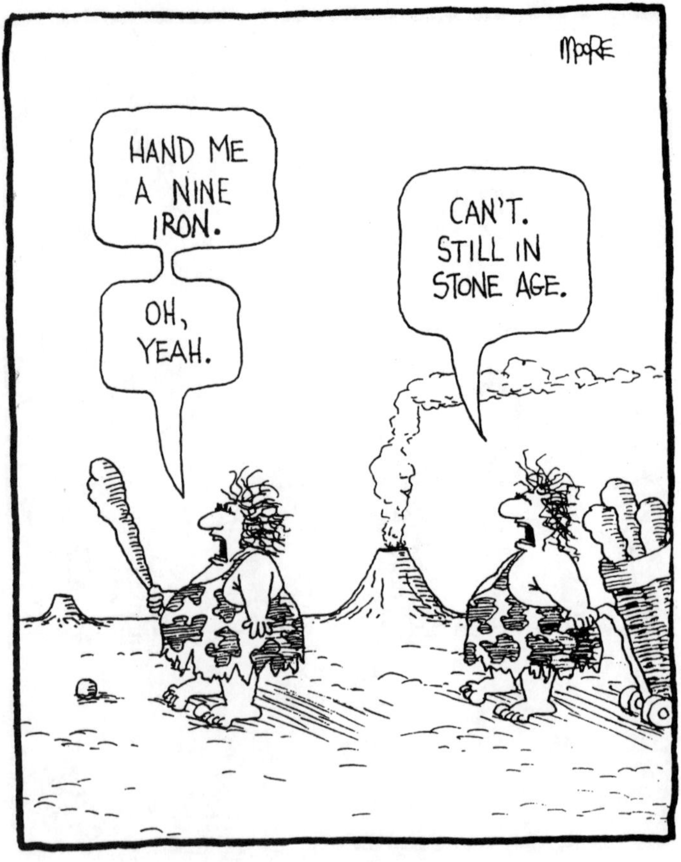
MOORE
HAND ME A NINE IRON.
OH, YEAH.
CAN'T. STILL IN STONE AGE.

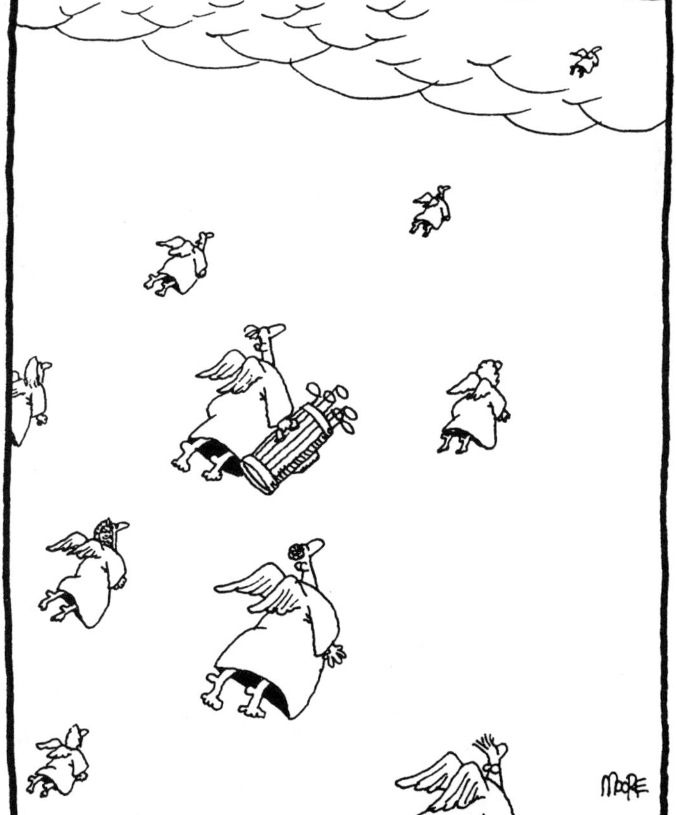
MOORE

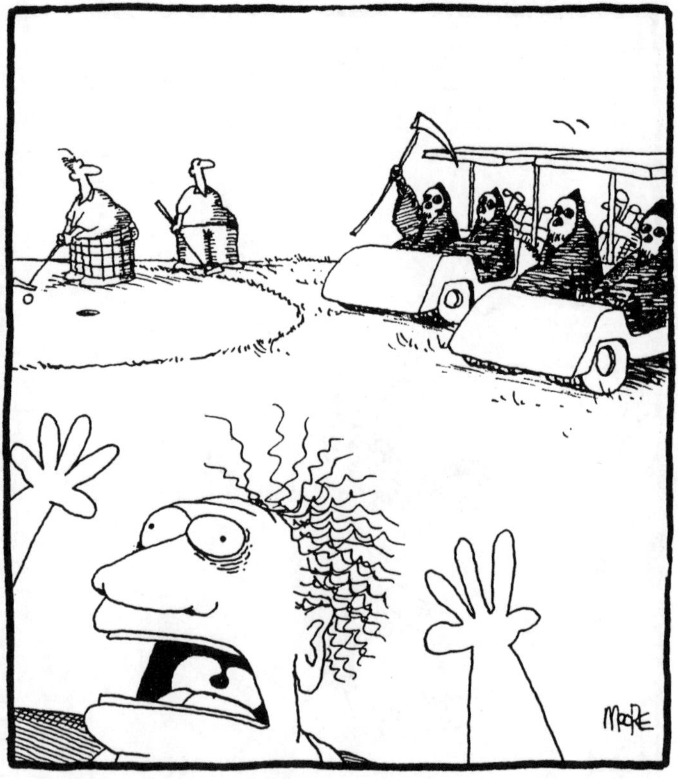
MOORE

"Aaaaaah! We're doomed!! It's the foursome of the Apocalypse!!!"

The tournament is postponed as golfballs the size of hail
begin to fall.

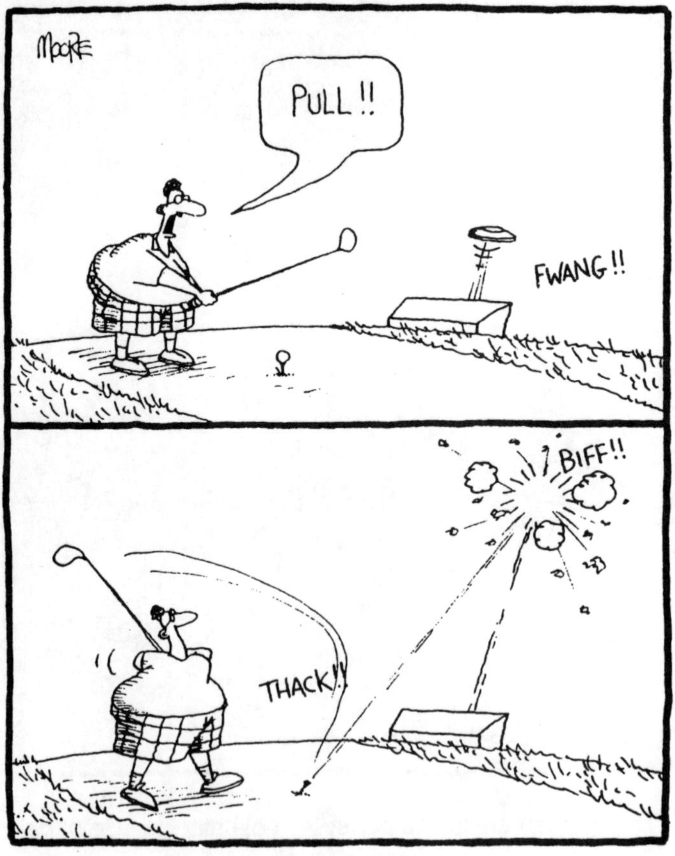
MOORE
PULL !!
FWANG !!
BIFF !!
THACK !!

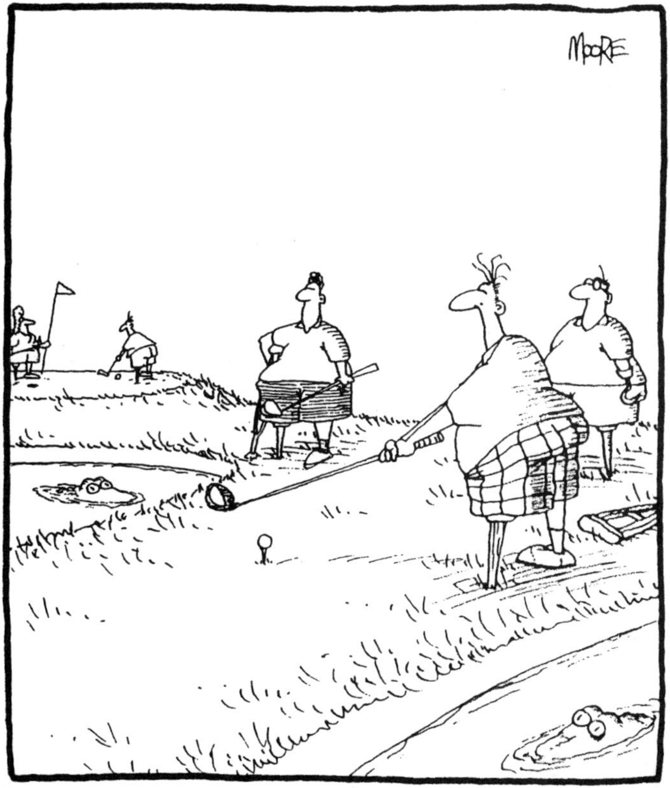
MOORE

Cypress Shoals Country Club and Crocodile Farm

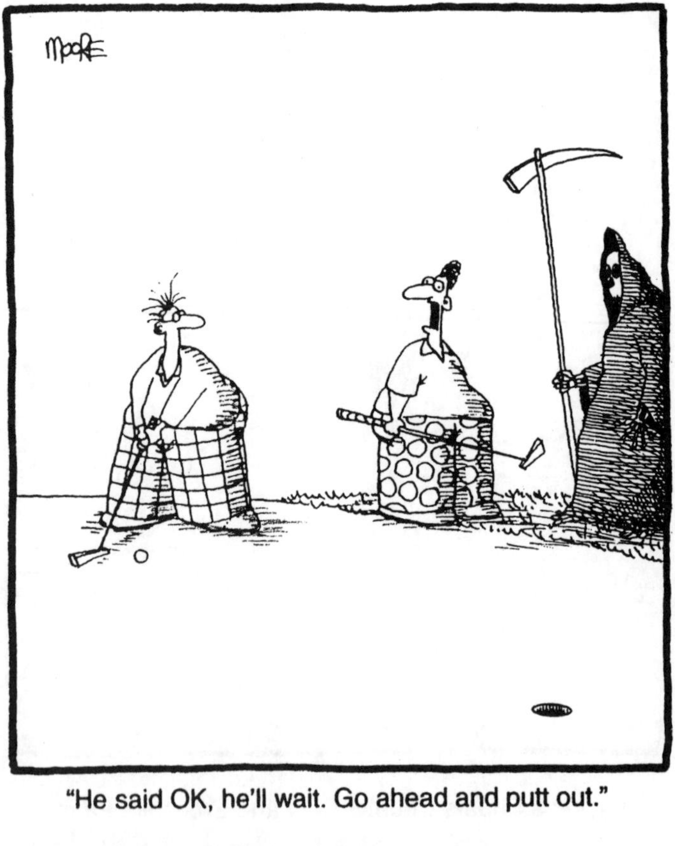
MOORE

"He said OK, he'll wait. Go ahead and putt out."

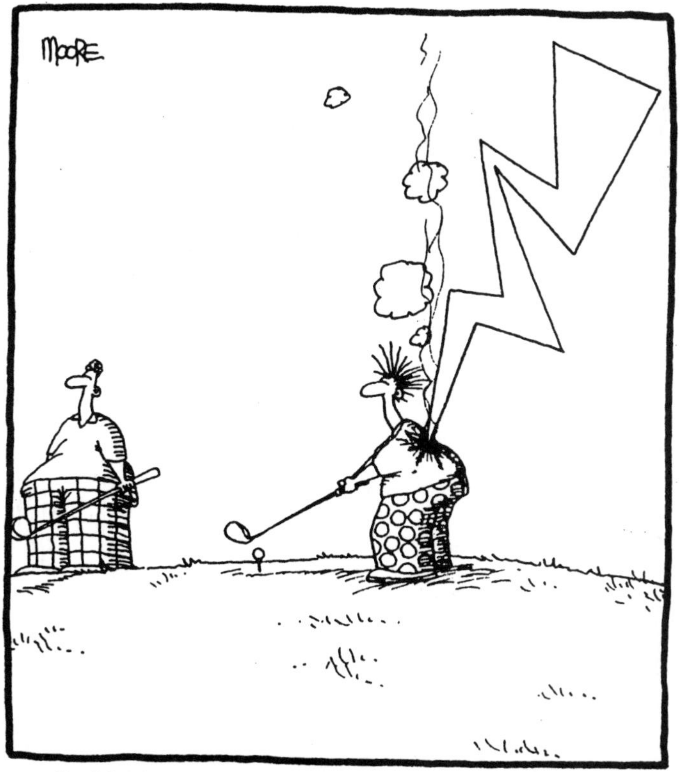
MOORE

. . . Suddenly, the skies cleared and Leonard decided to finish the round in spite of the pain.

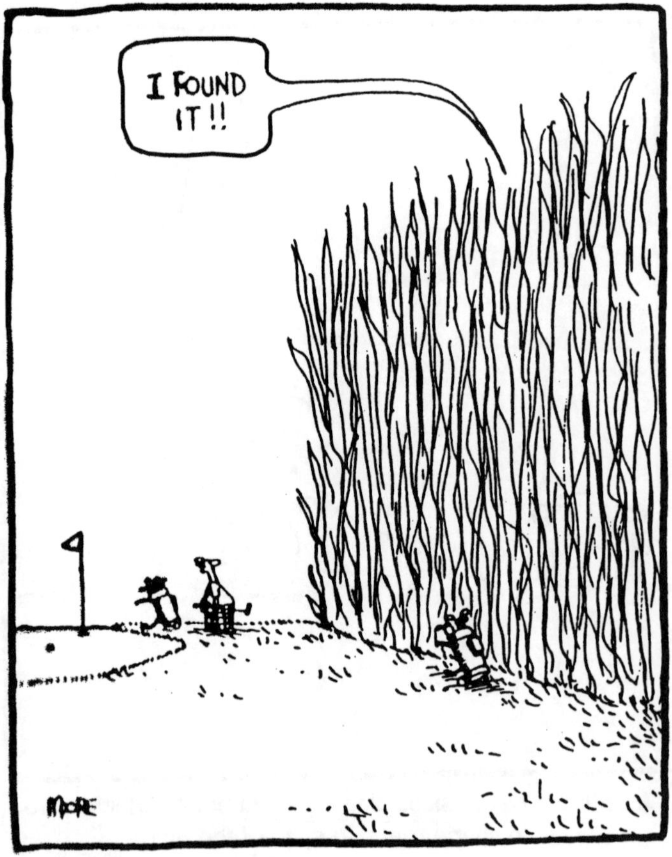
I FOUND IT !!

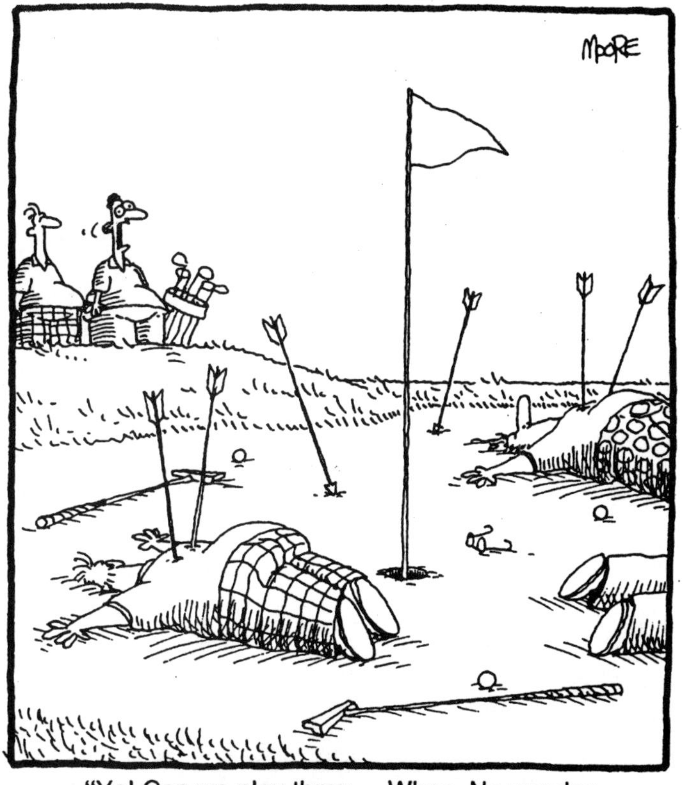
MOORE

"Yo! Can we play throu… Whoa. No wonder they were taking so long to putt out."

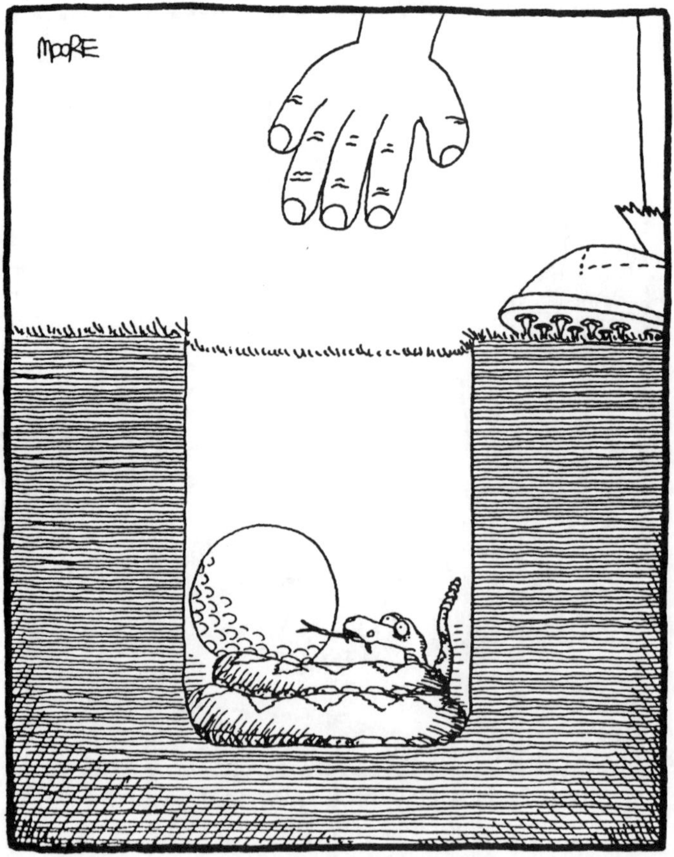
MOORE

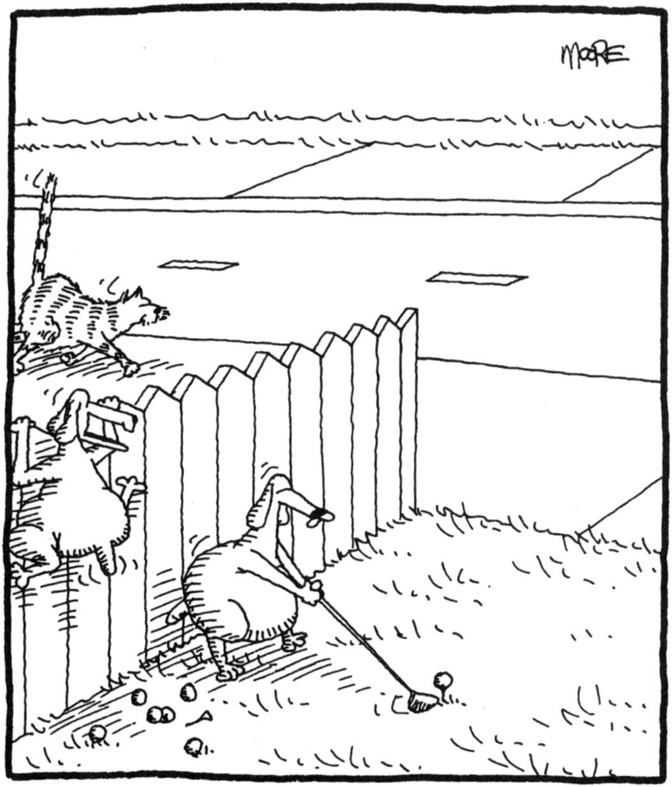
MOORE

"Ready... set..."

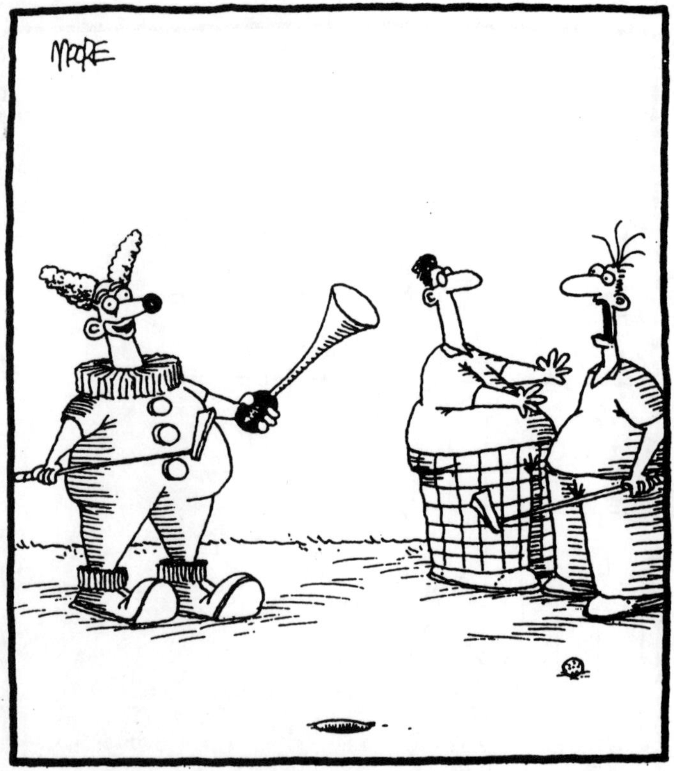
MOORE

"I *know* the horn is his only means of communication! Just tell him to quit talking when I'm trying to putt!!"

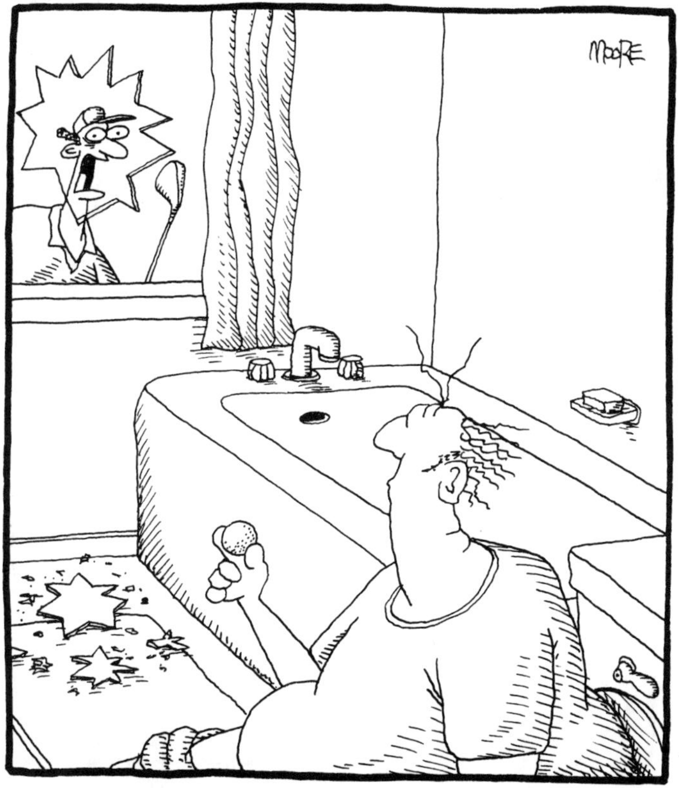
MOORE

"Top-Flite? Yeah, that's mine. Say, it must be nice living next to a golf course."

BEFORE
MOORE
AFTER*
*RESULTS MAY VARY

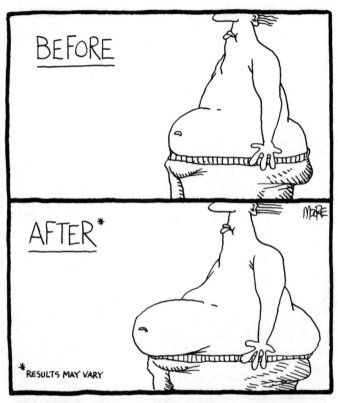

Play golf, and in just one month you will experience dramatic changes in fitness *or your money back*!!

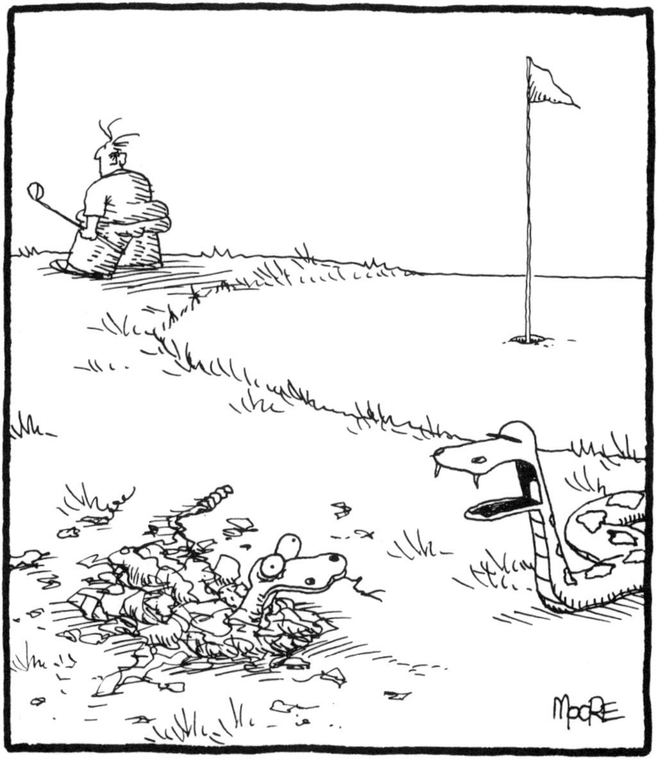
MOORE

"Live and learn, Sid. Never, ever coil and threaten to strike someone who's holding a golf club with a bubble shaft and oversize titanium head."

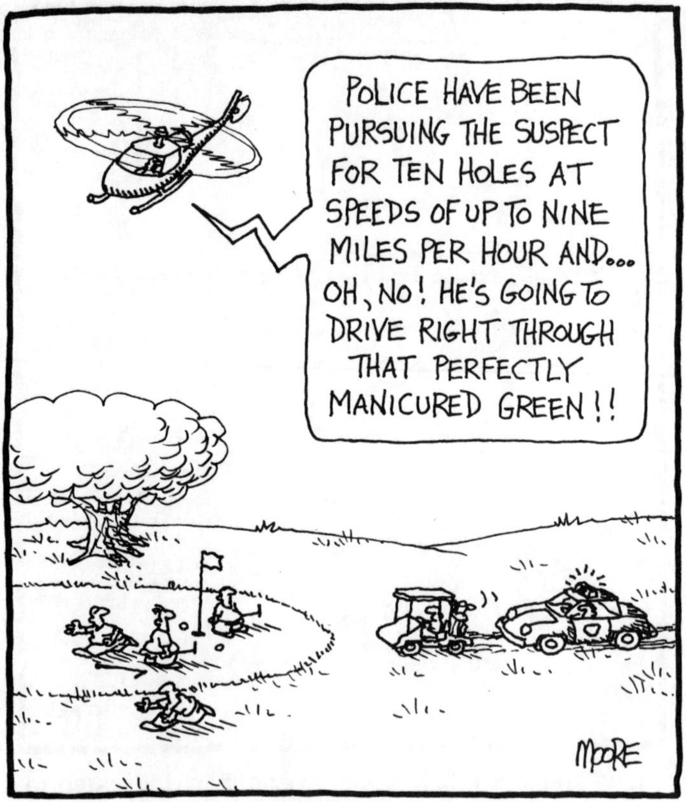
POLICE HAVE BEEN PURSUING THE SUSPECT FOR TEN HOLES AT SPEEDS OF UP TO NINE MILES PER HOUR AND... OH, NO! HE'S GOING TO DRIVE RIGHT THROUGH THAT PERFECTLY MANICURED GREEN!!
MOORE

World's Scariest Golf Cart Chases

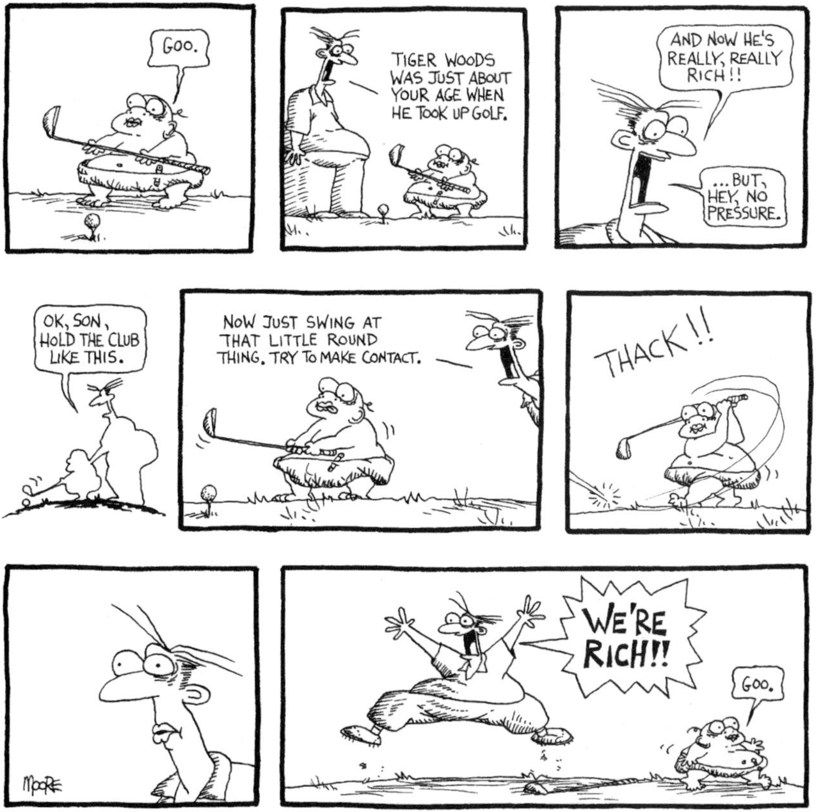
GOO.
TIGER WOODS WAS JUST ABOUT YOUR AGE WHEN HE TOOK UP GOLF.
AND NOW HE'S REALLY, REALLY RICH!!
...BUT, HEY, NO PRESSURE.
OK, SON, HOLD THE CLUB LIKE THIS.
NOW JUST SWING AT THAT LITTLE ROUND THING. TRY TO MAKE CONTACT.
THACK!!
MOORE
WE'RE RICH!!
GOO.

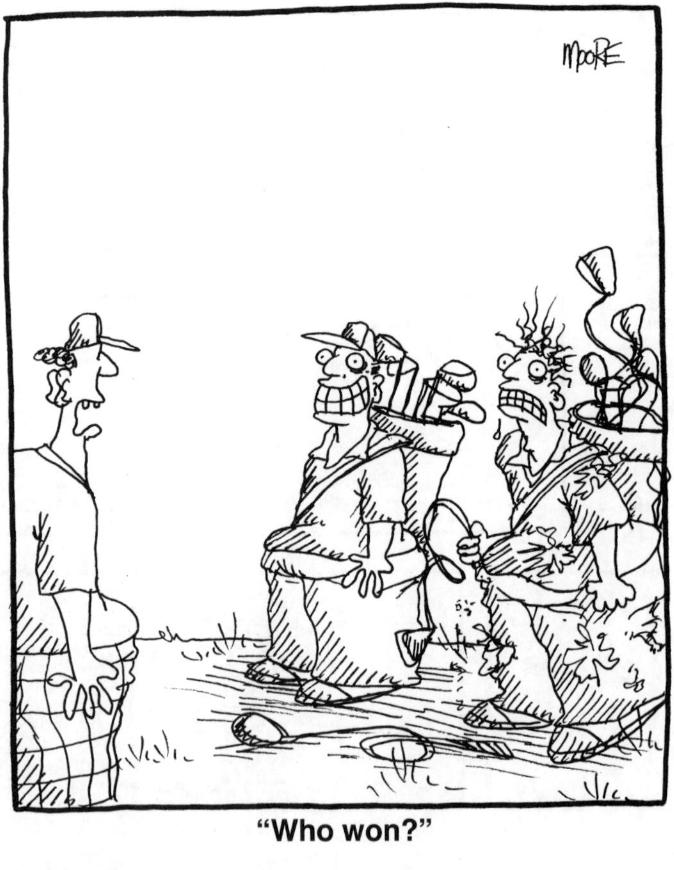
MOORE

"Who won?"

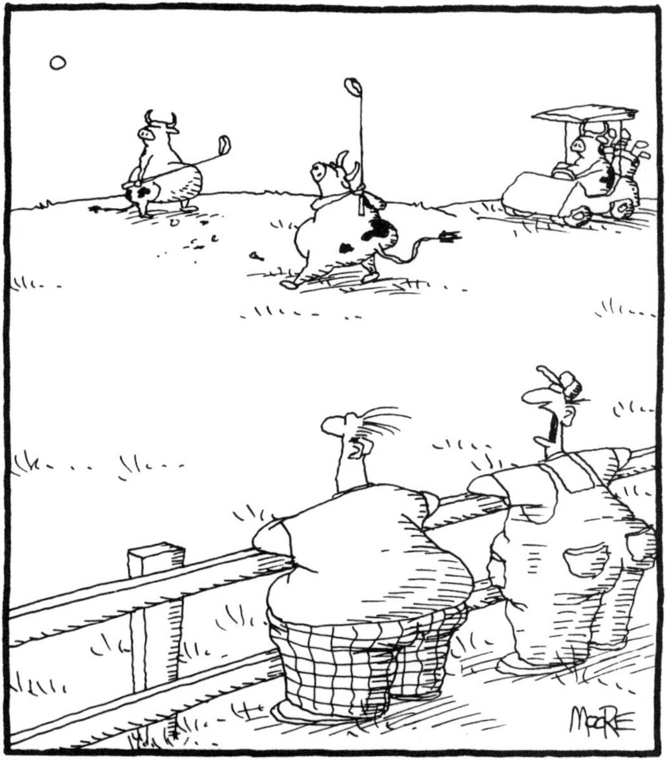
MOORE

"Shoot, yes. I encourage all my cattle to play golf. It fattens them up for the market."

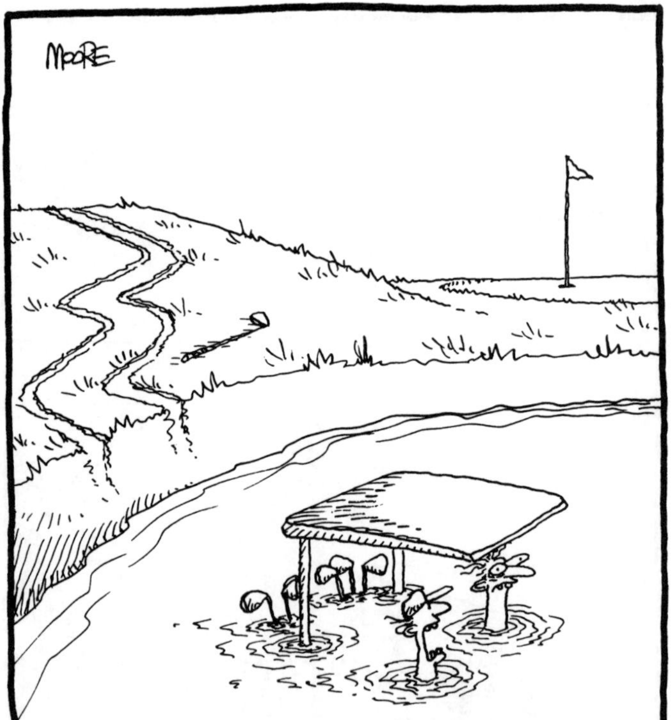
MOORE

"Step on pedal to go. Take foot off pedal to stop....
Golf carts are pretty simple machines, Lenny."

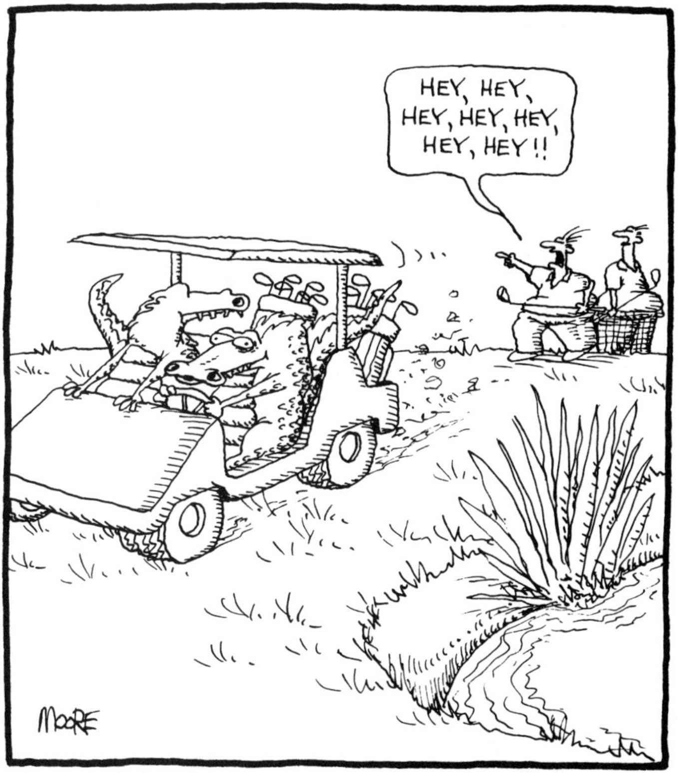
HEY, HEY,
HEY, HEY, HEY,
HEY, HEY!!
MOORE

The cart was later found stripped and abandoned in a bad part of the golf course.

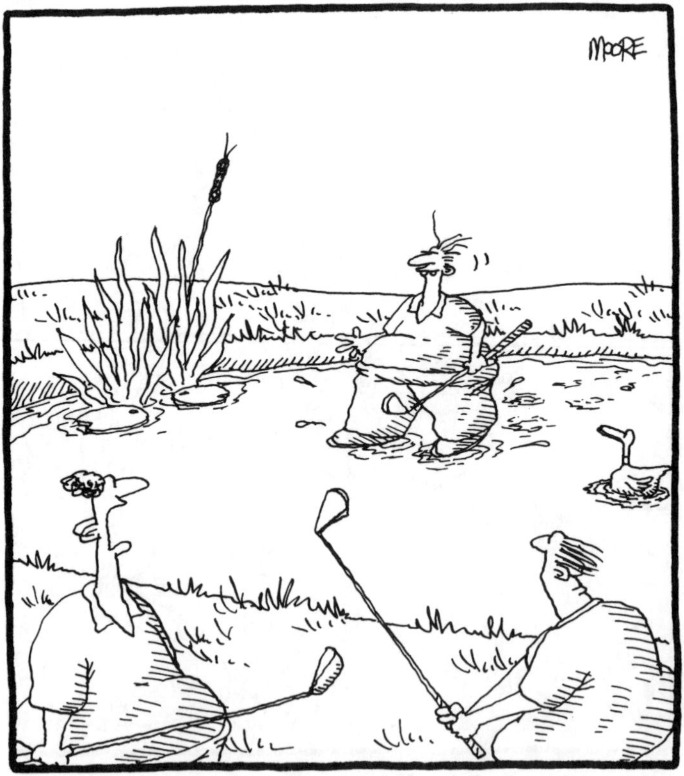
MOORE

"Well, well. Look who's here . . . God's gift to golf."

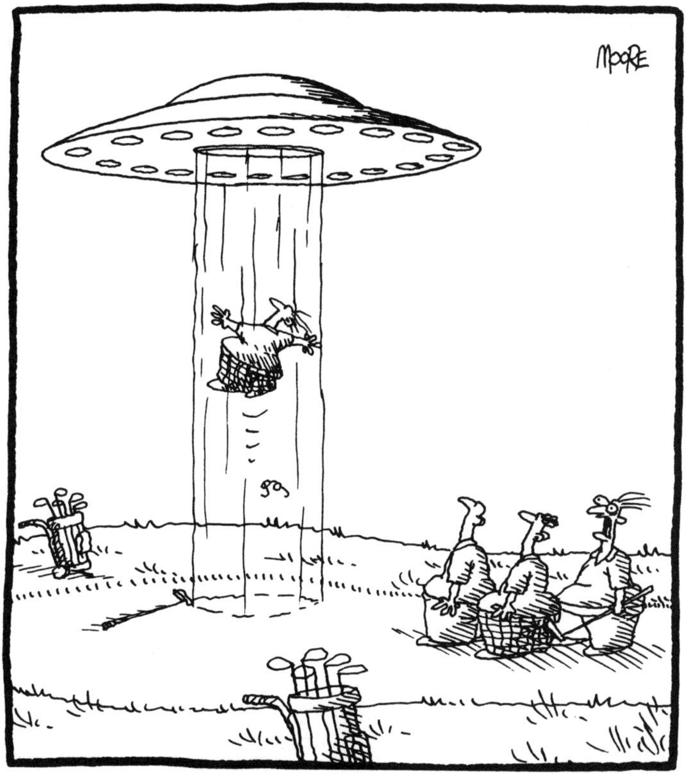
MOORE

"We saw nothing. Do you understand? Nothing! First of all, no one would believe us. Second, I've got dibs on his golf clubs."

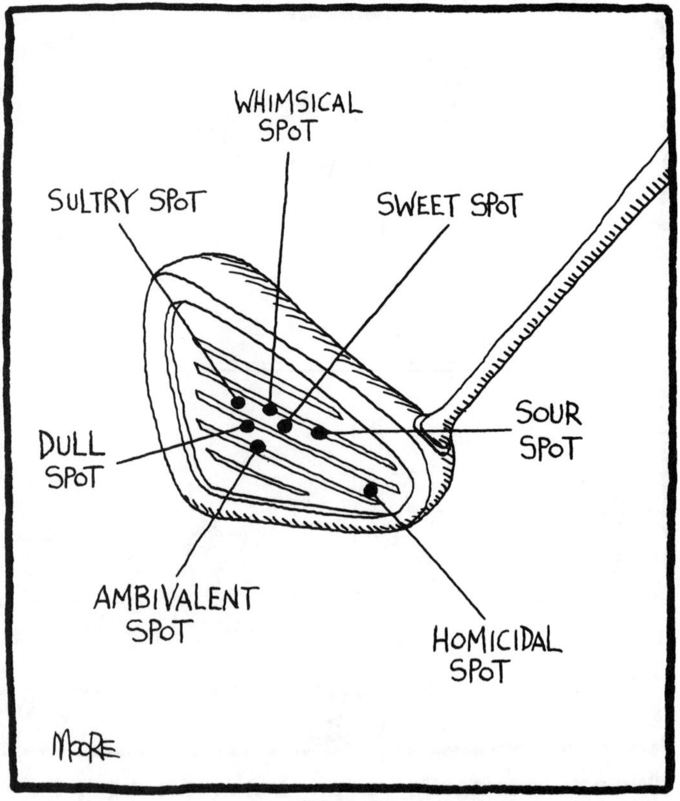
WHIMSICAL SPOT
SULTRY SPOT
SWEET SPOT
SOUR SPOT
DULL SPOT
AMBIVALENT SPOT
HOMICIDAL SPOT
MOORE

The mood spots of a golf club

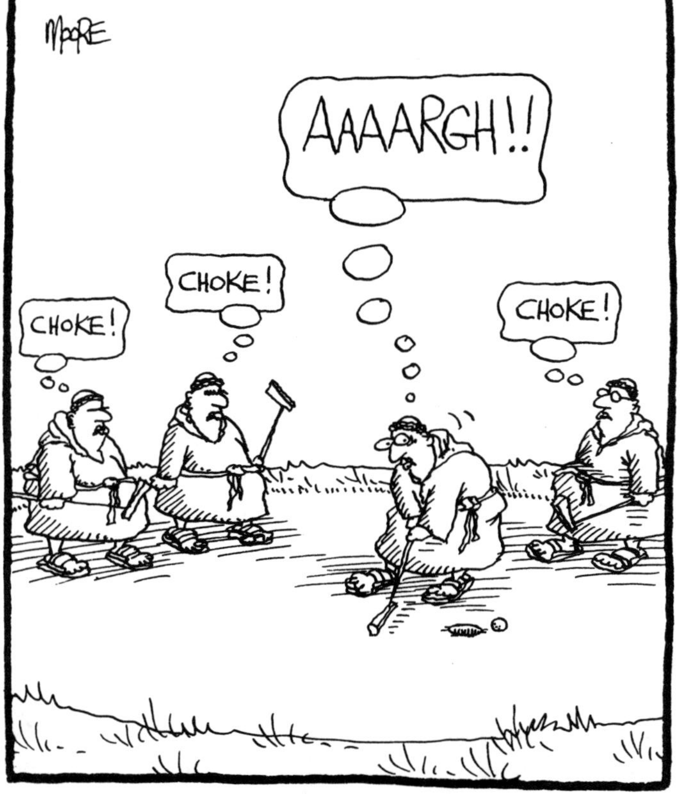
MOORE
AAAARGH!!
CHOKE!
CHOKE!
CHOKE!

Trappist monks in golf

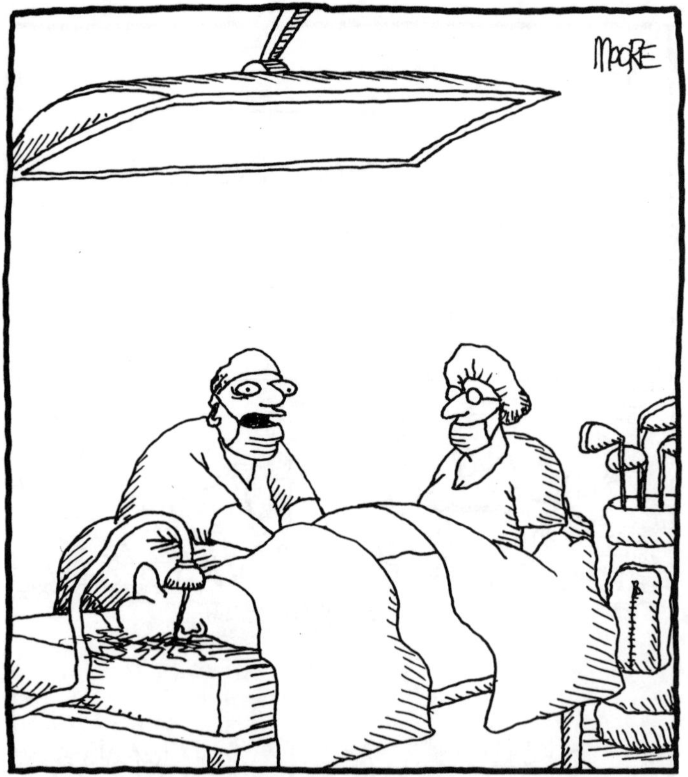
MOORE

“There it is next to the spleen. It’s about the size of a golf ball. . . . Well, this should be kind of fun. Hand me the 9-iron.”

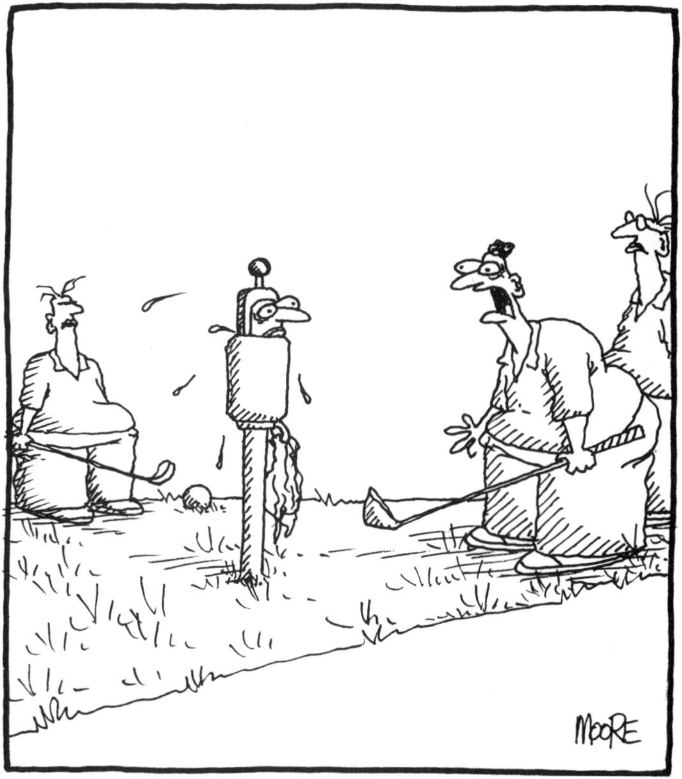
MOORE

"Craig, come out! You're embarrassing us! Those washers are just for golf balls!"

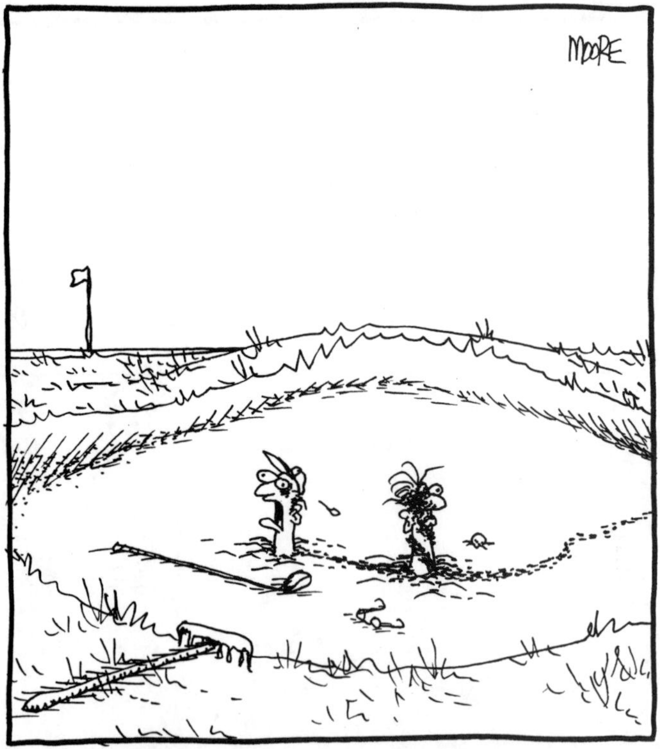
MOORE

"Buried up to our necks in a sand trap and abandoned by our so-called golf buddies. . . . Well, it could be worse, Bob. There could be ants."

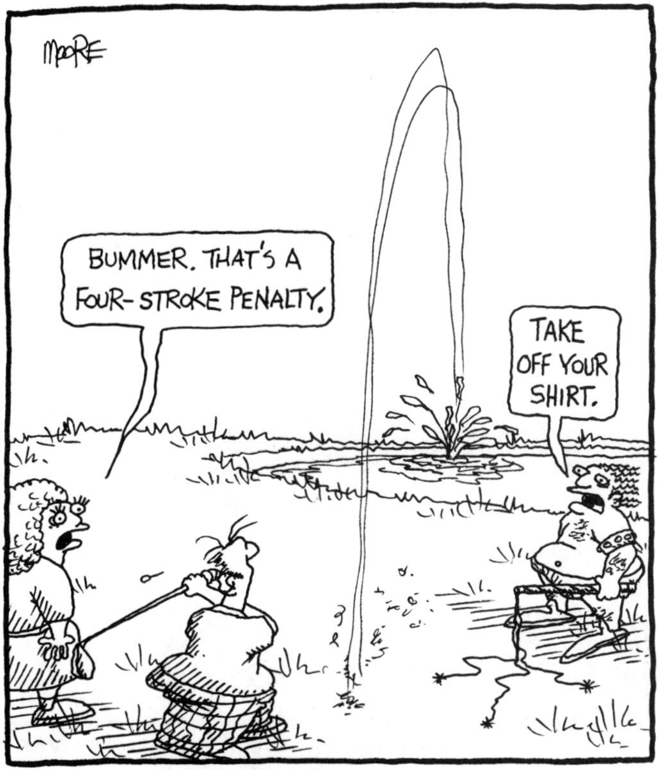
MOORE
BUMMER. THAT'S A FOUR-STROKE PENALTY.
TAKE OFF YOUR SHIRT.

The Corporal Punishment Golf and Country Club

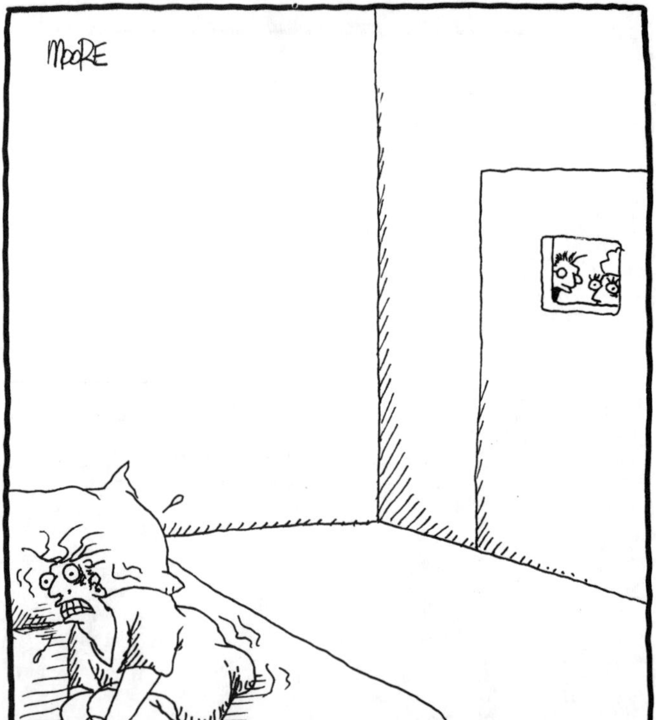
MOORE

"I know it's hard, ma'am, but the worst is over. The vomiting and severe shakes are nearly gone, and soon your husband's body will no longer crave golf."

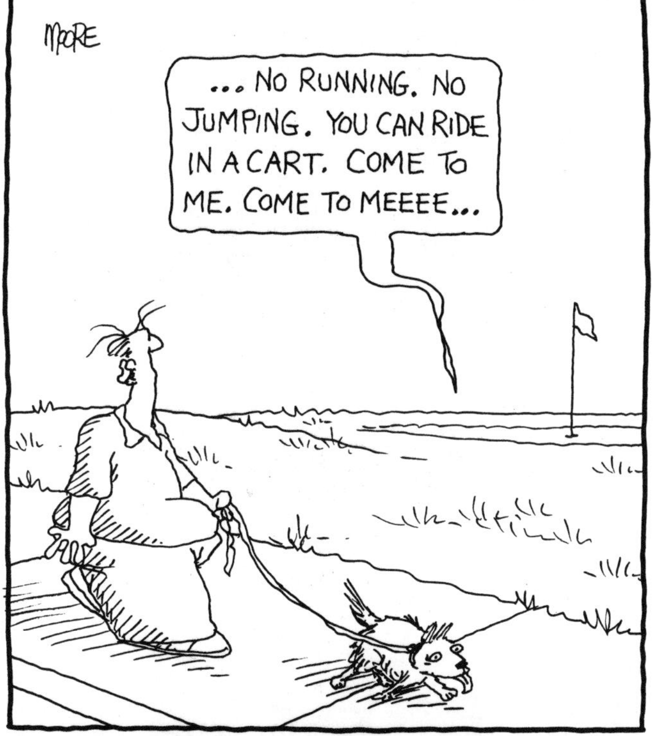
MOORE
... NO RUNNING. NO JUMPING. YOU CAN RIDE IN A CART. COME TO ME. COME TO MEEEE...

With his football, basketball, and baseball days a fading memory, another middle-aged man is seduced by the game of golf.

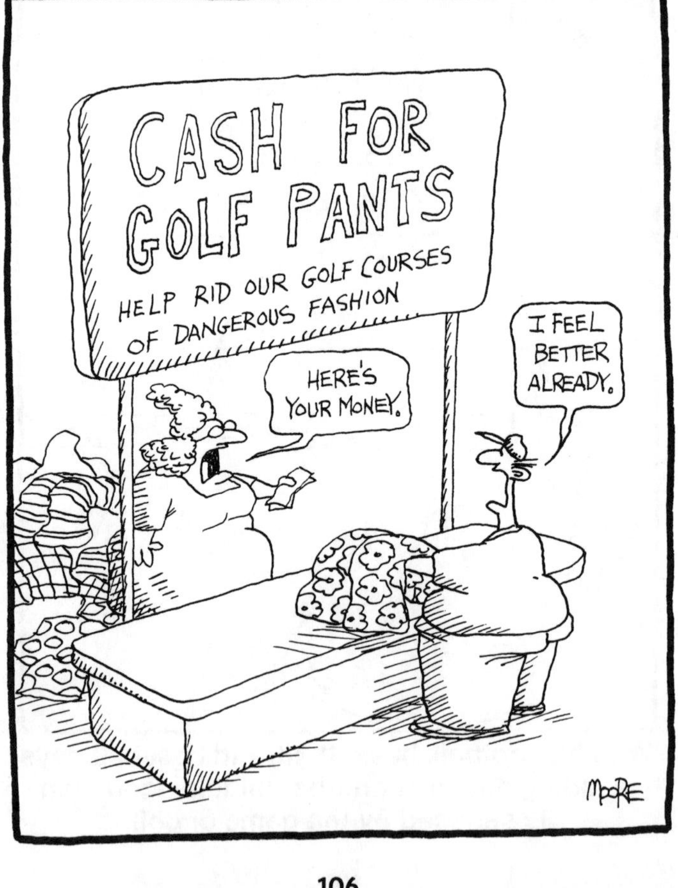
CASH FOR GOLF PANTS
HELP RID OUR GOLF COURSES OF DANGEROUS FASHION
HERE'S YOUR MONEY.
I FEEL BETTER ALREADY.
MOORE

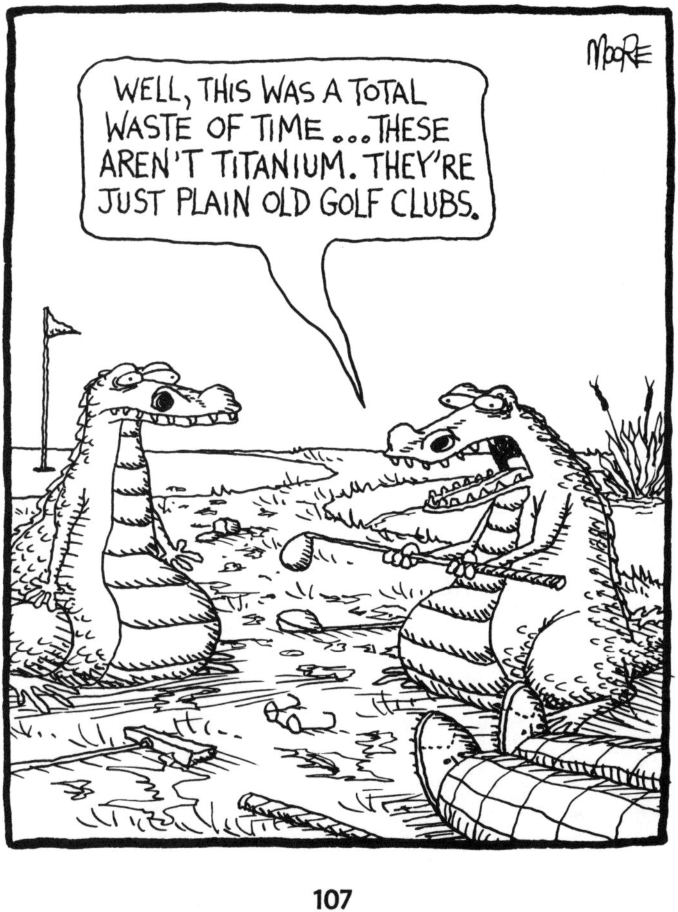
MOORE
WELL, THIS WAS A TOTAL WASTE OF TIME...THESE AREN'T TITANIUM. THEY'RE JUST PLAIN OLD GOLF CLUBS.

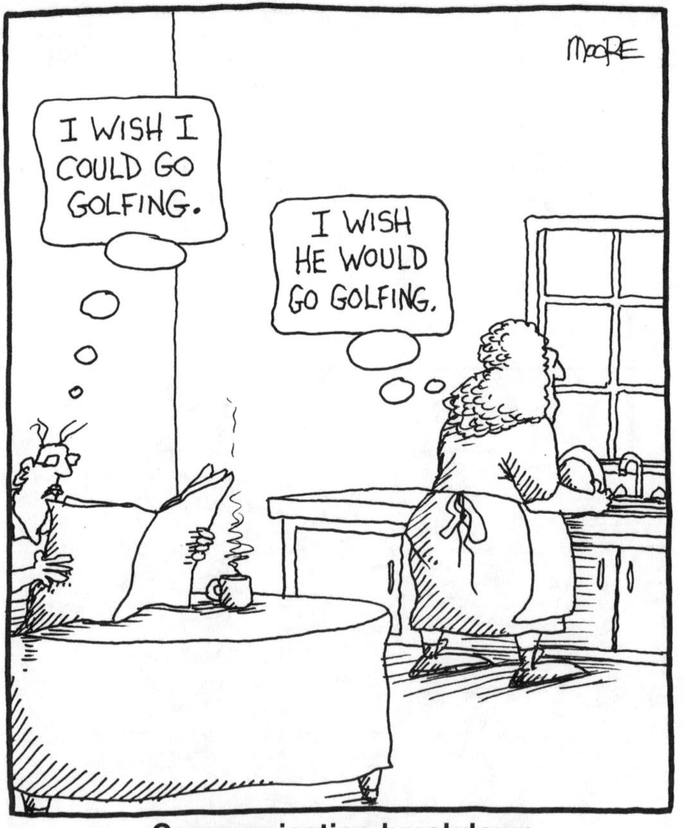
MOORE
I WISH I COULD GO GOLFING.
I WISH HE WOULD GO GOLFING.

Communication breakdown

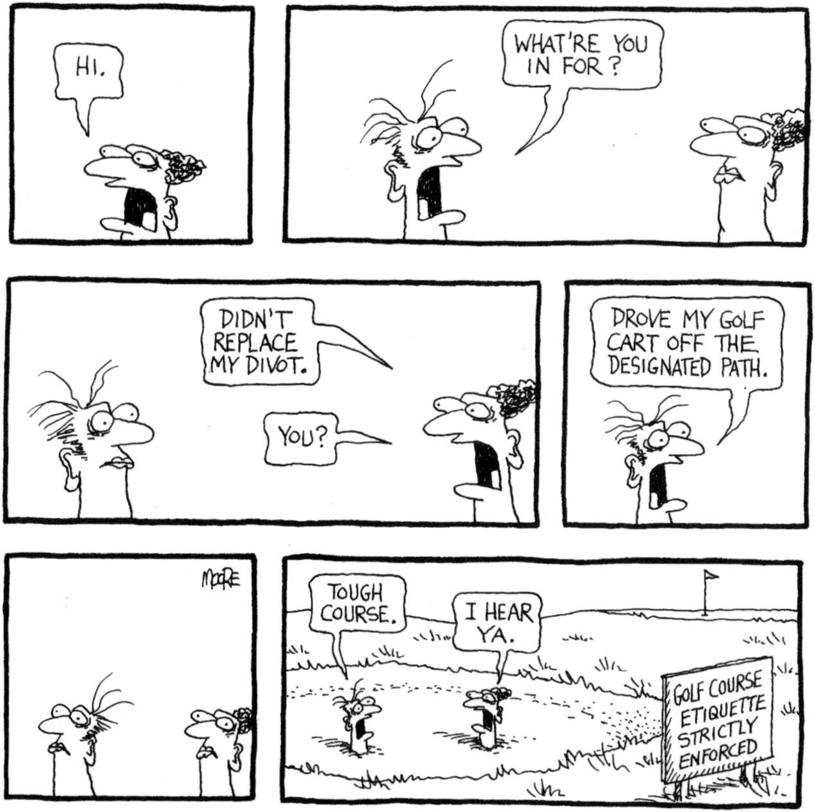
HI.
WHAT'RE YOU IN FOR?
DIDN'T REPLACE MY DIVOT.
YOU?
DROVE MY GOLF CART OFF THE DESIGNATED PATH.
MOORE
TOUGH COURSE.
I HEAR YA.
GOLF COURSE ETIQUETTE STRICTLY ENFORCED

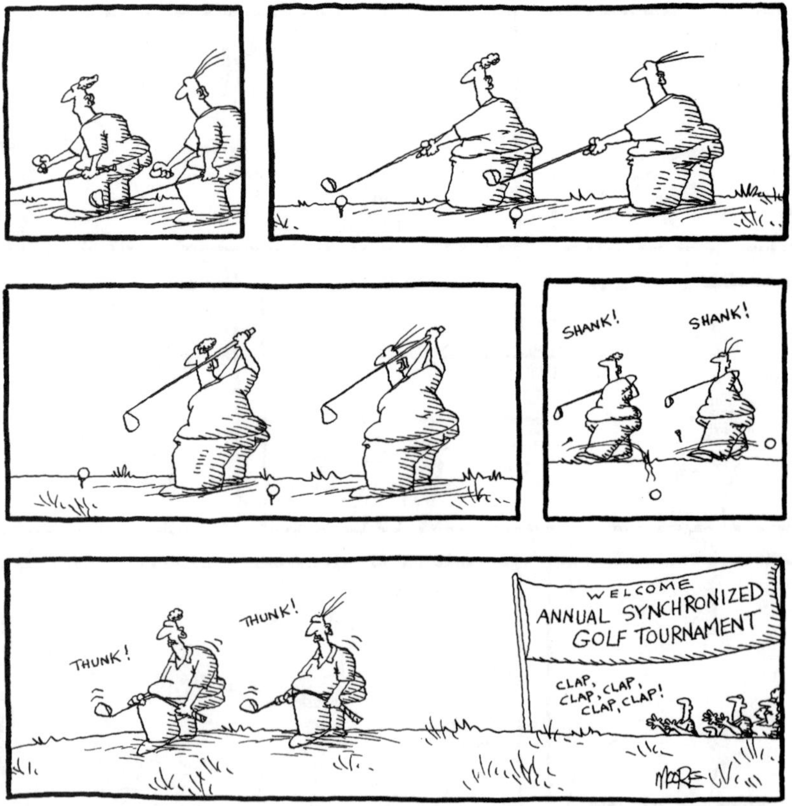
SHANK!
SHANK!
THUNK!
THUNK!
WELCOME
ANNUAL SYNCHRONIZED
GOLF TOURNAMENT
CLAP, CLAP, CLAP, CLAP, CLAP!
MOORE

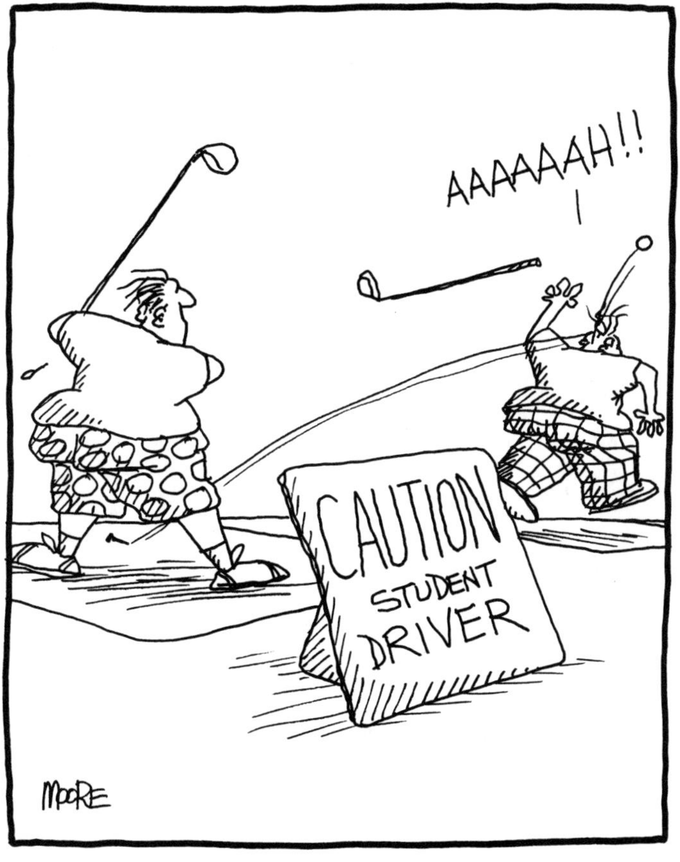
AAAAAAH!!
CAUTION
STUDENT
DRIVER
MOORE

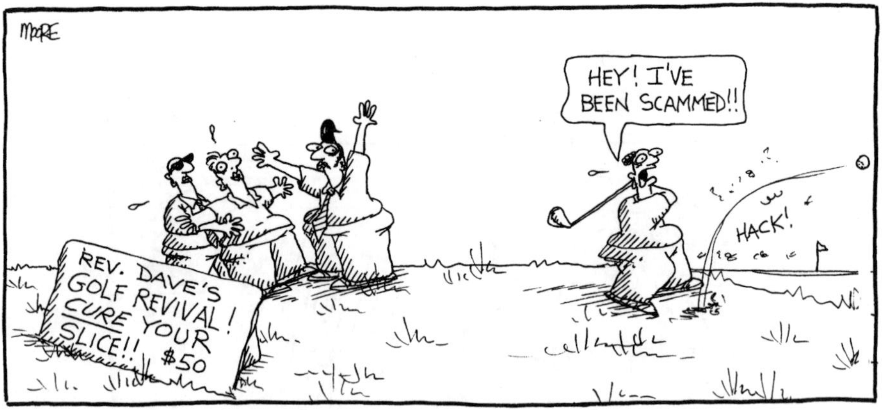
MOORE
HEY! I'VE BEEN SCAMMED!!
HACK!
REV. DAVE'S GOLF REVIVAL! CURE YOUR SLICE!! $50

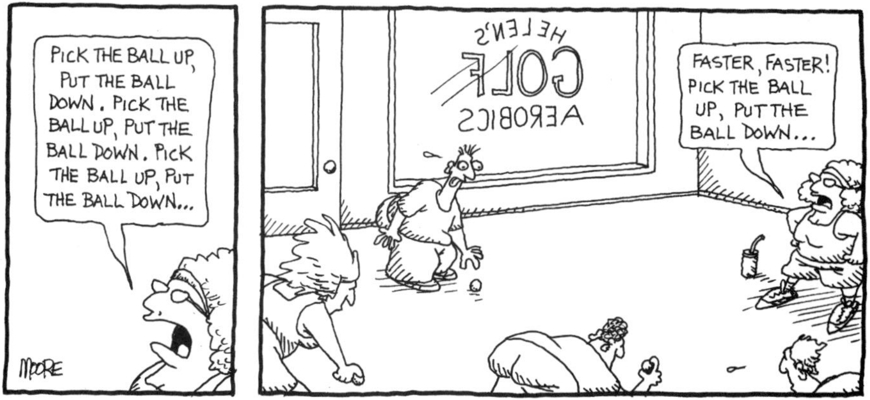
PICK THE BALL UP, PUT THE BALL DOWN. PICK THE BALL UP, PUT THE BALL DOWN. PICK THE BALL UP, PUT THE BALL DOWN...
MOORE
HELEN'S GOLF AEROBICS
FASTER, FASTER! PICK THE BALL UP, PUT THE BALL DOWN...

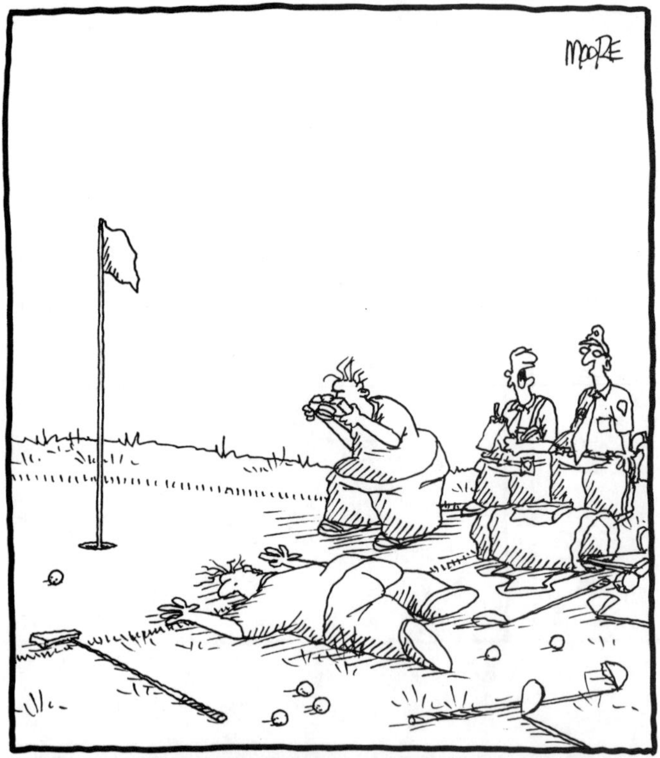
MOORE

"We won't know, Cooper, until forensic tests are complete. So quit making wild speculations that he was struck by some kind of metallic, club-like object."

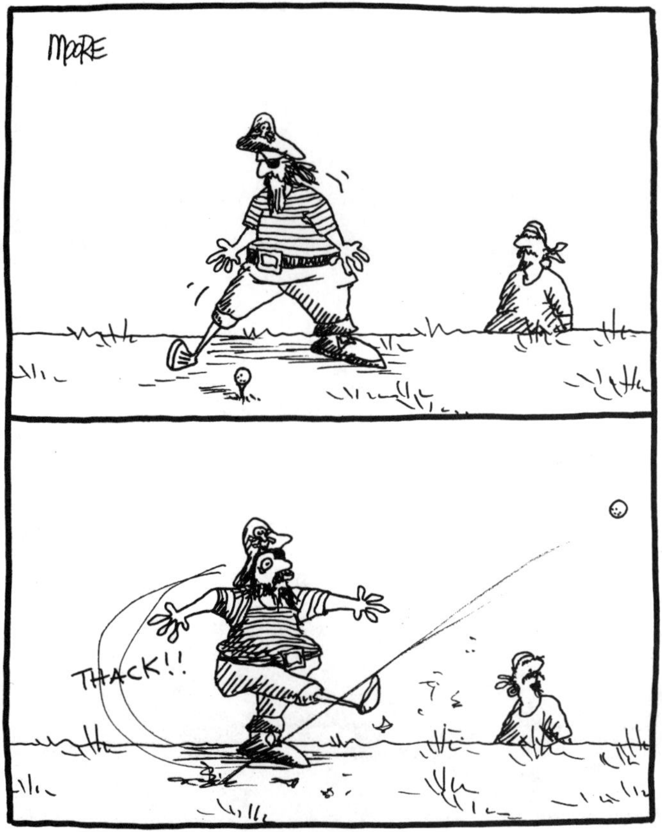
MOORE
THACK!!

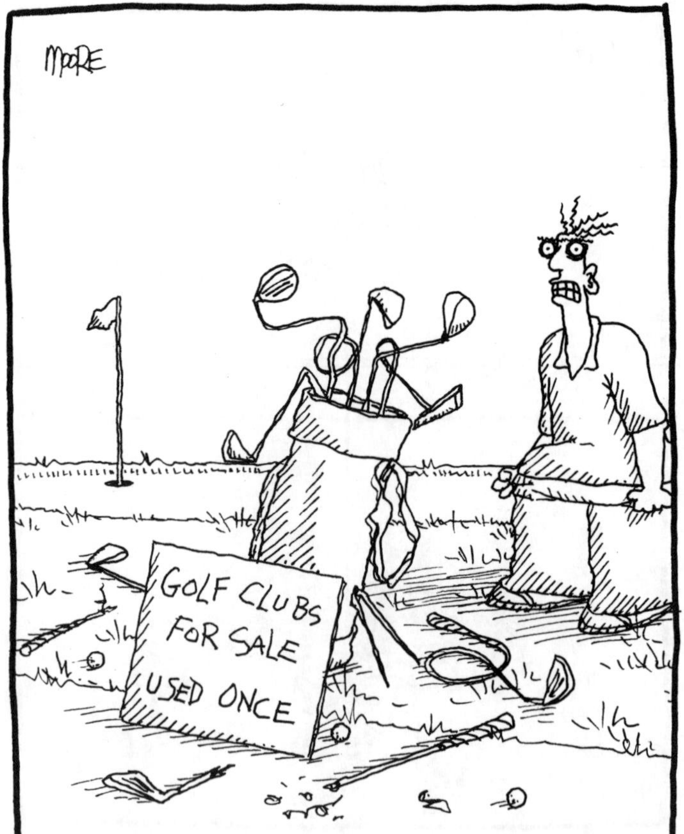
MOORE
GOLF CLUBS
FOR SALE
USED ONCE

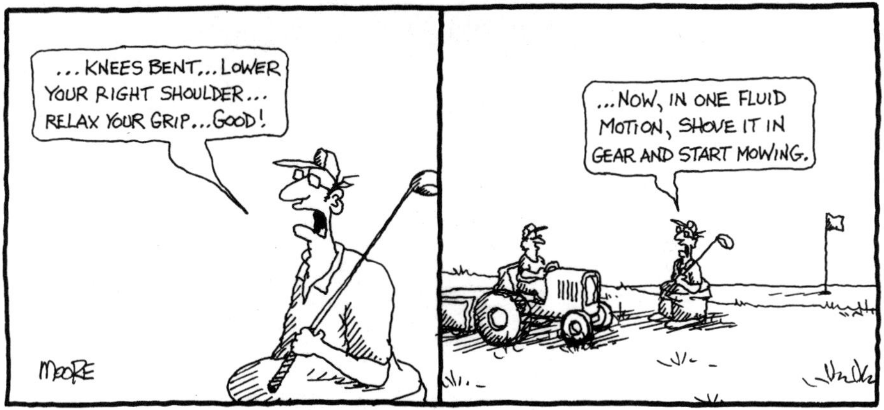
...KNEES BENT,...LOWER YOUR RIGHT SHOULDER... RELAX YOUR GRIP...GOOD!
MOORE
...NOW, IN ONE FLUID MOTION, SHOVE IT IN GEAR AND START MOWING.

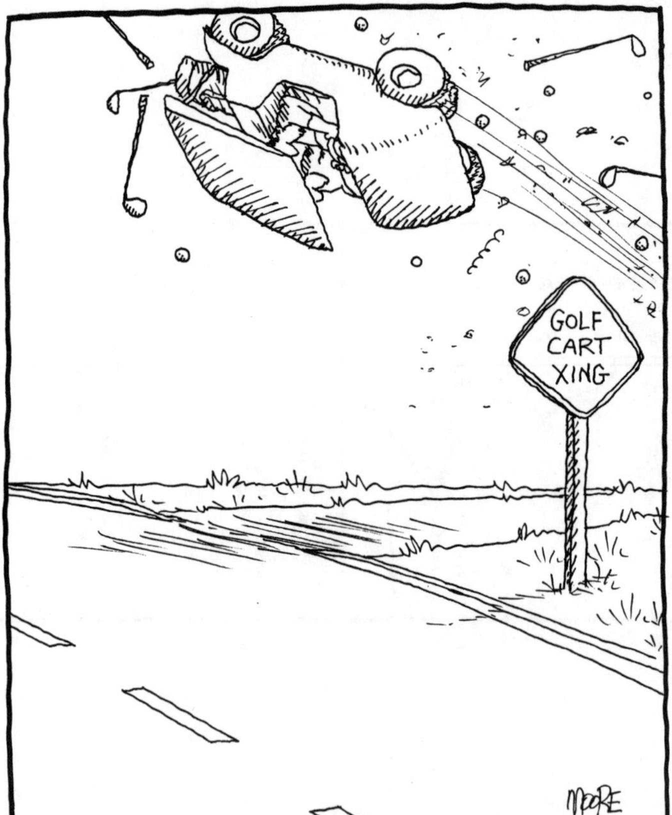
GOLF
CART
XING
MOORE

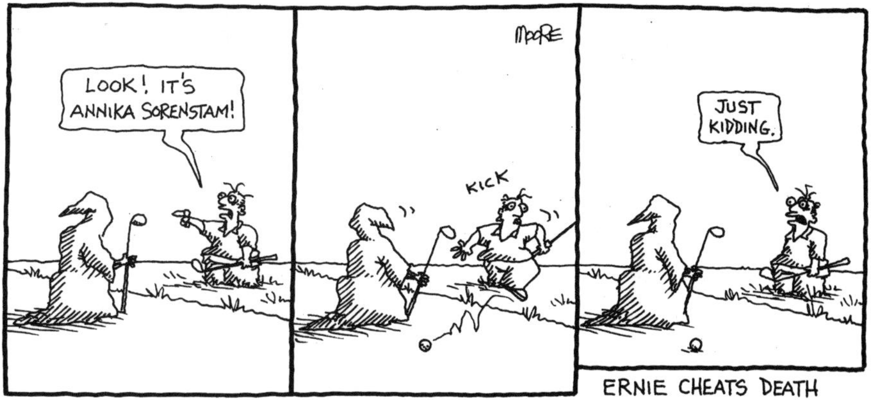
LOOK! IT'S ANNIKA SORENSTAM!
KICK
MOORE
JUST KIDDING.

ERNIE CHEATS DEATH

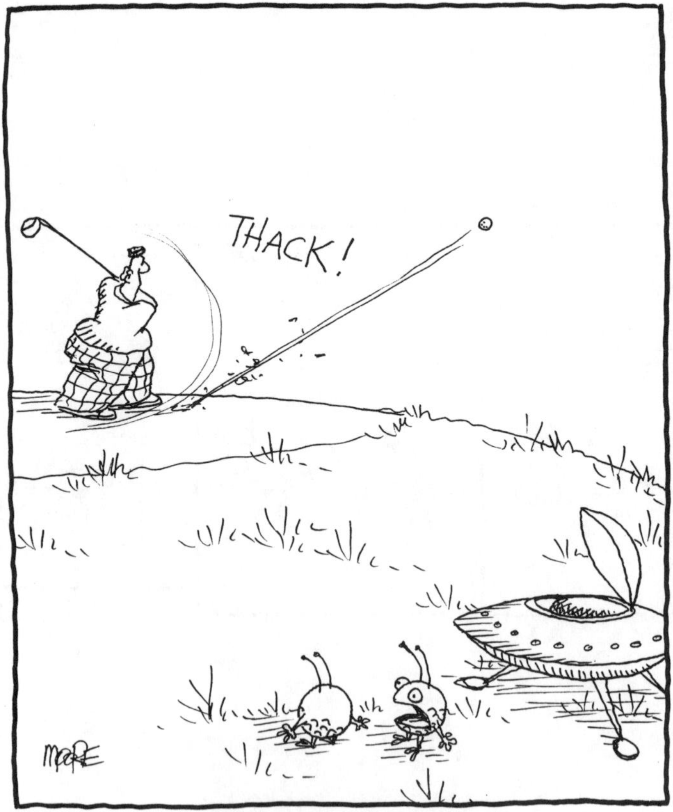
THACK!
MOORE
"Let's get out of here!"

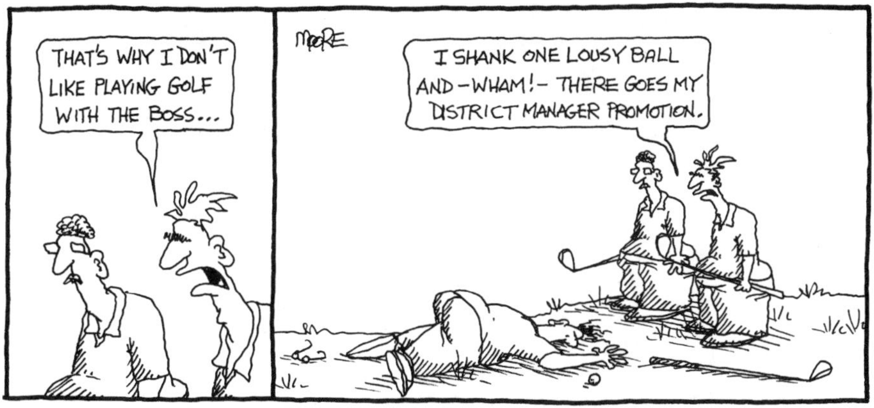
THAT'S WHY I DON'T LIKE PLAYING GOLF WITH THE BOSS...
MOORE
I SHANK ONE LOUSY BALL AND -WHAM!- THERE GOES MY DISTRICT MANAGER PROMOTION.

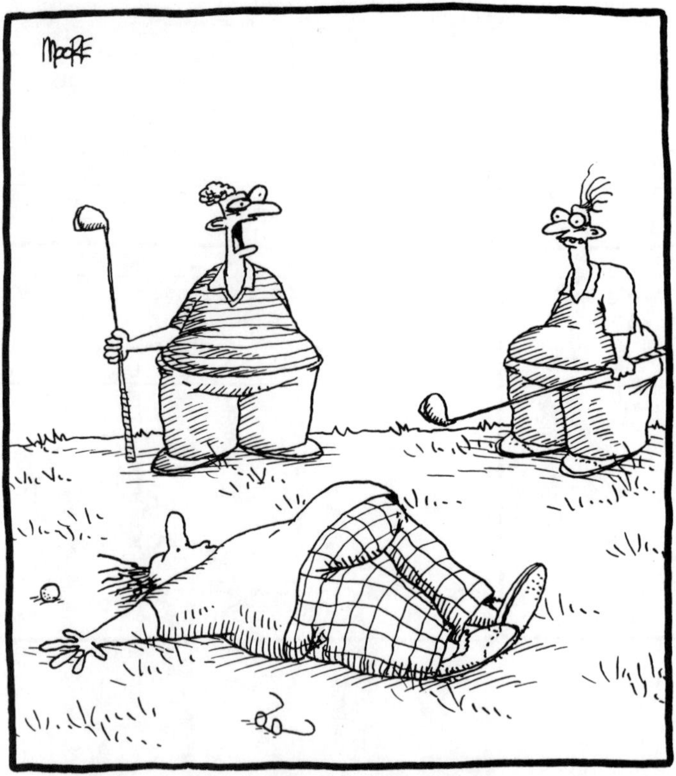
MOORE

"'Heads up'? No one responds to 'heads up' on a golf course, Leonard! The proper term is 'fore.' I'm so embarrassed for you, Leonard."

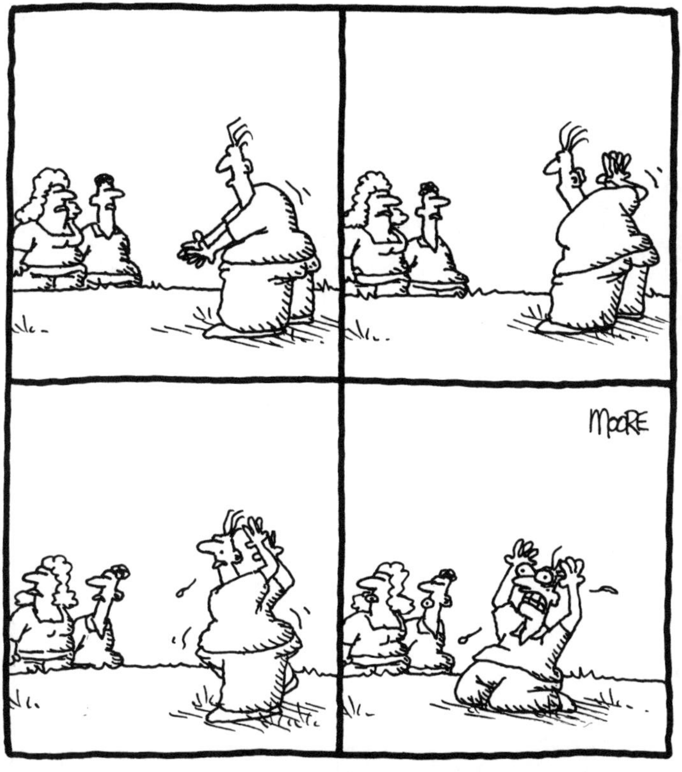
MOORE

Frank hits an imaginary drive into a bunker and falls two strokes behind in the U.S. Open Air Golf Championship.

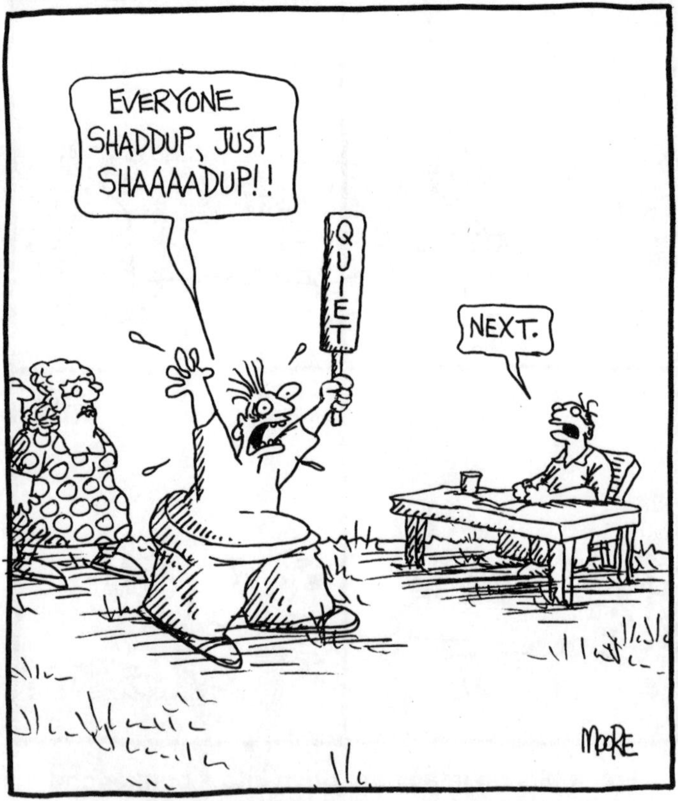
EVERYONE SHADDUP, JUST SHAAAADUP!!
QUIET
NEXT.
MOORE

Golf tournament marshal tryouts

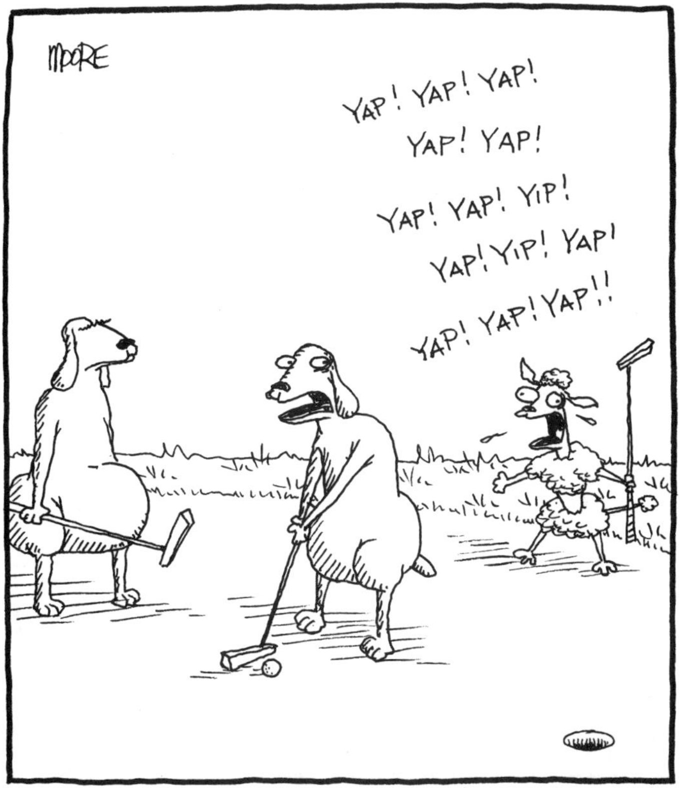
MOORE
YAP! YAP! YAP!
YAP! YAP!
YAP! YAP! YIP!
YAP! YIP! YAP!
YAP! YAP! YAP!!

"This is the last time I play golf with a small, high-strung breed."

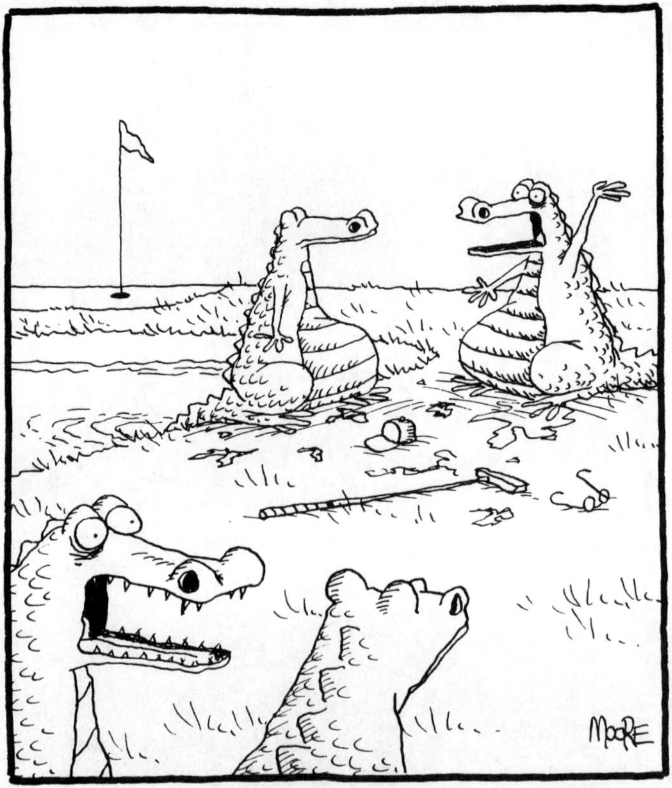
MOORE

"Every time he tells that story, the golfer grows a little bigger."

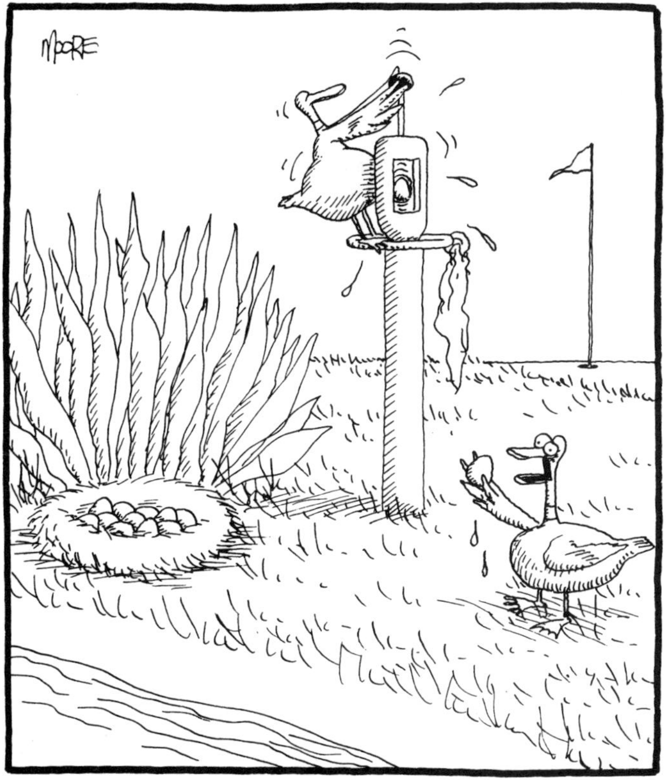
MOORE

"Wow. Squeaky clean."

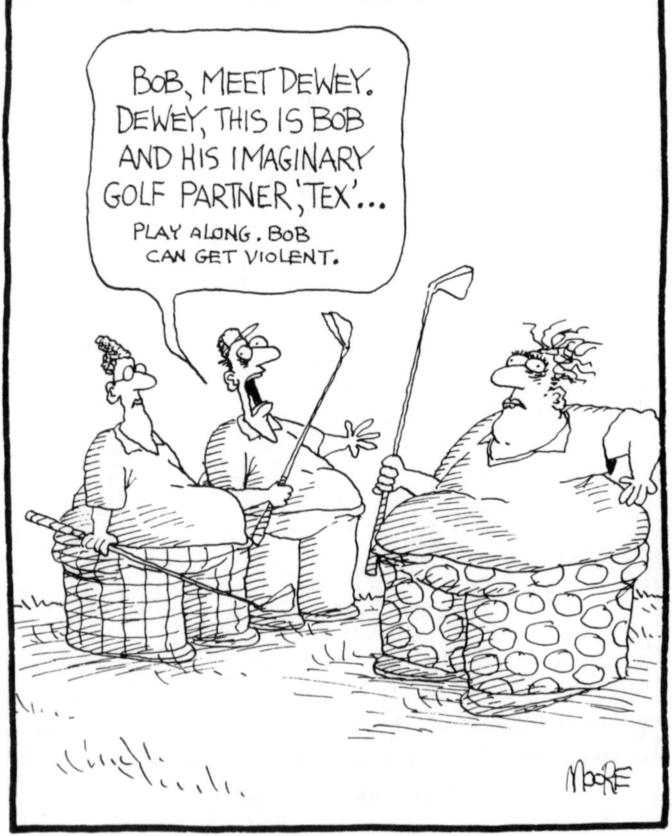
BOB, MEET DEWEY. DEWEY, THIS IS BOB AND HIS IMAGINARY GOLF PARTNER, 'TEX'... PLAY ALONG. BOB CAN GET VIOLENT.
MOORE

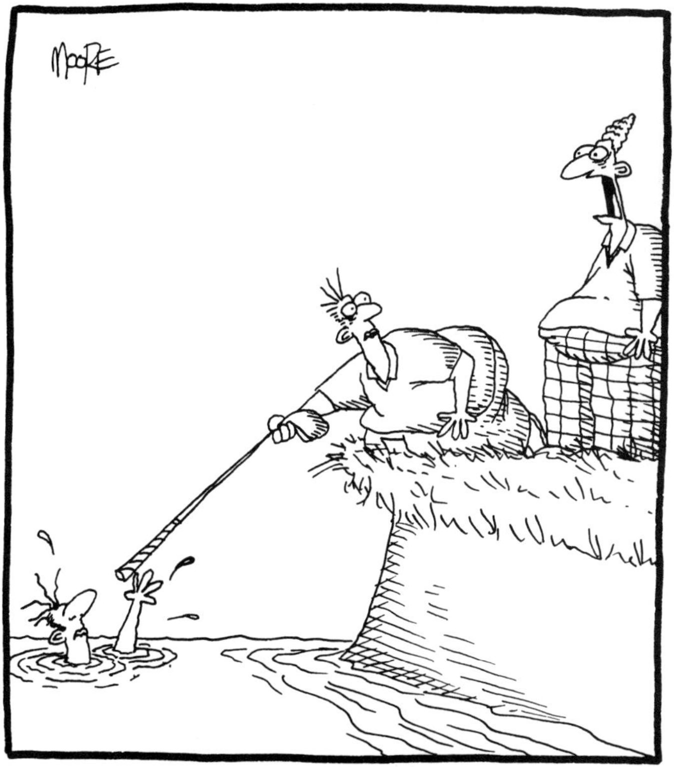
MOORE

"Don't be a fool, Dewey! Put that 9-iron back in your bag. . . . You want to use a wedge in a situation like this."

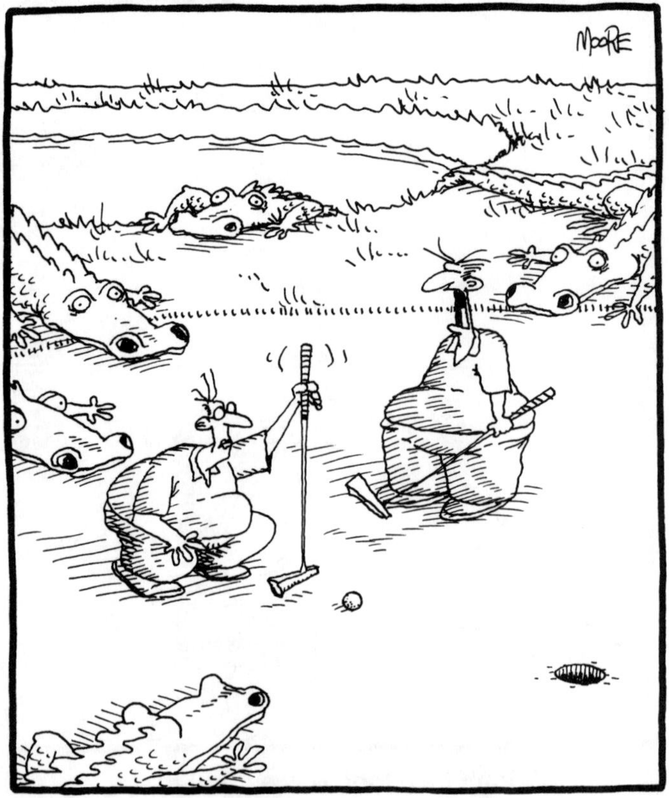
MOORE

"Putt the stinkin' ball already!"

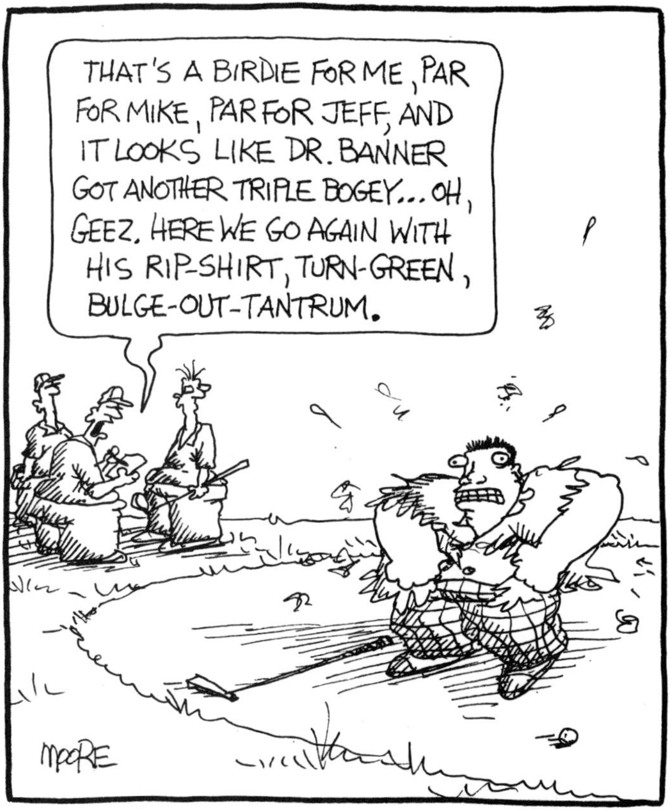
THAT'S A BIRDIE FOR ME, PAR FOR MIKE, PAR FOR JEFF, AND IT LOOKS LIKE DR. BANNER GOT ANOTHER TRIPLE BOGEY... OH, GEEZ. HERE WE GO AGAIN WITH HIS RIP-SHIRT, TURN-GREEN, BULGE-OUT-TANTRUM.
MOORE

Golfing with the Incredible Hulk

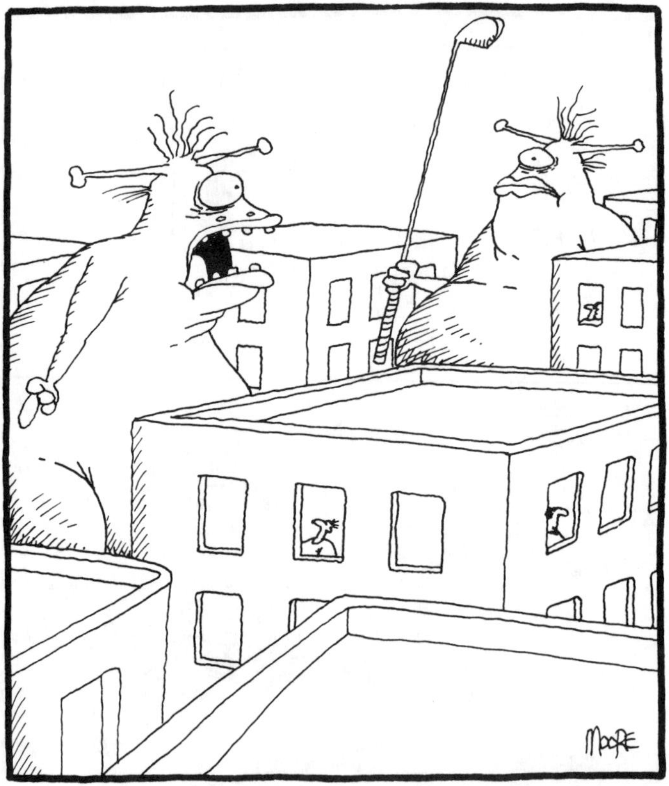
MOORE

"Here's your ball, Larry. You gonna try to hit it out of the city or take a penalty stroke?

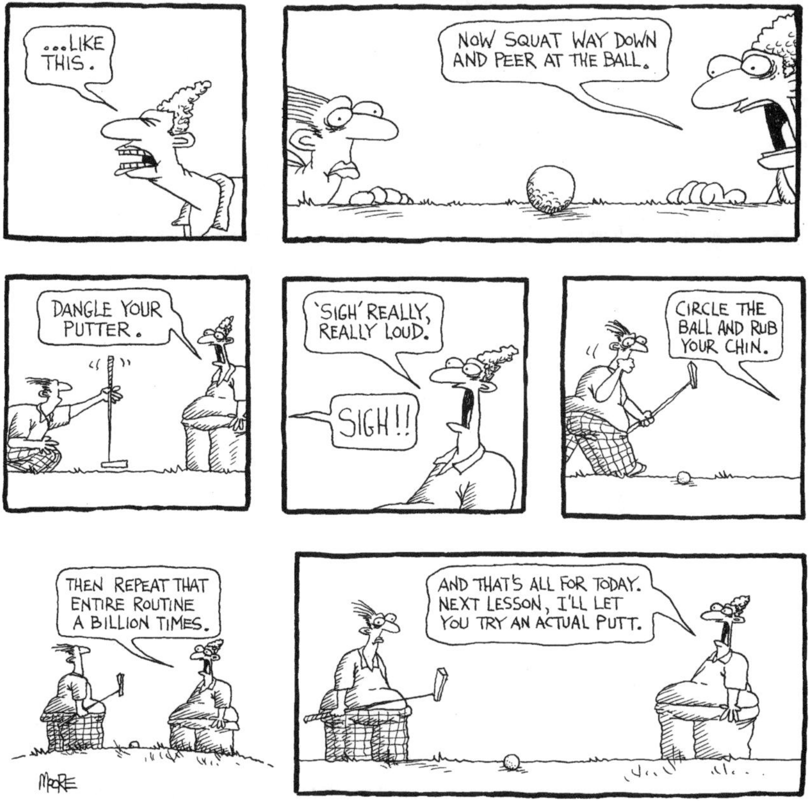
...LIKE THIS.
NOW SQUAT WAY DOWN AND PEER AT THE BALL.
DANGLE YOUR PUTTER.
'SIGH' REALLY, REALLY LOUD.
SIGH!!
CIRCLE THE BALL AND RUB YOUR CHIN.
THEN REPEAT THAT ENTIRE ROUTINE A BILLION TIMES.
MOORE
AND THAT'S ALL FOR TODAY. NEXT LESSON, I'LL LET YOU TRY AN ACTUAL PUTT.

WE'RE SAVED!!
I SEE SOMEONE! QUICK, GIVE ME THE FLARE GUN!!
BOONT!!
WELL, WE'RE DOOMED. THEY DIDN'T SEE US, AND THAT WAS OUR LAST FLARE.
MOORE

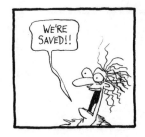

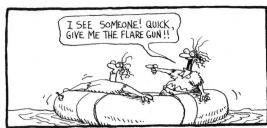

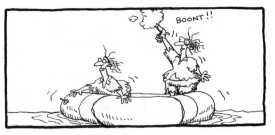

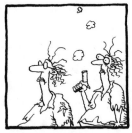

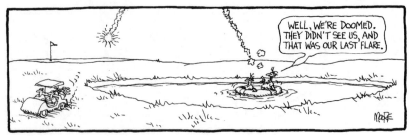

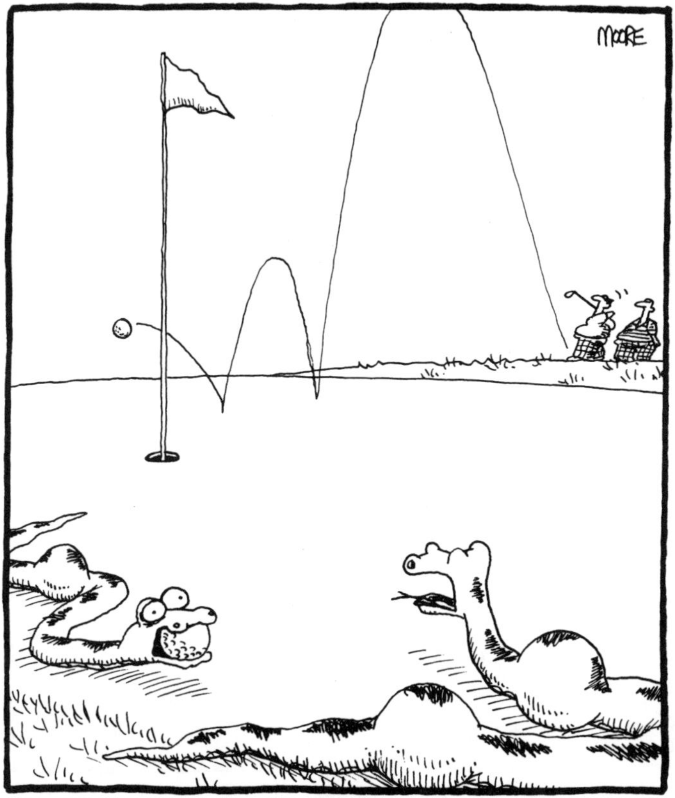
MOORE

"There's another one!"

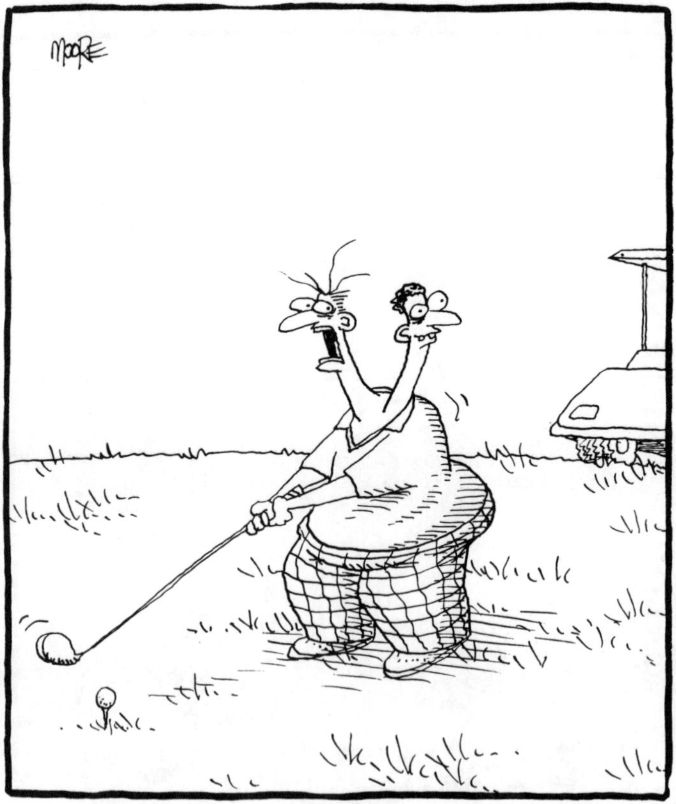
MOORE

"Keep your eyes on the ball! Criminy, do you want me to teach you this game or not?"

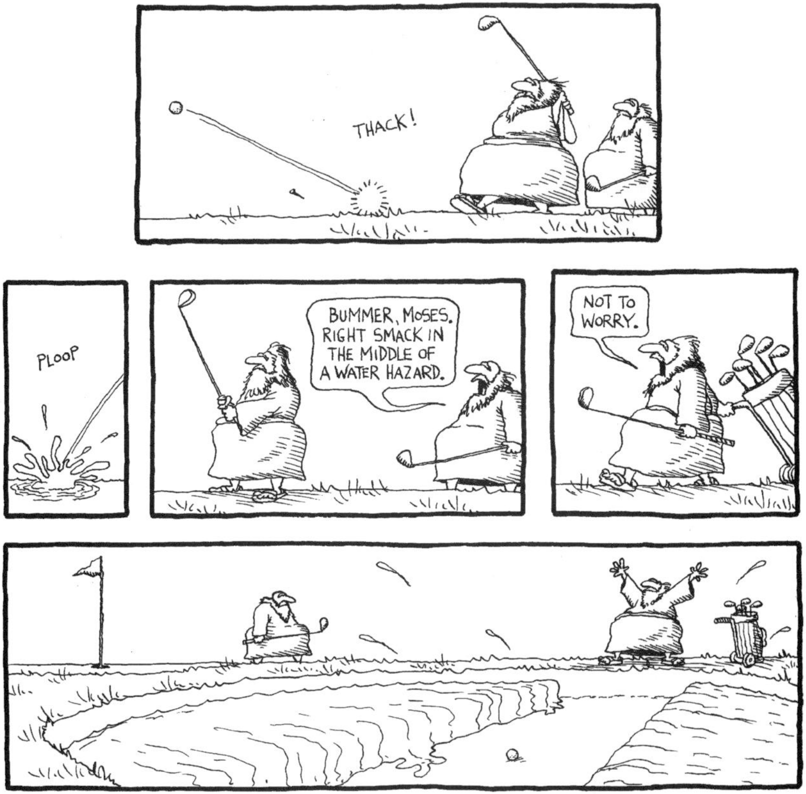
THACK!
PLOOP
BUMMER, MOSES. RIGHT SMACK IN THE MIDDLE OF A WATER HAZARD.
NOT TO WORRY.

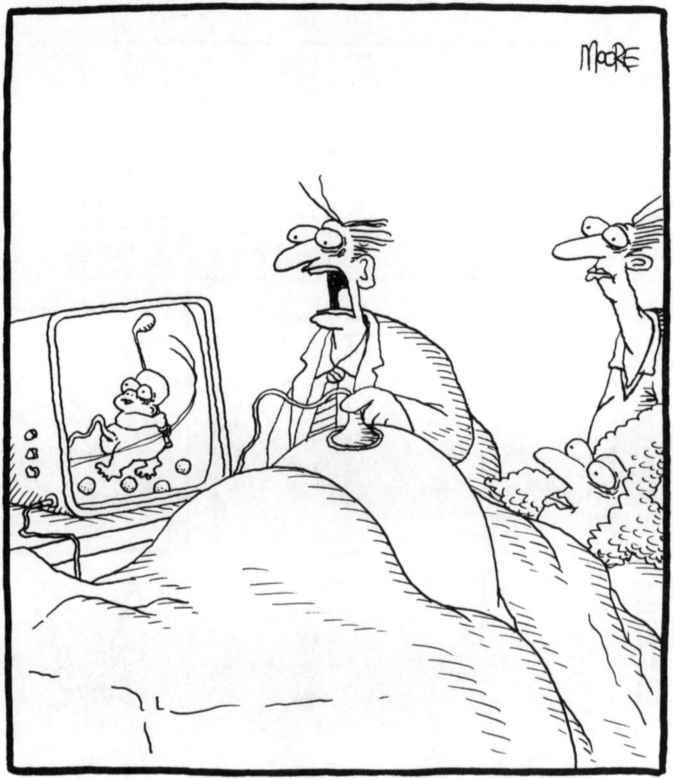
MOORE

"From this angle, it's hard to say if it's a boy or a girl... either way, you and your husband should consider hiring a good agent."

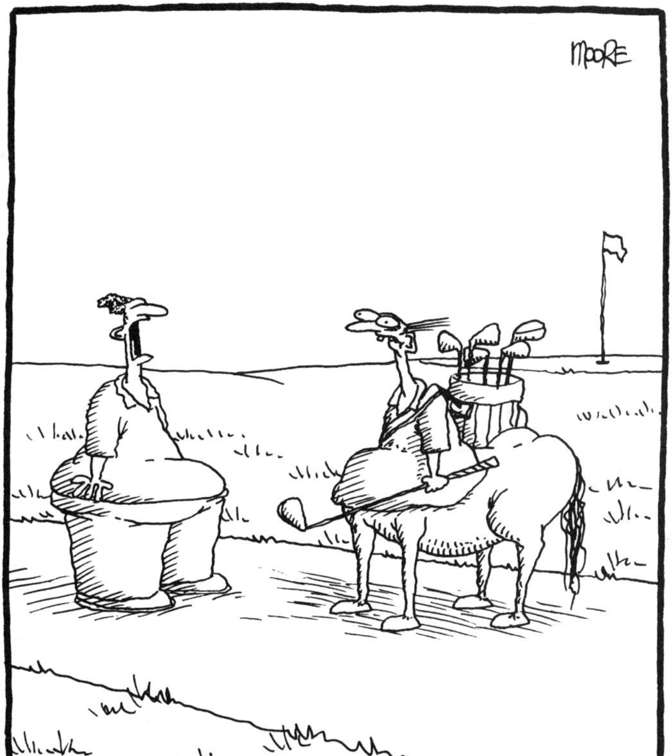
MOORE

"Sorry, club rules . . . no hooves."

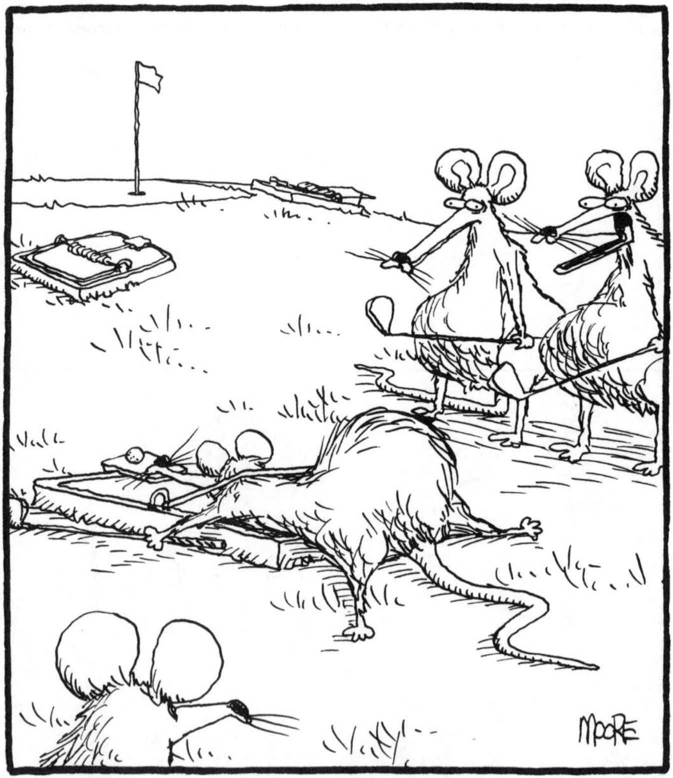
MOORE

"OK, from now on, if anyone's ball lands in a trap, just take the penalty strokes."

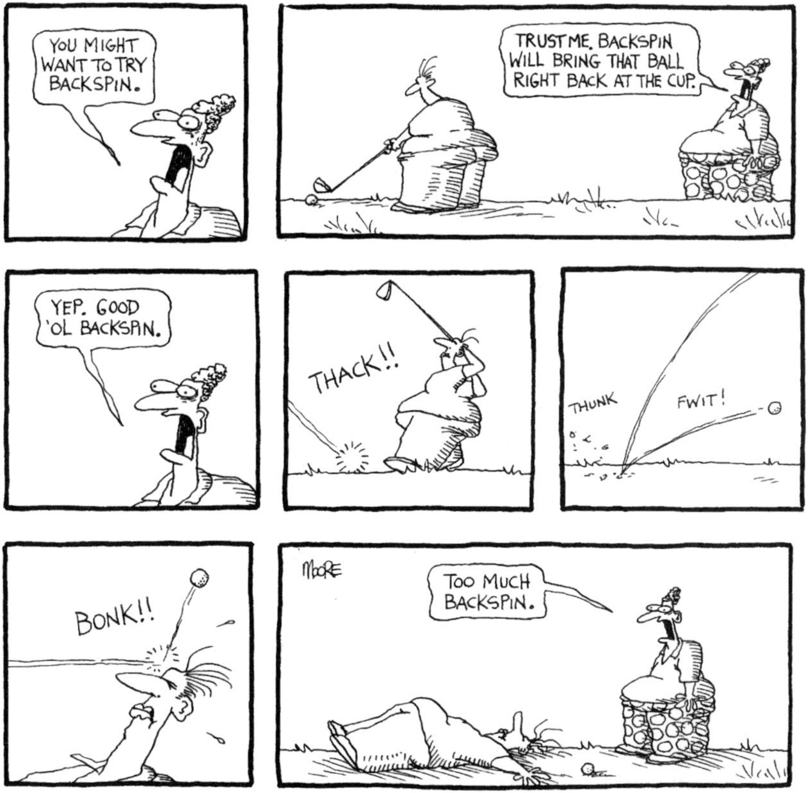
YOU MIGHT WANT TO TRY BACKSPIN.
TRUST ME. BACKSPIN WILL BRING THAT BALL RIGHT BACK AT THE CUP.
YEP. GOOD 'OL BACKSPIN.
THACK!!
THUNK
FWIT!
BONK!!
MOORE
TOO MUCH BACKSPIN.

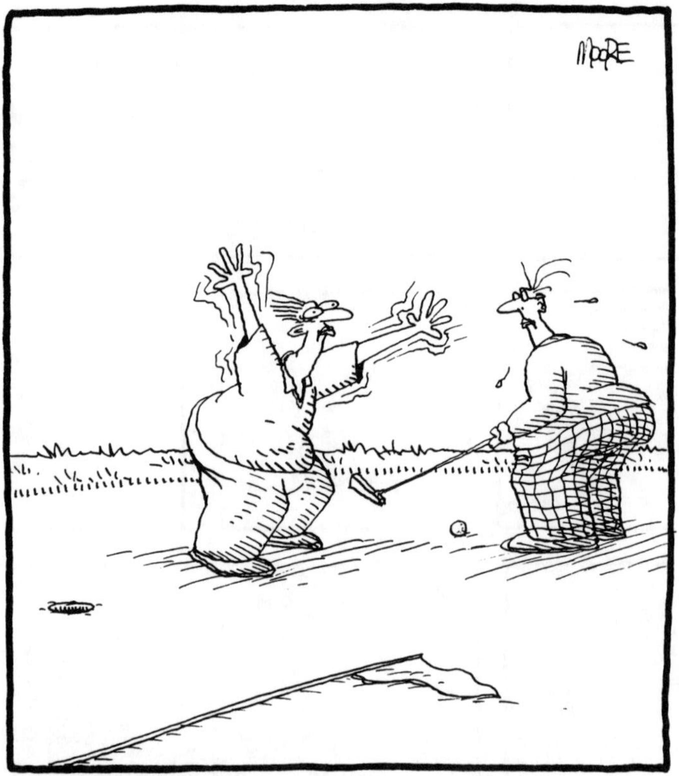
MOORE

Trailing by three strokes with only two holes to go, Mark switches to a man-to-man, full-course press.

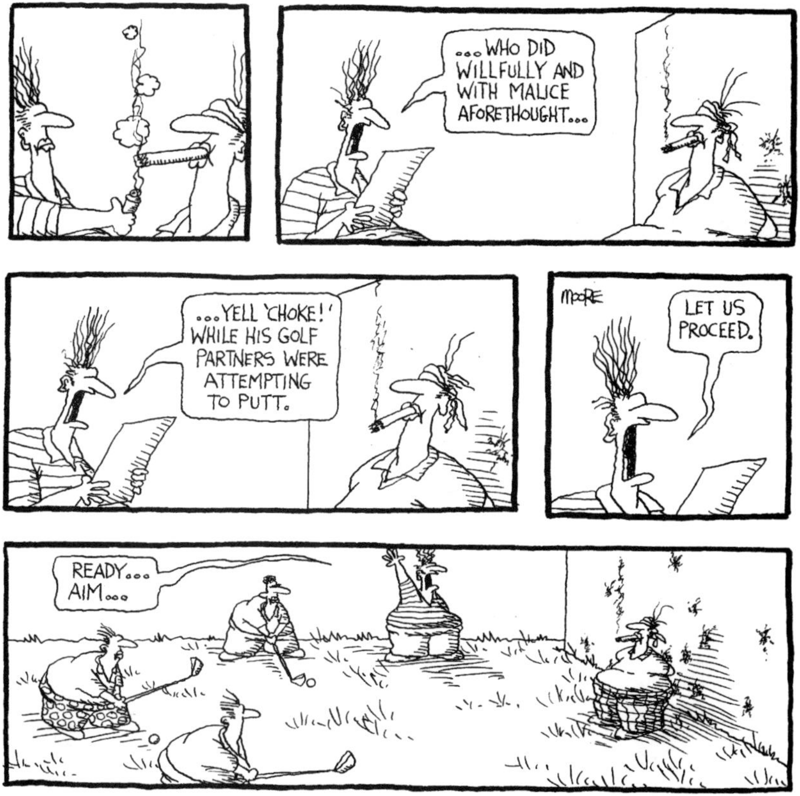
...WHO DID WILLFULLY AND WITH MALICE AFORETHOUGHT...
...YELL 'CHOKE!' WHILE HIS GOLF PARTNERS WERE ATTEMPTING TO PUTT.
MOORE
LET US PROCEED.
READY... AIM...

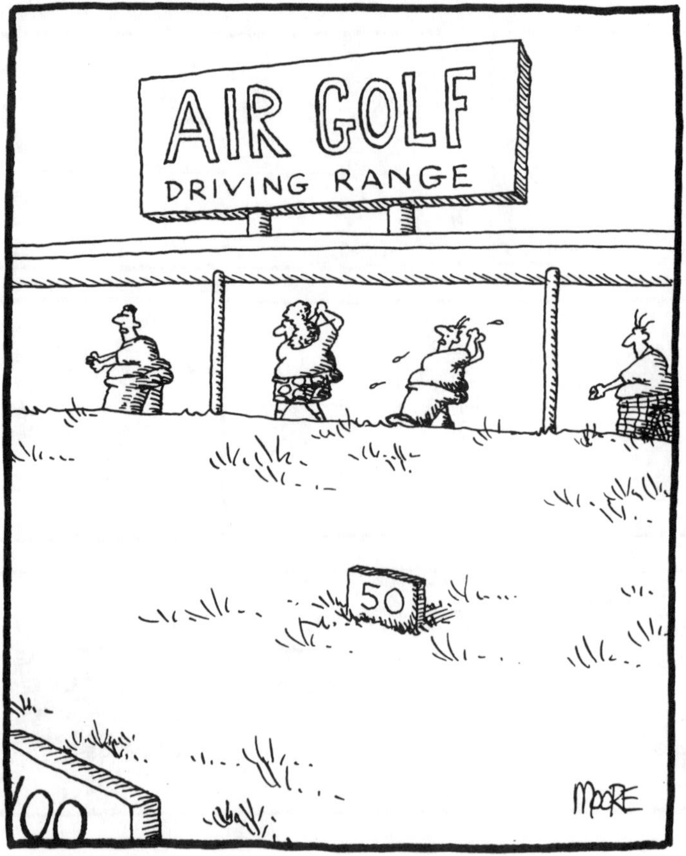
AIR GOLF
DRIVING RANGE
50
100
MOORE

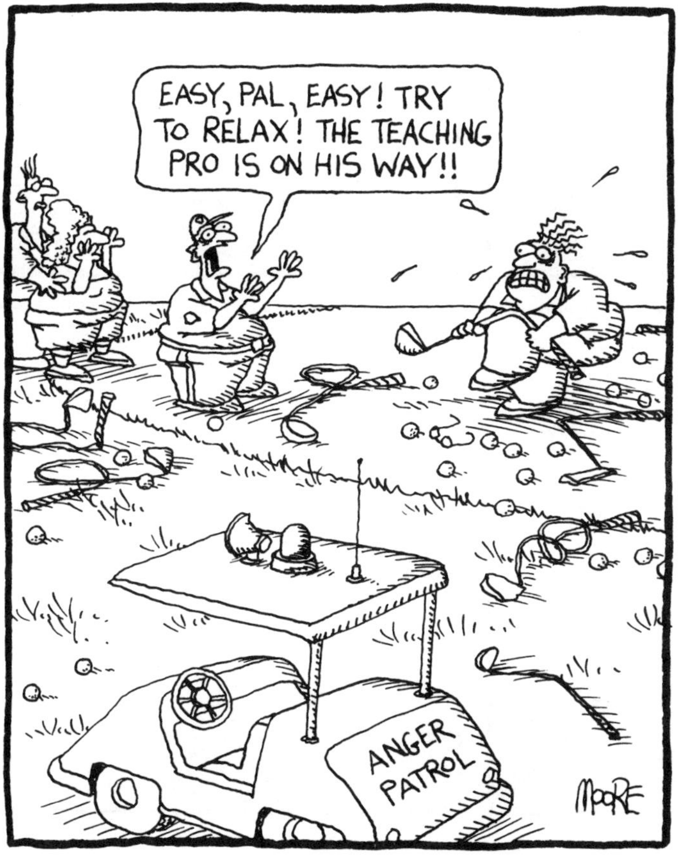
EASY, PAL, EASY! TRY TO RELAX! THE TEACHING PRO IS ON HIS WAY!!
ANGER PATROL
MOORE

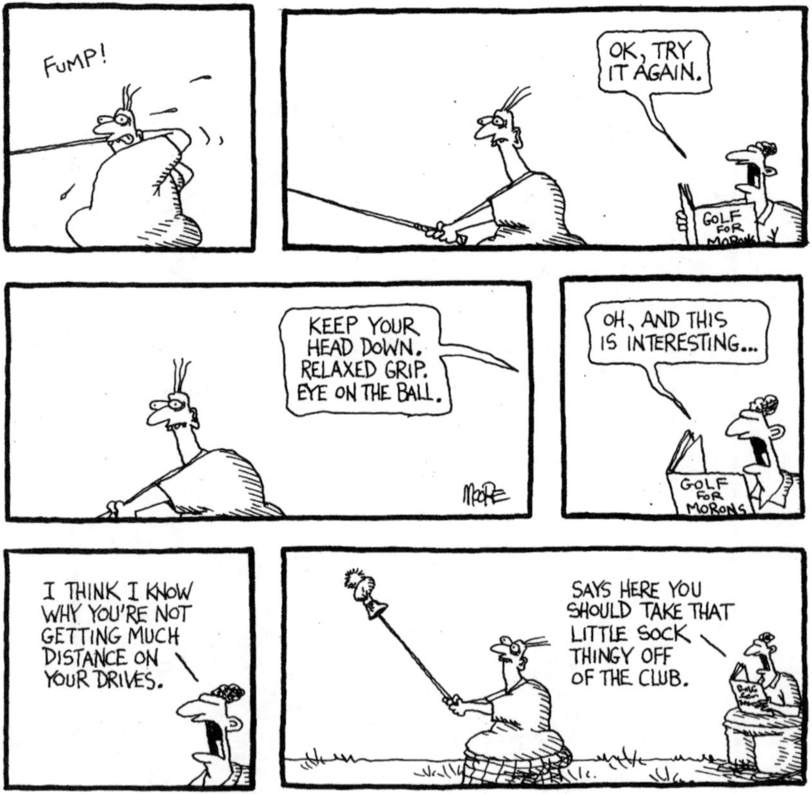
FUMP!
OK, TRY IT AGAIN.
GOLF FOR MORONS
KEEP YOUR HEAD DOWN. RELAXED GRIP. EYE ON THE BALL.
MOORE
OH, AND THIS IS INTERESTING...
GOLF FOR MORONS
I THINK I KNOW WHY YOU'RE NOT GETTING MUCH DISTANCE ON YOUR DRIVES.
SAYS HERE YOU SHOULD TAKE THAT LITTLE SOCK THINGY OFF OF THE CLUB.

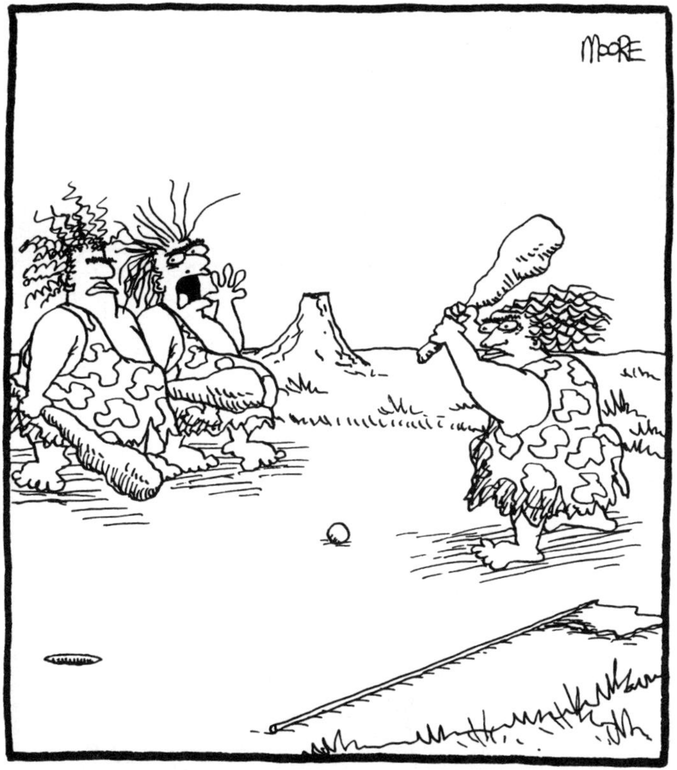
MOORE

"Gronk can crush ball off tee, but finesse game pretty much down toilet."

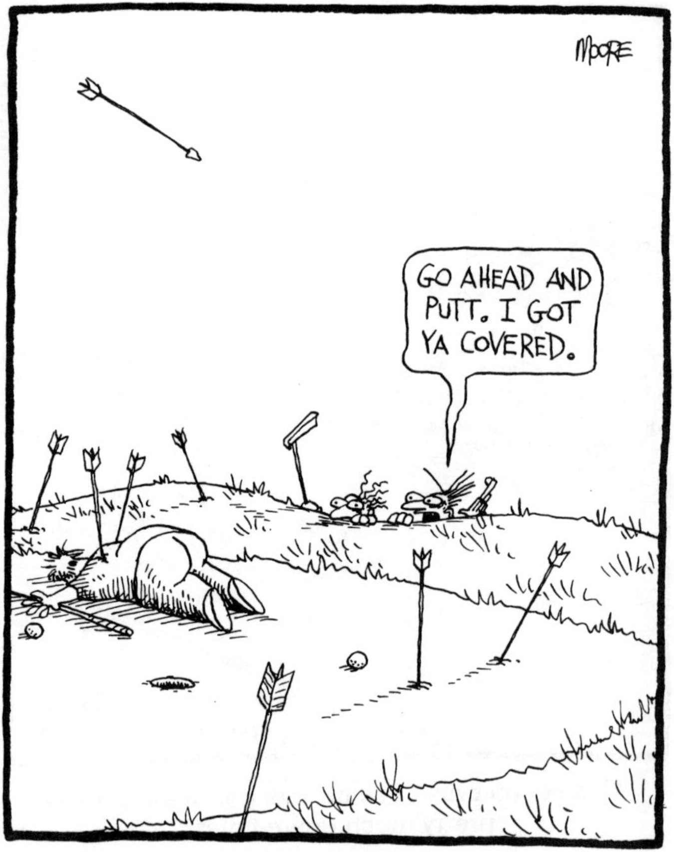
MOORE
GO AHEAD AND PUTT. I GOT YA COVERED.

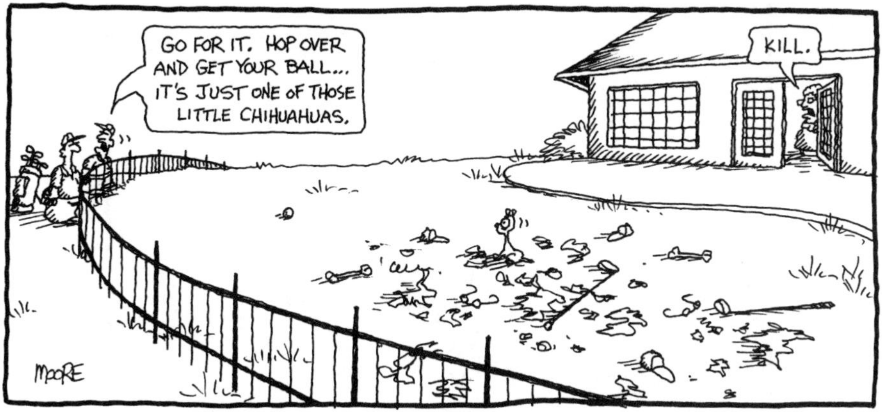
GO FOR IT. HOP OVER AND GET YOUR BALL... IT'S JUST ONE OF THOSE LITTLE CHIHUAHUAS.
KILL.
MOORE

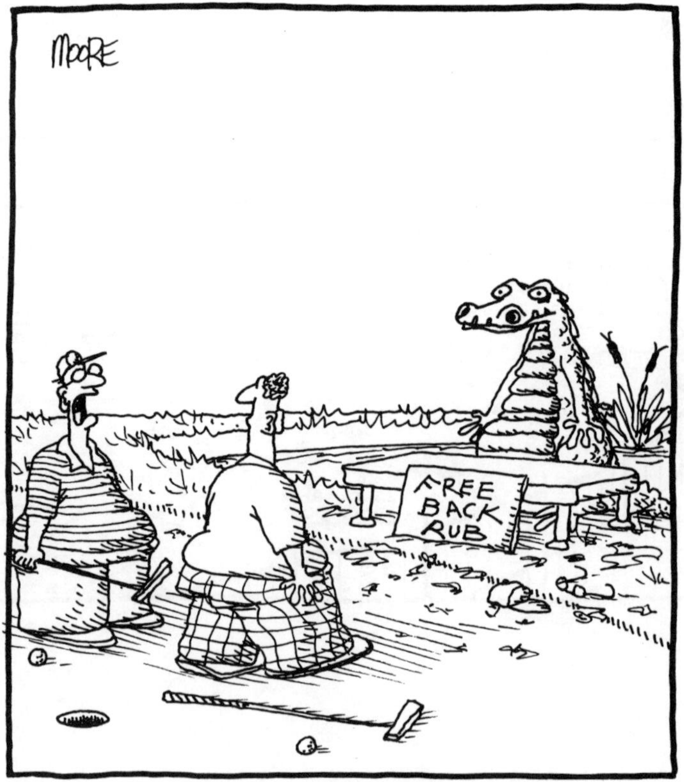
MOORE
FREE BACK RUB

"Careful, Tom. Could be a trick."

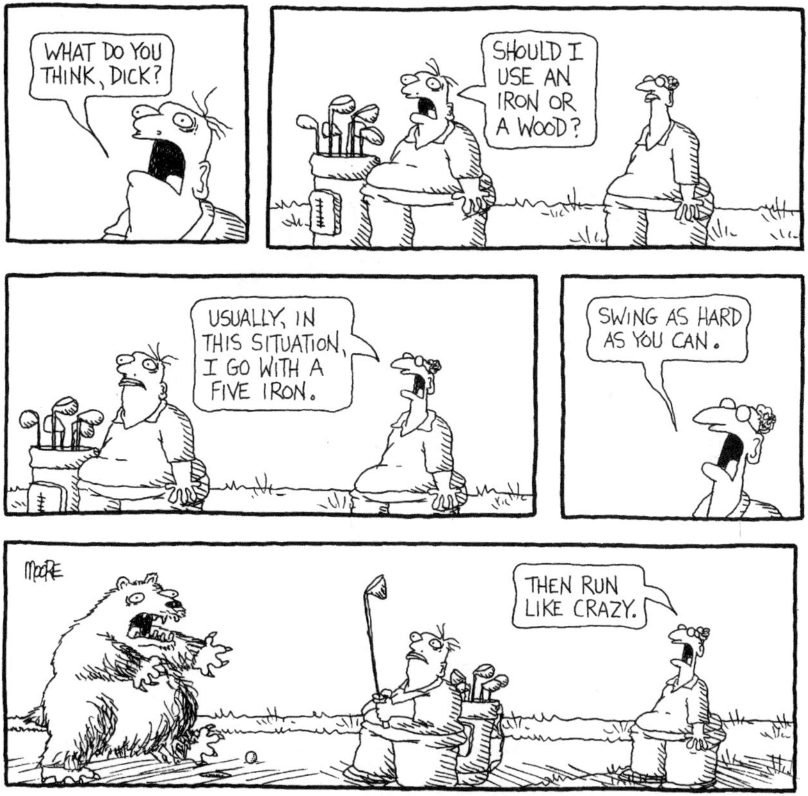
WHAT DO YOU THINK, DICK?
SHOULD I USE AN IRON OR A WOOD?
USUALLY, IN THIS SITUATION, I GO WITH A FIVE IRON.
SWING AS HARD AS YOU CAN.
MOORE
THEN RUN LIKE CRAZY.

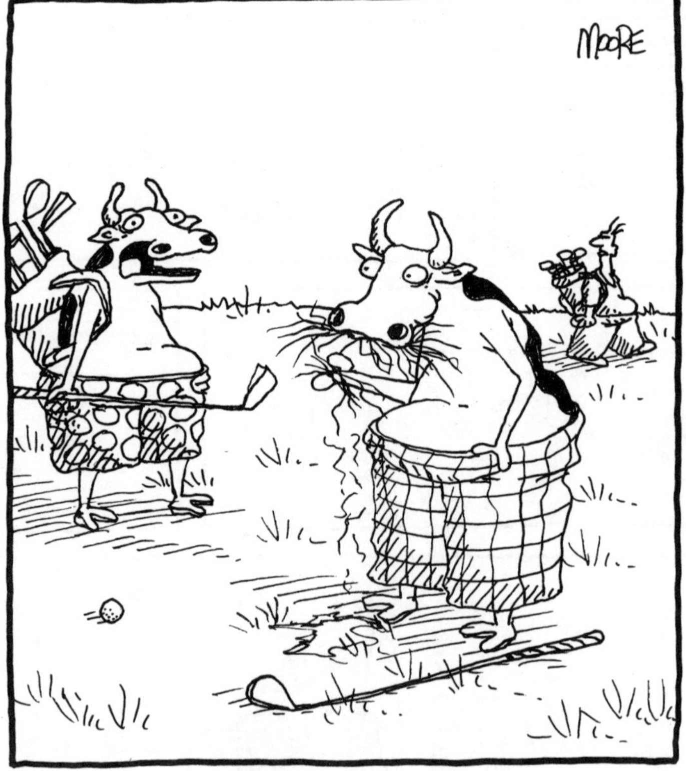
MOORE

"Stop grazing, Sid! You'll get us kicked off the course!!"

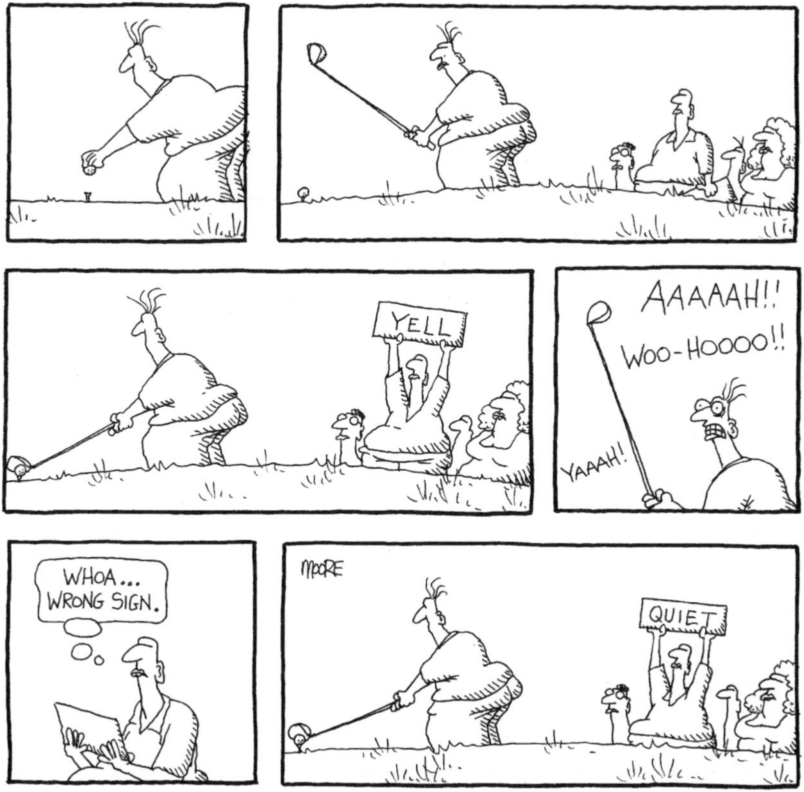
YELL
AAAAAH!!
WOO-HOOOO!!
YAAAH!
WHOA...
WRONG SIGN.
MOORE
QUIET

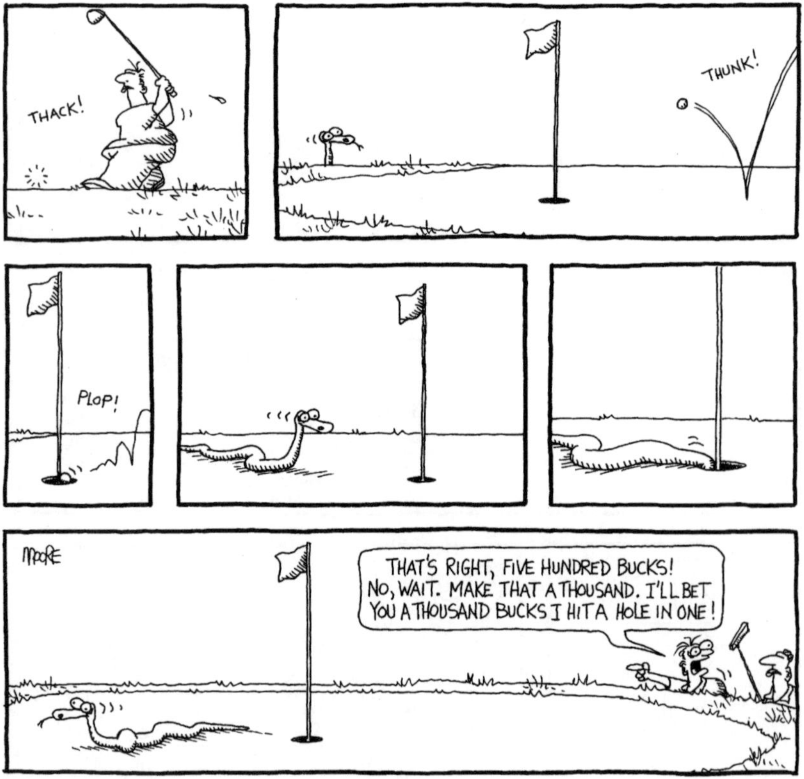
THACK!
THUNK!
PLOP!
MOORE
THAT'S RIGHT, FIVE HUNDRED BUCKS! NO, WAIT. MAKE THAT A THOUSAND. I'LL BET YOU A THOUSAND BUCKS I HIT A HOLE IN ONE!

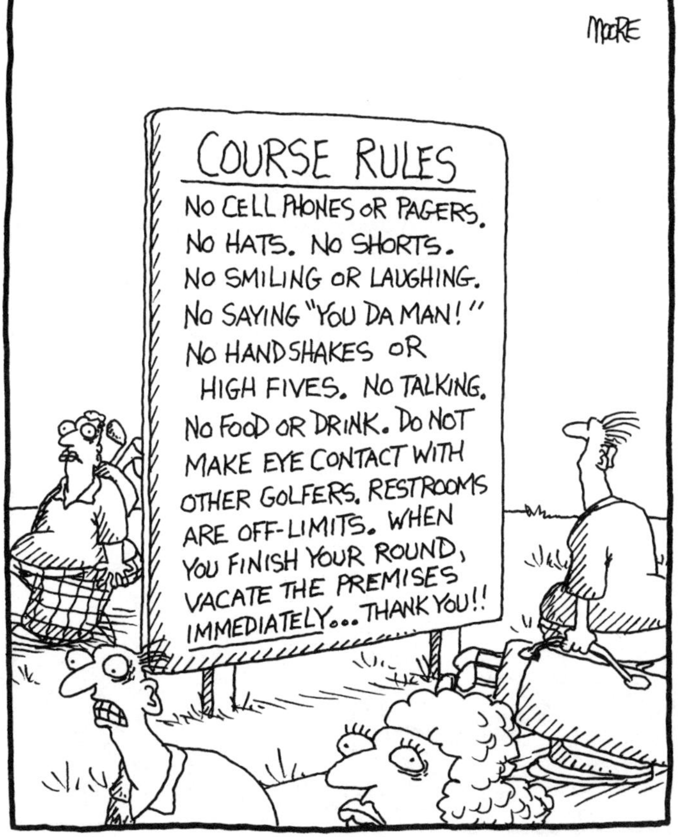
MOORE
COURSE RULES
NO CELL PHONES OR PAGERS.
NO HATS. NO SHORTS.
NO SMILING OR LAUGHING.
NO SAYING "YOU DA MAN!"
NO HANDSHAKES OR
HIGH FIVES. NO TALKING.
NO FOOD OR DRINK. DO NOT
MAKE EYE CONTACT WITH
OTHER GOLFERS. RESTROOMS
ARE OFF-LIMITS. WHEN
YOU FINISH YOUR ROUND,
VACATE THE PREMISES
IMMEDIATELY... THANK YOU!!

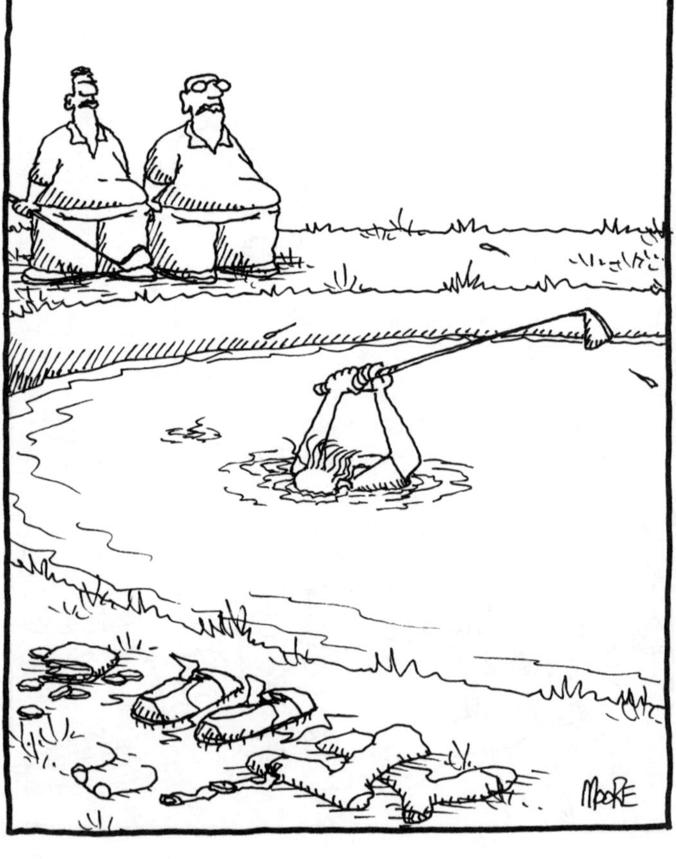
MOORE

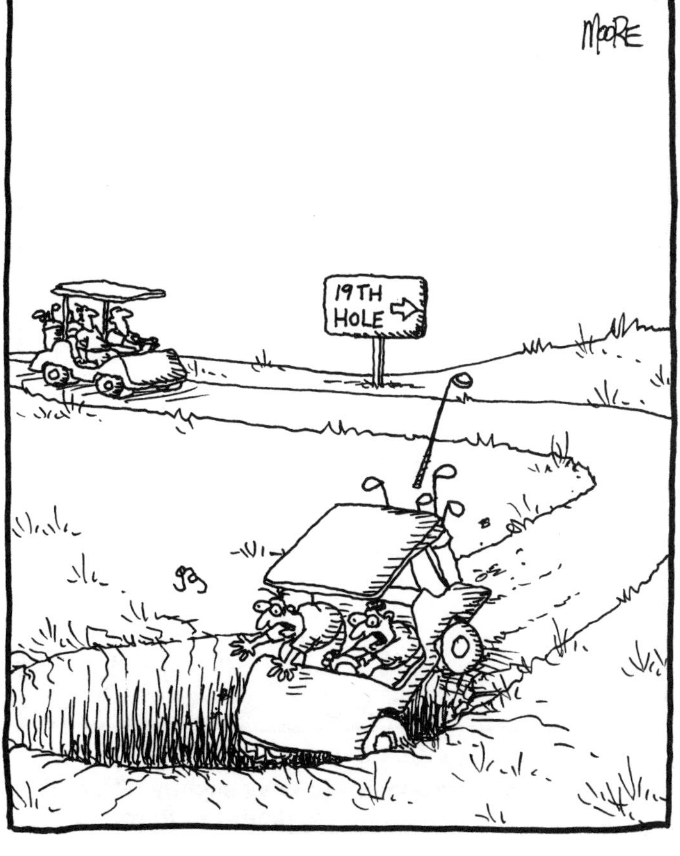
MOORE
19TH
HOLE

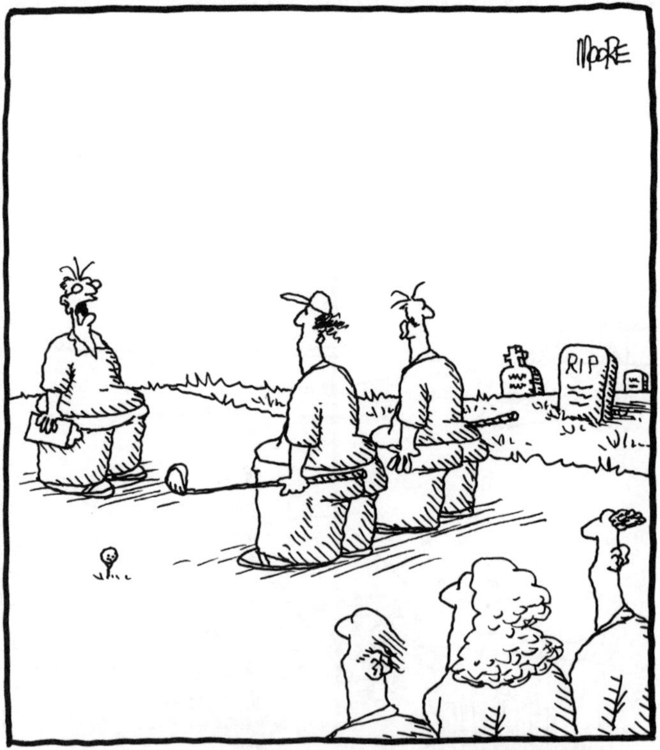
MOORE
RIP

"Oh, and before we begin the playoff, a word of caution: This tournament follows slightly different rules when it comes to a sudden-death round."

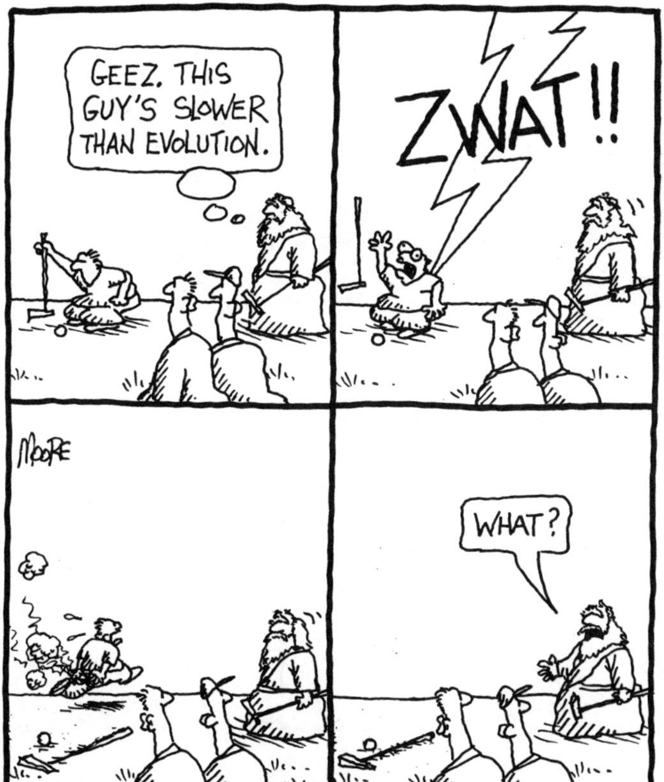
GEEZ. THIS GUY'S SLOWER THAN EVOLUTION.
ZWAT!!
MOORE
WHAT?

Golfing with God

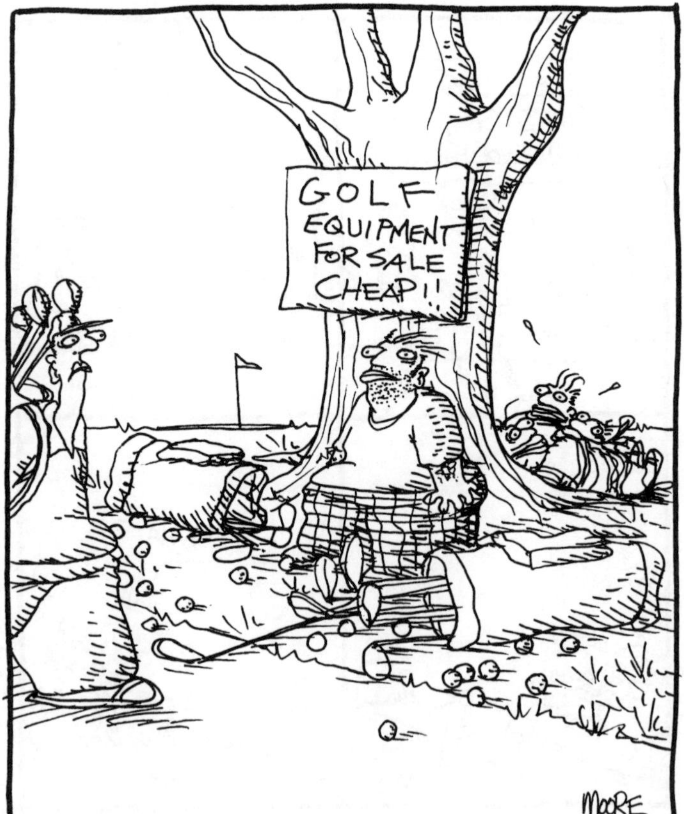
GOLF
EQUIPMENT
FOR SALE
CHEAP!!
MOORE

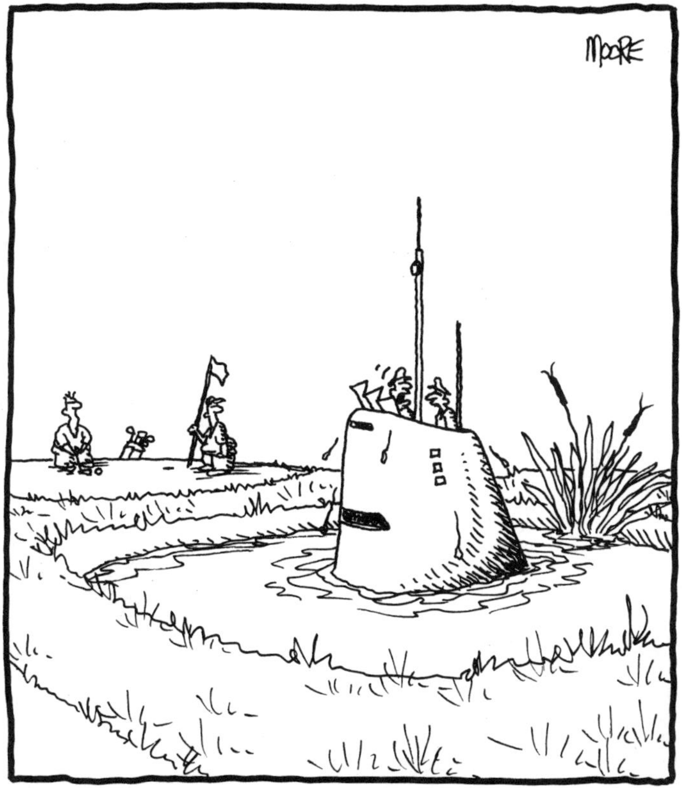
MOORE

"I said 35 degrees *latitude*, 60 degrees *longitude*, you brainless clam."

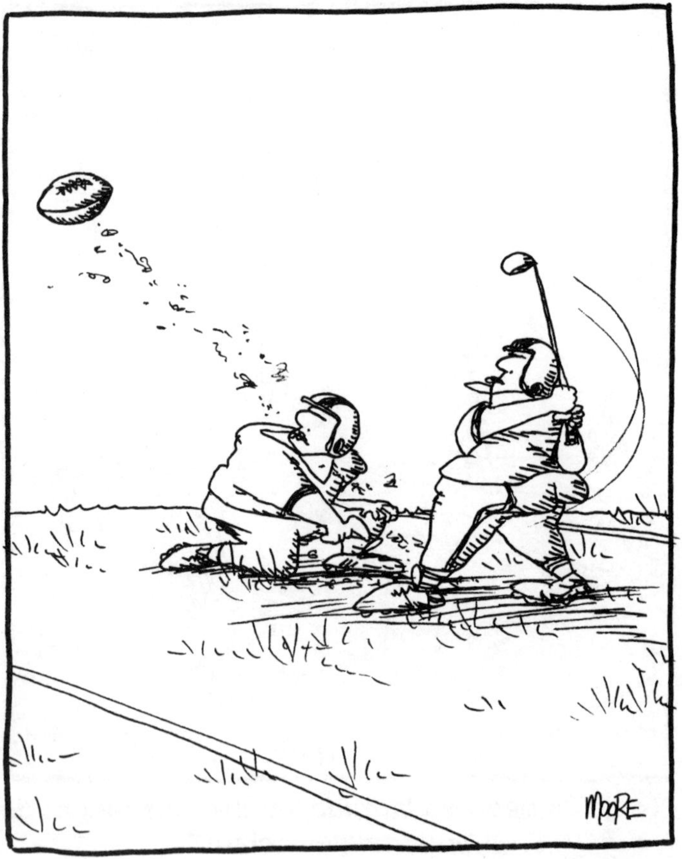
MOORE

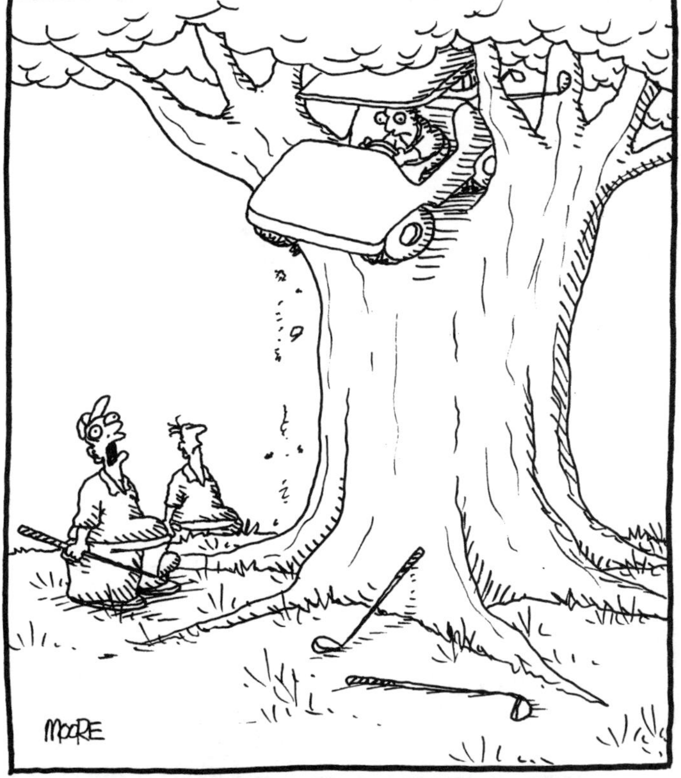
MOORE

"Try putting it in forward, then quickly shove it into reverse."

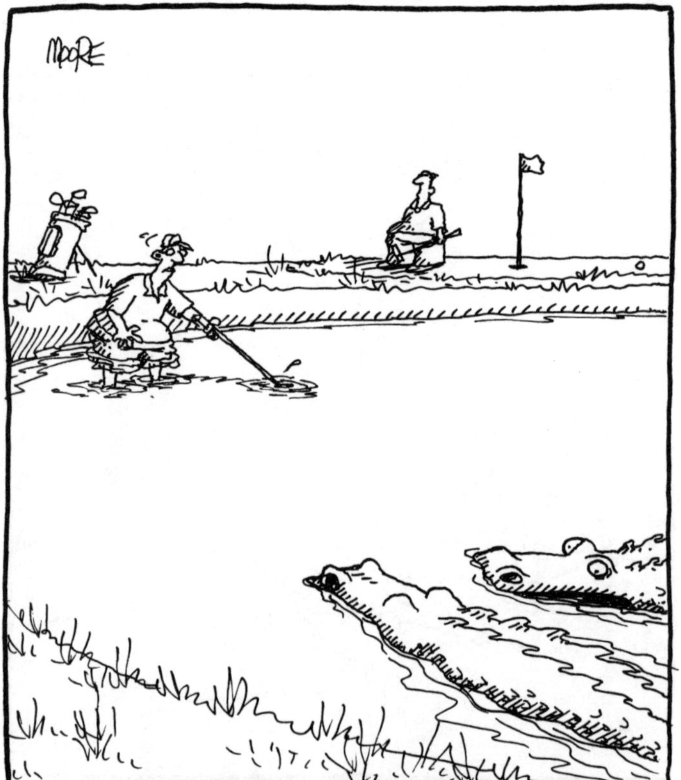
MOORE

"If it weren't for bad golfers, we'd starve."

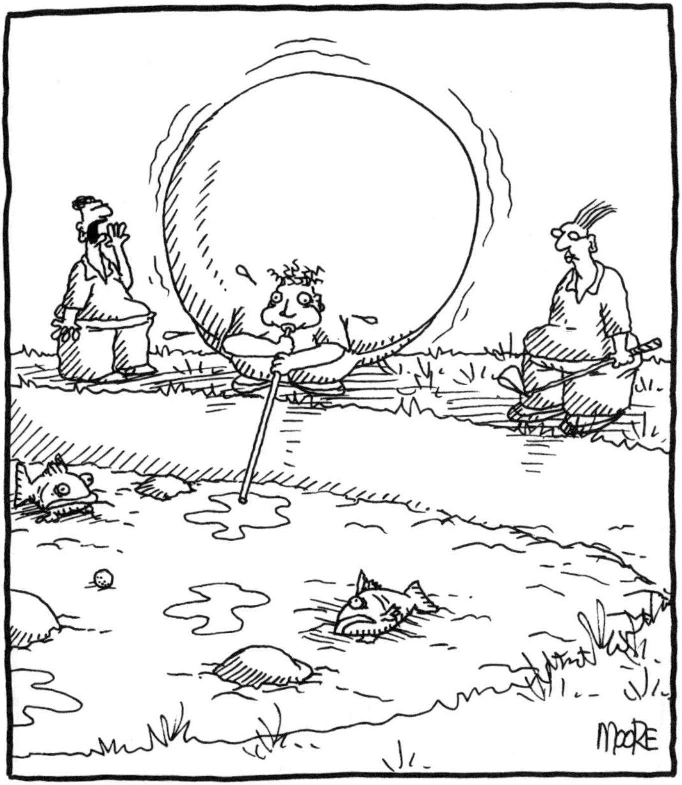
MOORE

"OK, go get your ball . . . but hurry!"

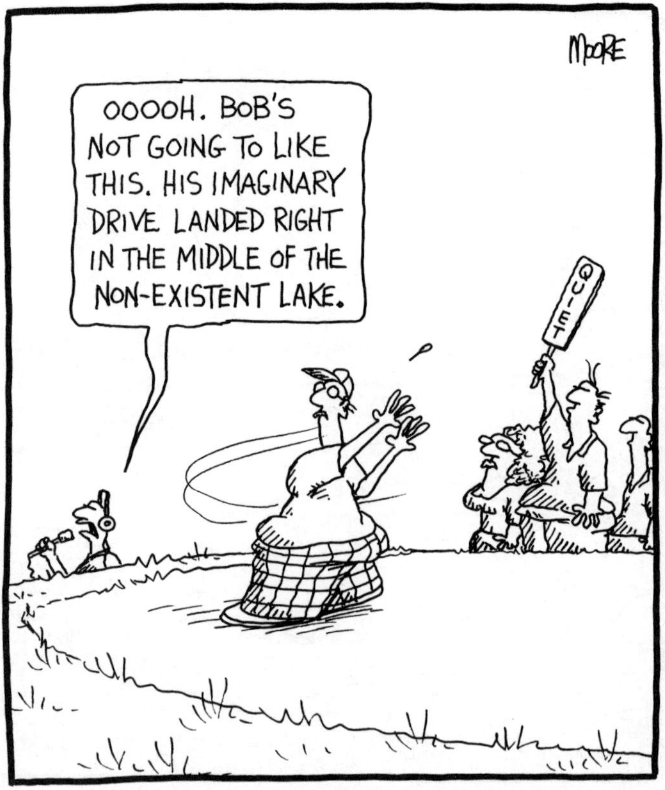
MOORE
OOOOH. BOB'S NOT GOING TO LIKE THIS. HIS IMAGINARY DRIVE LANDED RIGHT IN THE MIDDLE OF THE NON-EXISTENT LAKE.
QUIET

On the Professional Air Golfers Association tour

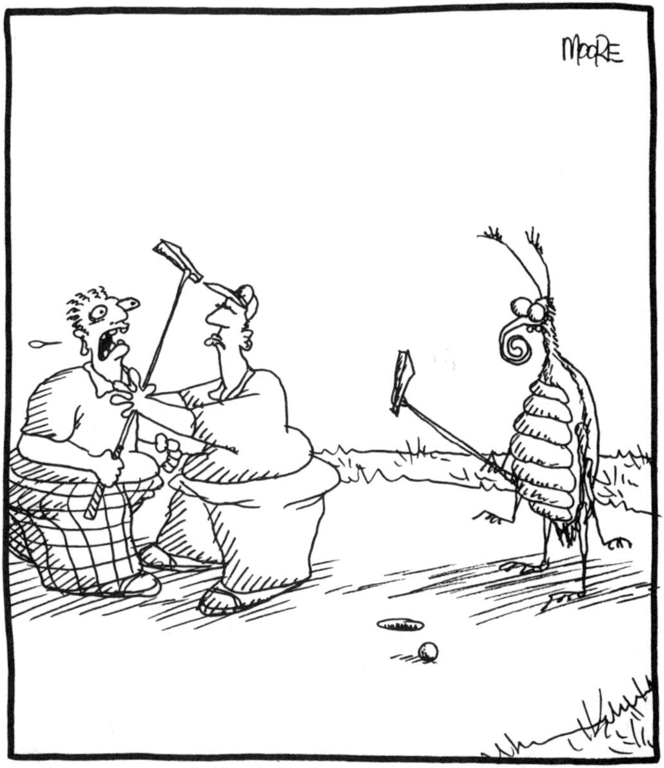
MOORE

"Hey, I don't care if he's trying to attract a mate! If he makes that obnoxious high-pitched sound again, I'm gonna smash him!"

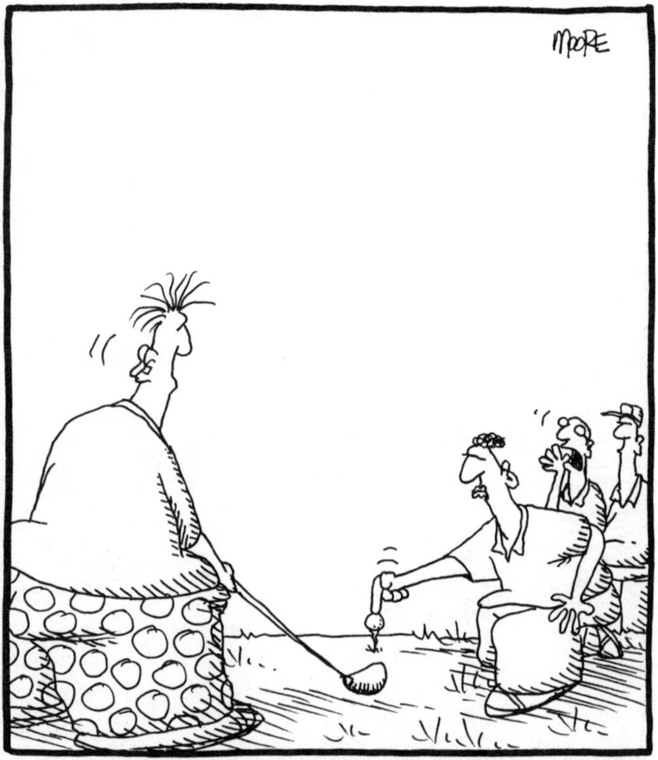
MOORE

"That's the only way Gordon can tee off. He spent 10 years in the NFL as a field-goal kicker."

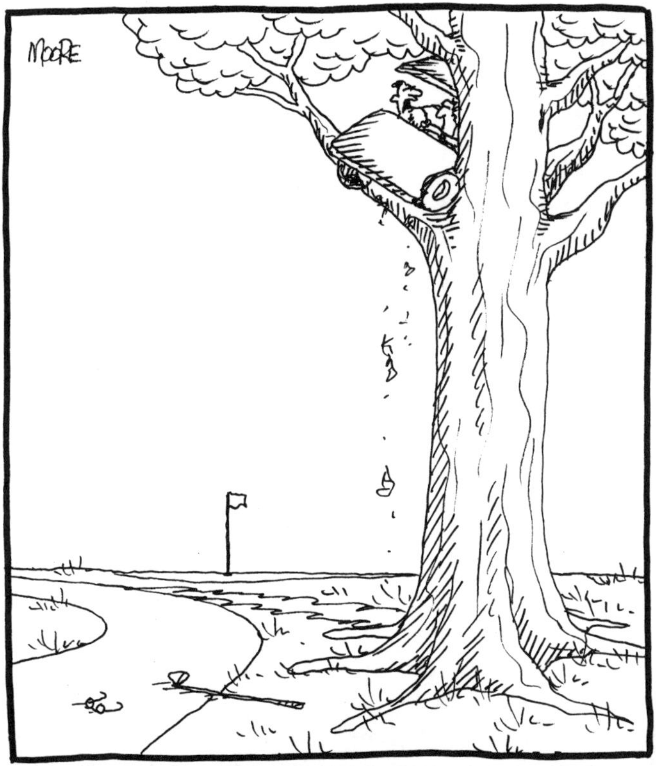
MOORE

"That's it, Wilson! I'm driving the cart the rest of the way!"

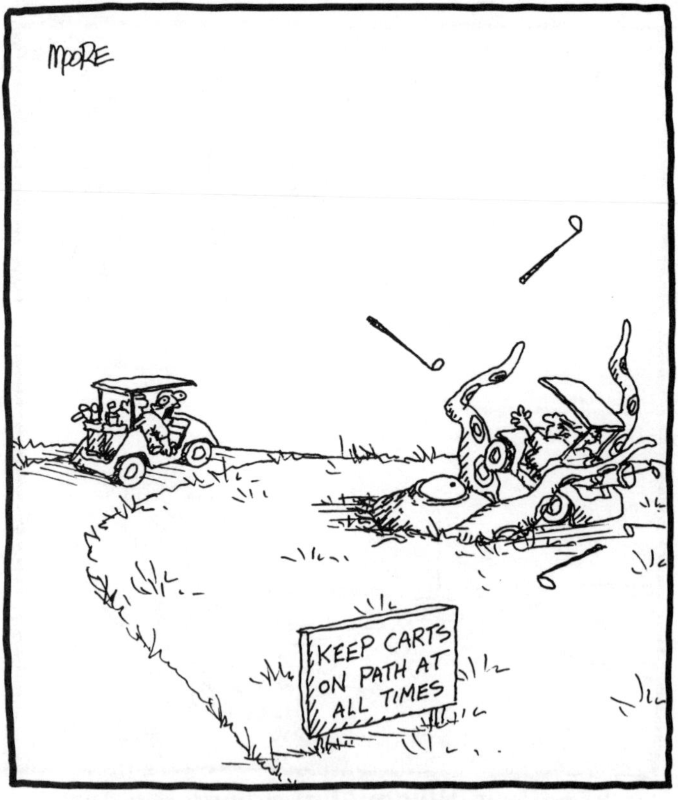
MOORE
KEEP CARTS ON PATH AT ALL TIMES

"Frank! Get back on the cart path! You'll get us kicked off the course!"

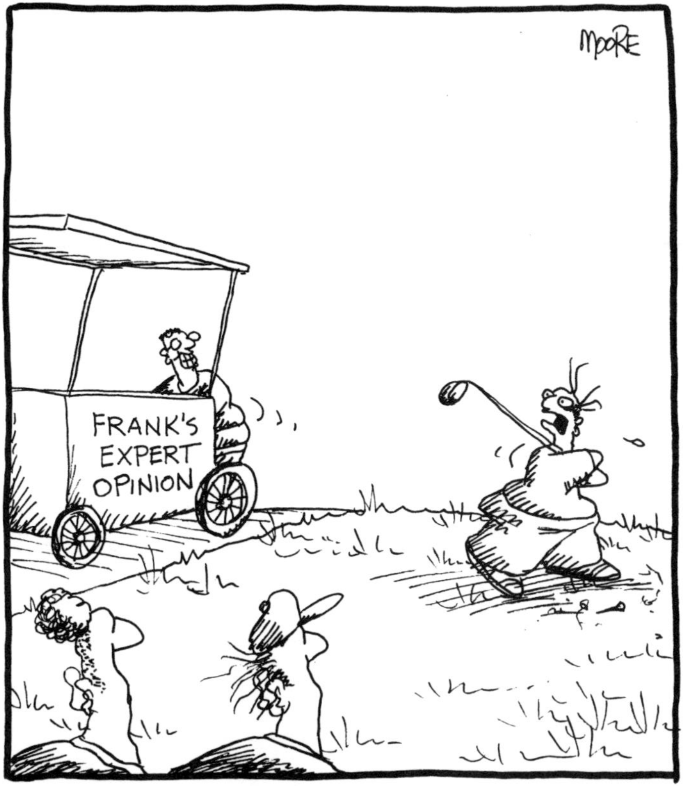
MOORE
FRANK'S
EXPERT
OPINION

"I'm *still* slicing my drive! What I need is a frank opinion from an expert and . . . oh, thank God!"

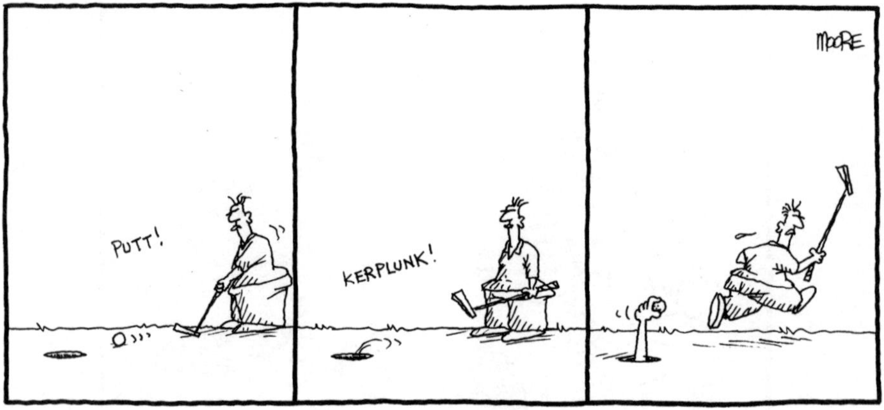
PUTT!
KERPLUNK!
MOORE

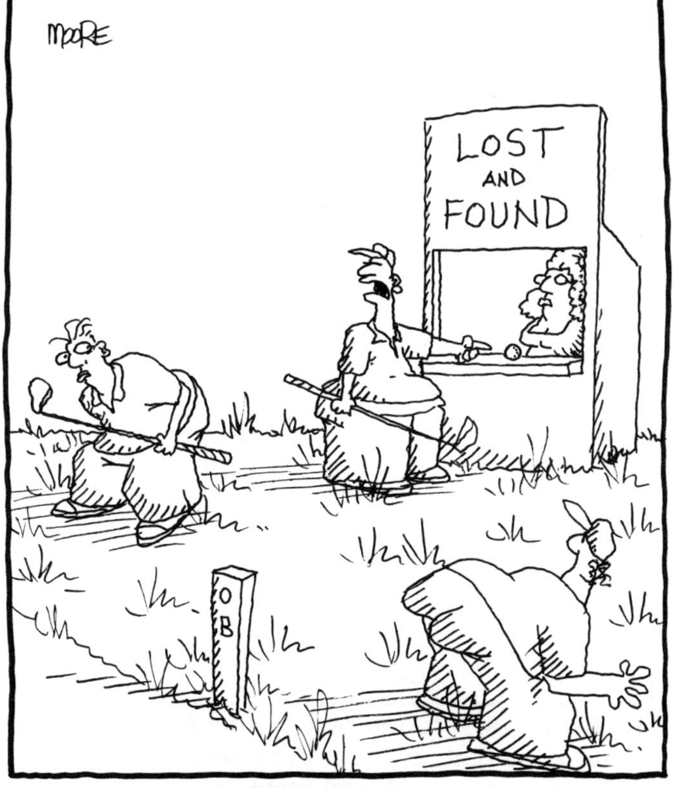
MOORE
LOST
AND
FOUND
O
B

"Here it is!"

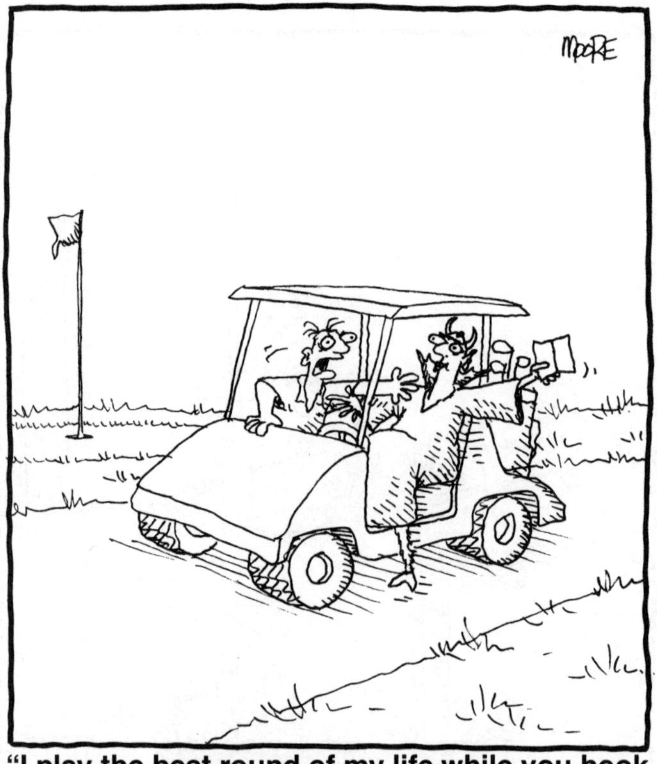
MOORE

"I play the best round of my life while you hook and slice balls all over the course, and now you say you *won* by 10 strokes? Let me see that scorecard!"

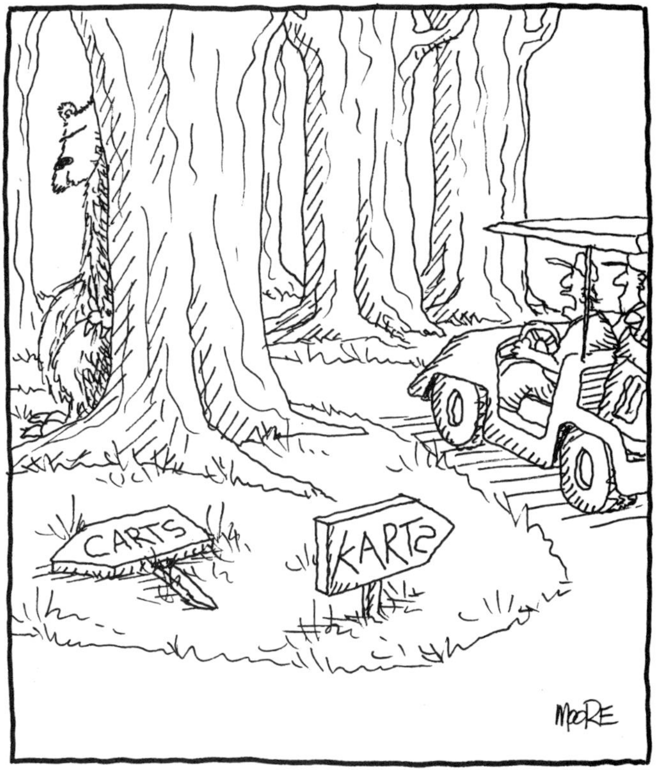
CARTS
KARTS
MOORE

"What kind of an idiot spells 'carts' with a 'k'?"

QUIT WHINING.
MOORE
YOU TOLD ME TO TAKE YOU TO YOUR BALL.

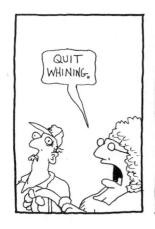

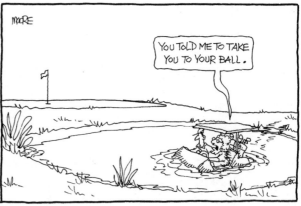

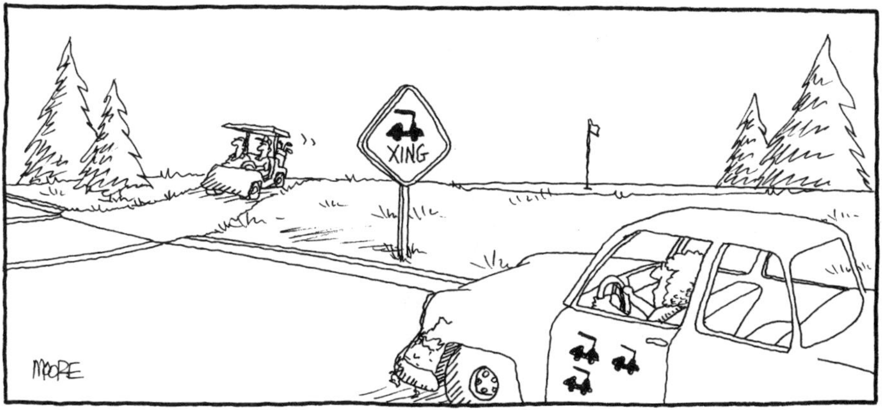
XING
MOORE

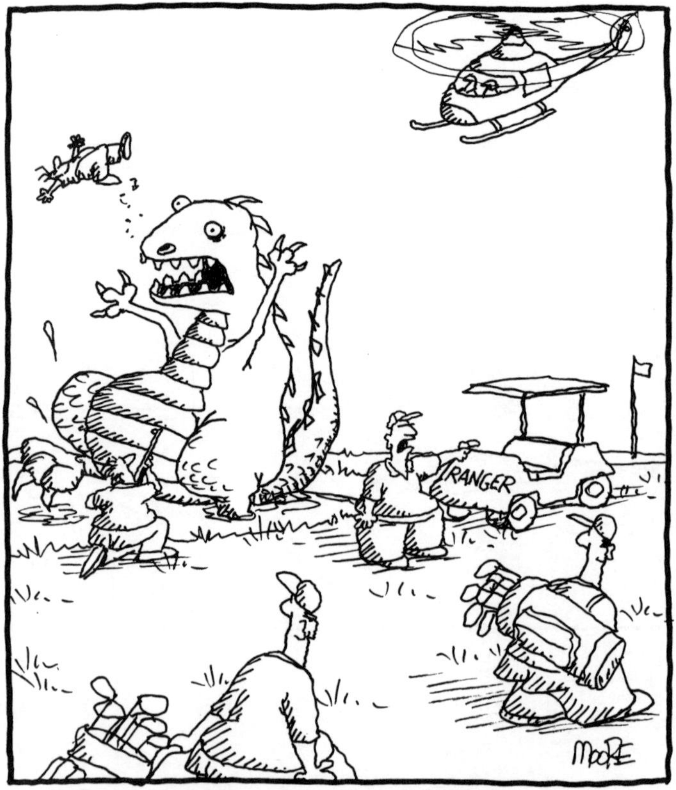
RANGER
MOORE

"Move along, move along! Nothing to see here! Don't hold up play!"

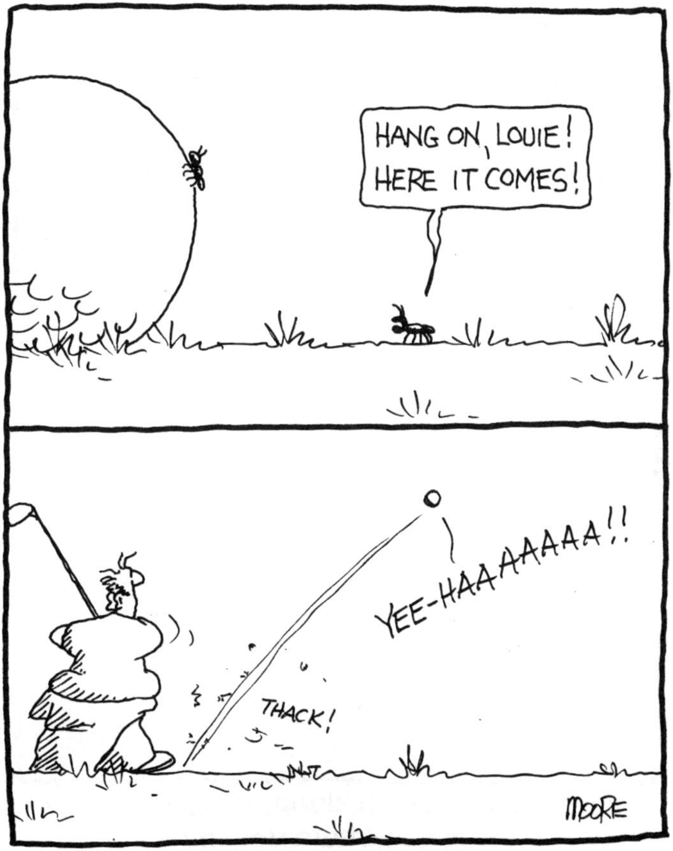
HANG ON, LOUIE! HERE IT COMES!
YEE-HAAAAAAAA!!
THACK!
MOORE

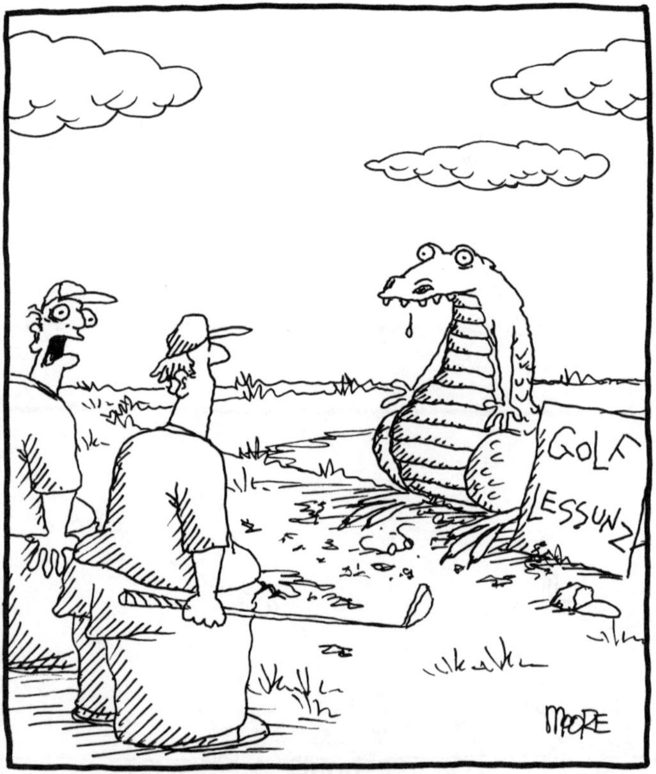
GOLF
LESSUNZ
MOORE

"Don't be a fool, Bob! How do you know he's even *qualified* to teach?"

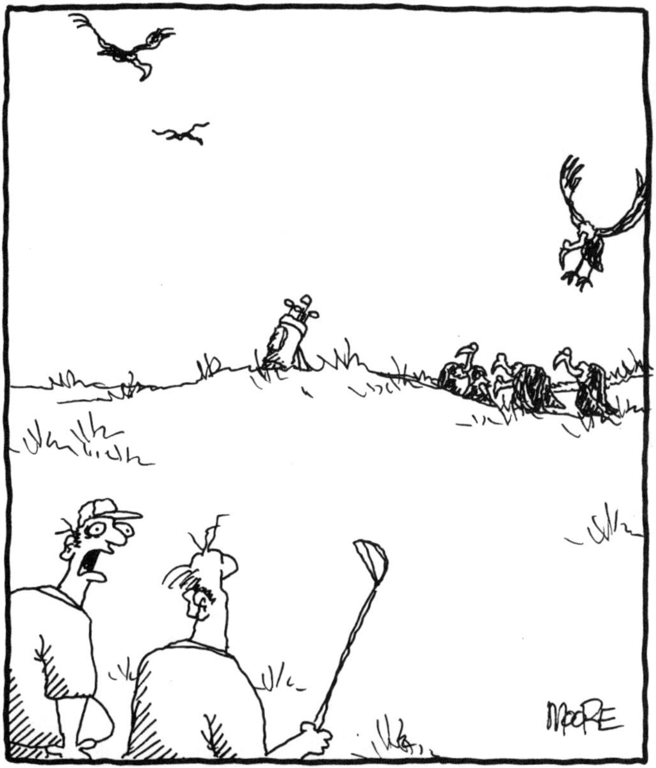
MOORE

"Maybe one of us should go check on Floyd. I think he's having trouble hitting out of the bunker."

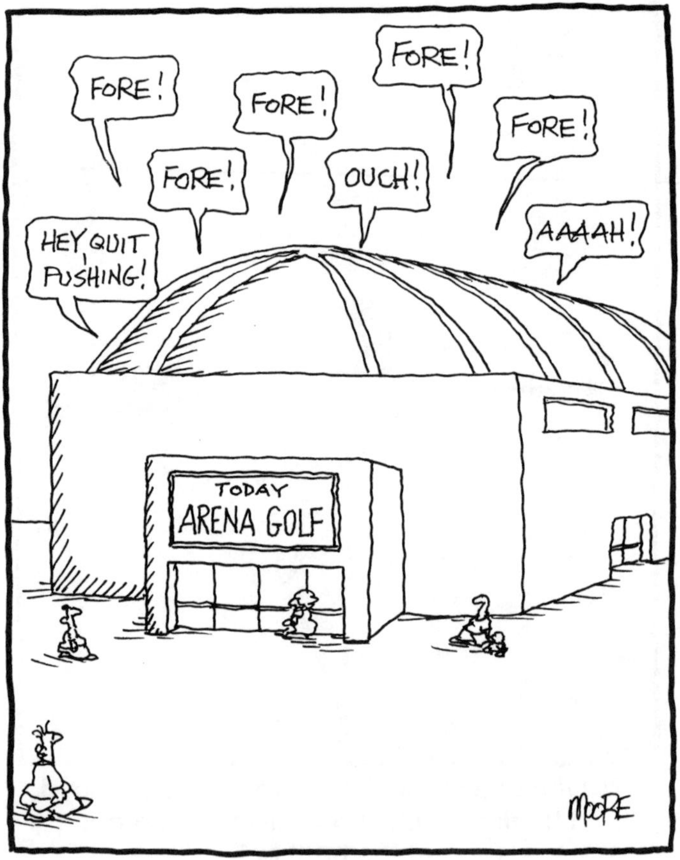
HEY, QUIT PUSHING!
FORE!
FORE!
FORE!
OUCH!
FORE!
FORE!
AAAAH!
TODAY
ARENA GOLF
MOORE

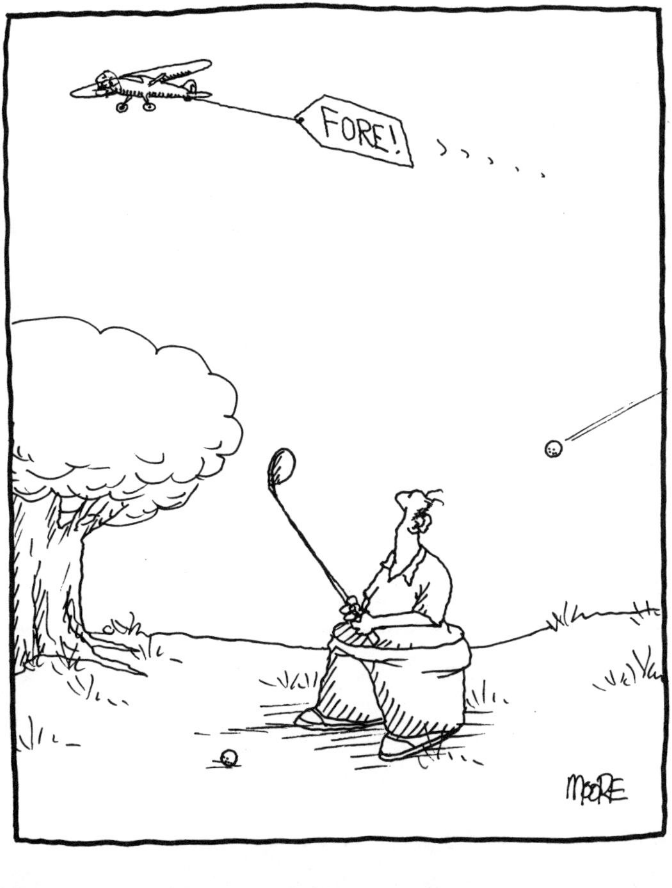
FORE!
MOORE

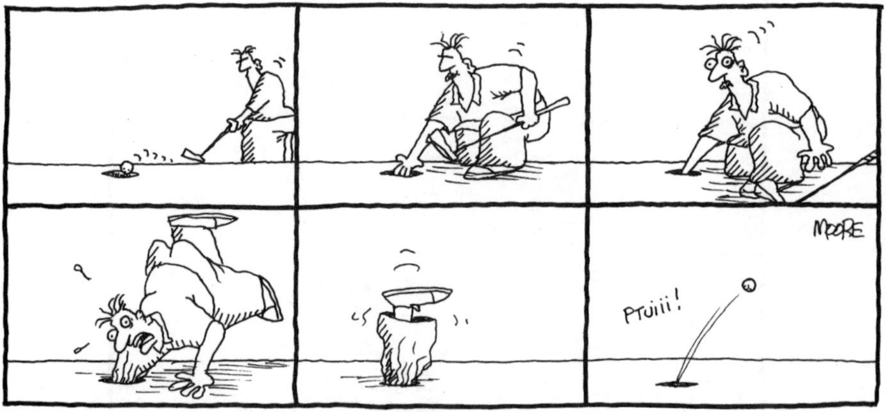
MOORE
PTUIII!

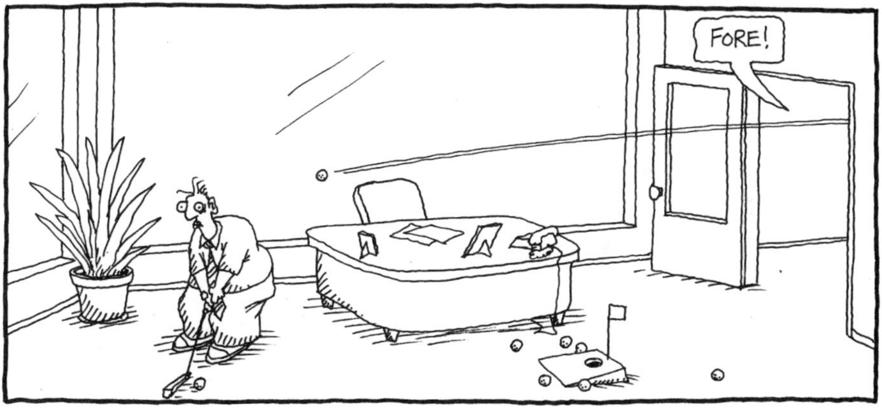
FORE!

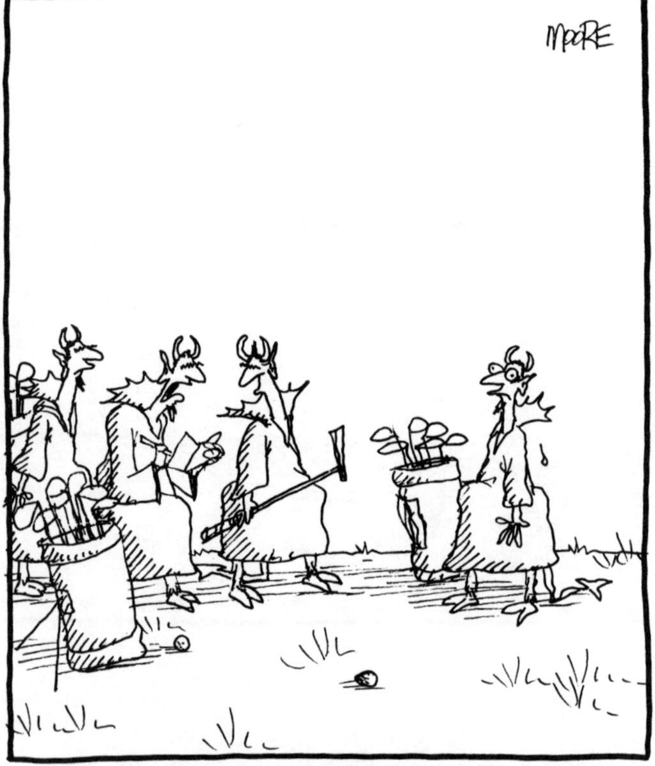
MOORE

"We all scored a course-record 65, except Bob, who finished at 109 and... What the... Hey! *Bob* didn't cheat!"

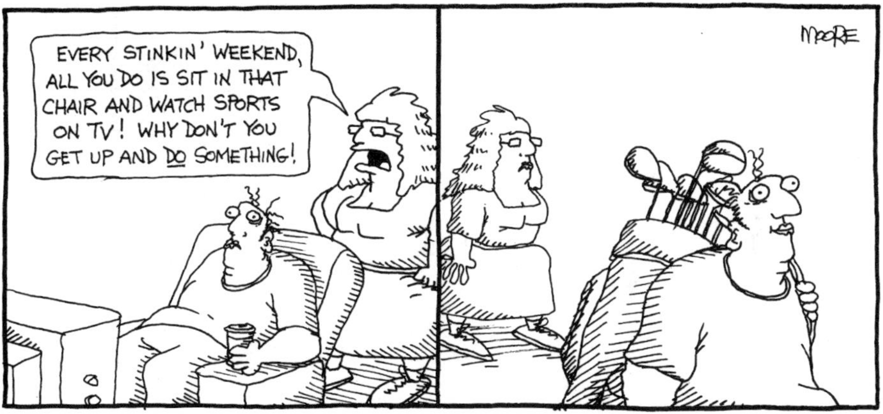
EVERY STINKIN' WEEKEND, ALL YOU DO IS SIT IN THAT CHAIR AND WATCH SPORTS ON TV! WHY DON'T YOU GET UP AND DO SOMETHING!
MOORE

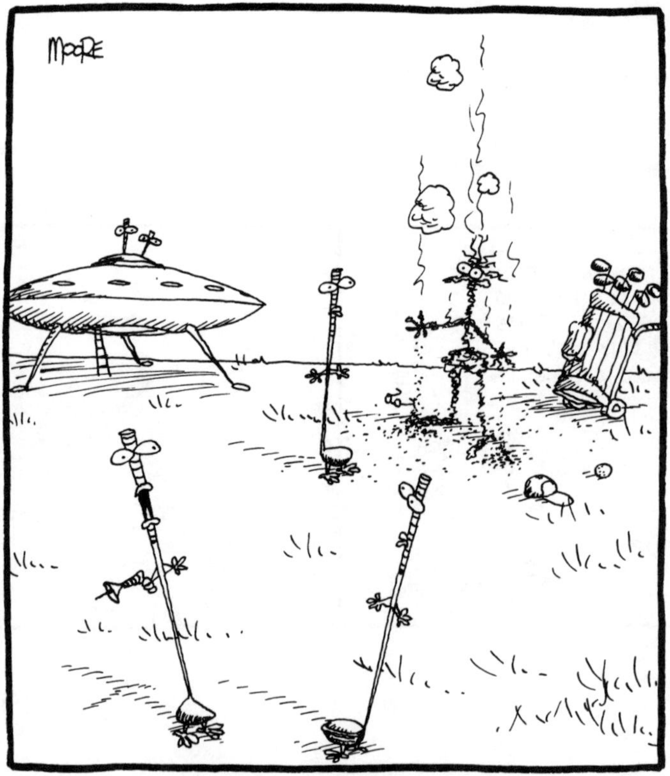
MOORE

"He grabbed me and swung me around . . . so I blasted him."

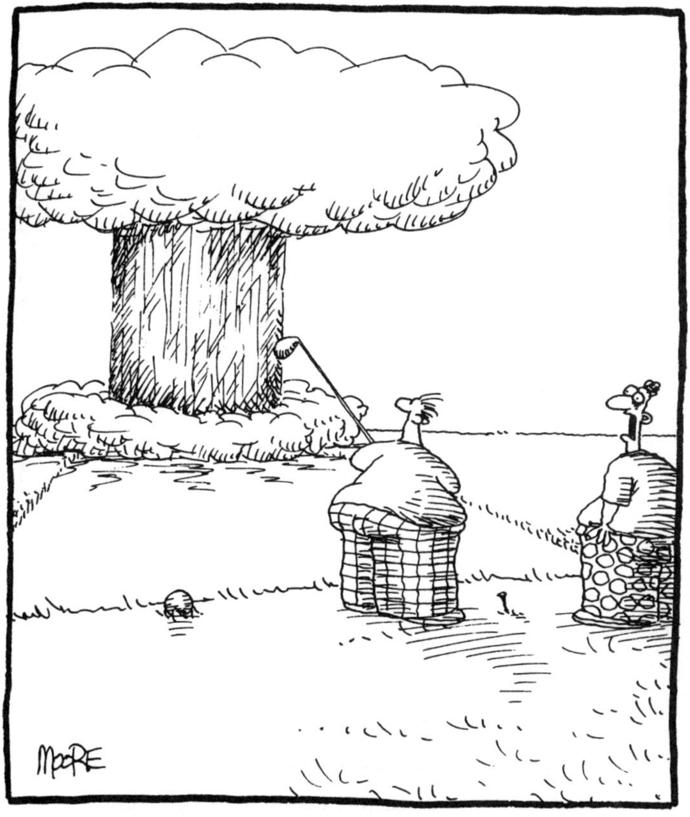
MOORE

"Nice shot, man!"

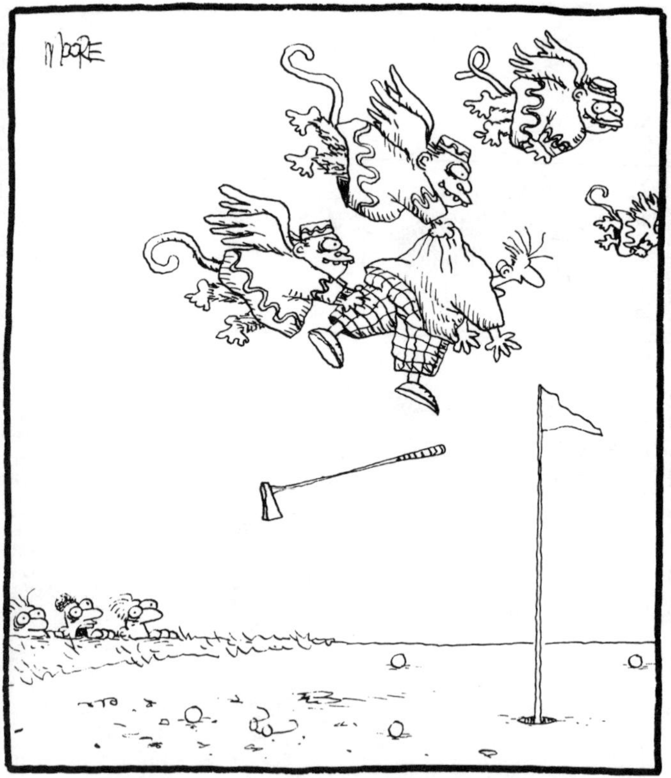
MOORE

"Maybe we shouldn't mention this when we get back to the clubhouse."

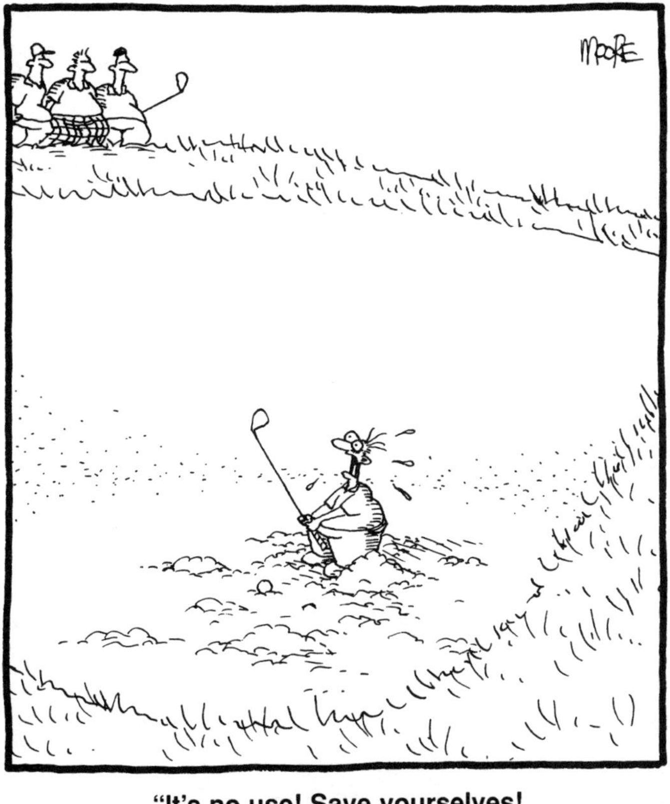
MOORE

"It's no use! Save yourselves!
Go on to the next hole!"

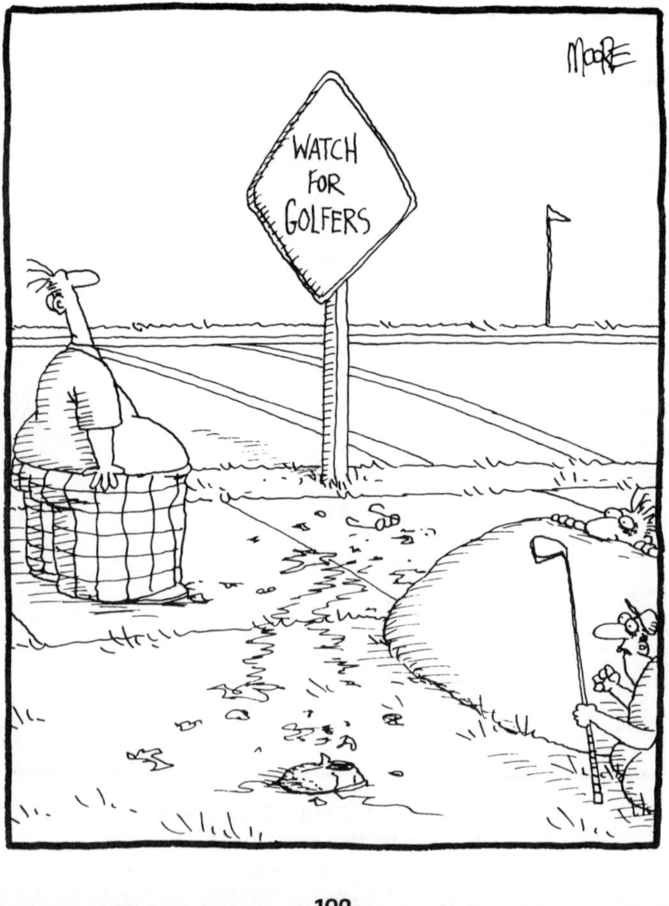
MOORE
WATCH FOR GOLFERS

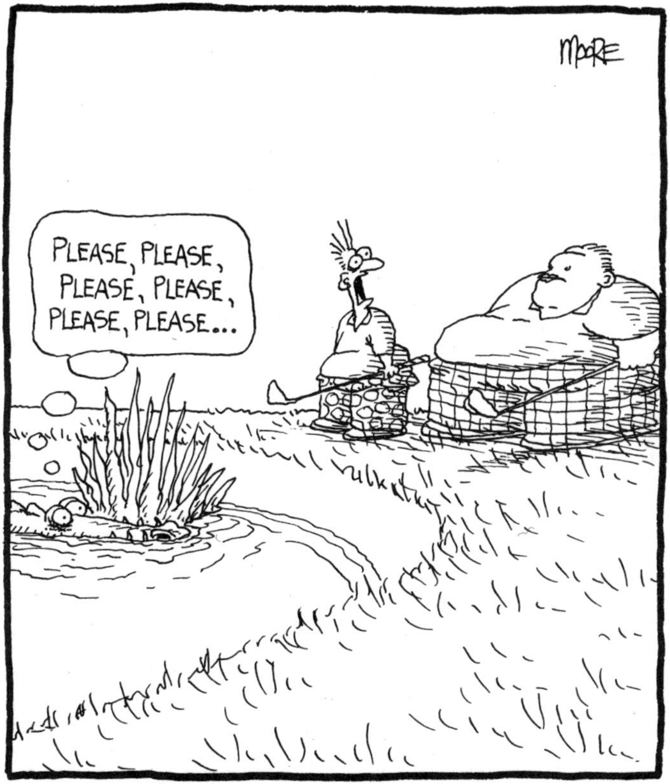
MOORE
PLEASE, PLEASE, PLEASE, PLEASE, PLEASE, PLEASE...

"Your ball landed in the water. You want to play another ball or wade in and get it?"

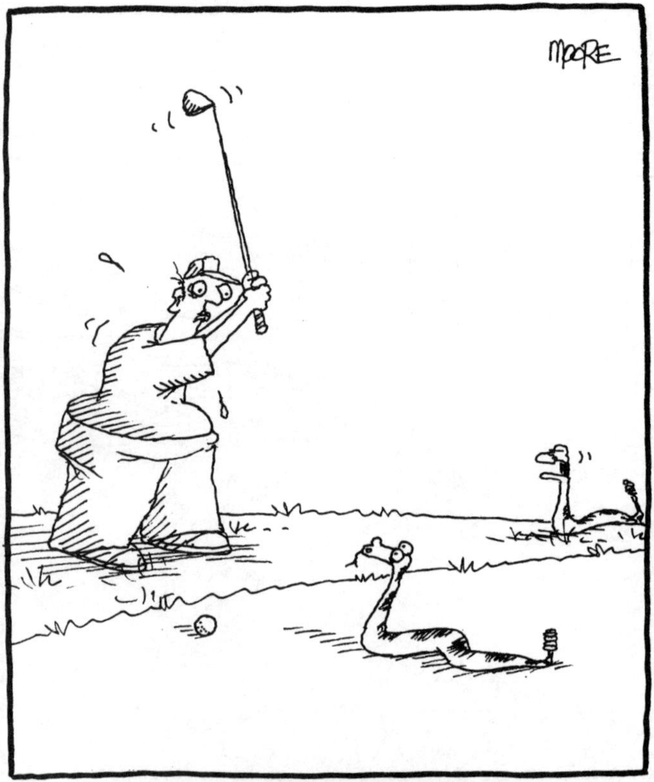
MOORE

"No sudden moves, Lenny! Just turn and crawl away reeeeal slow, and he probably won't strike."

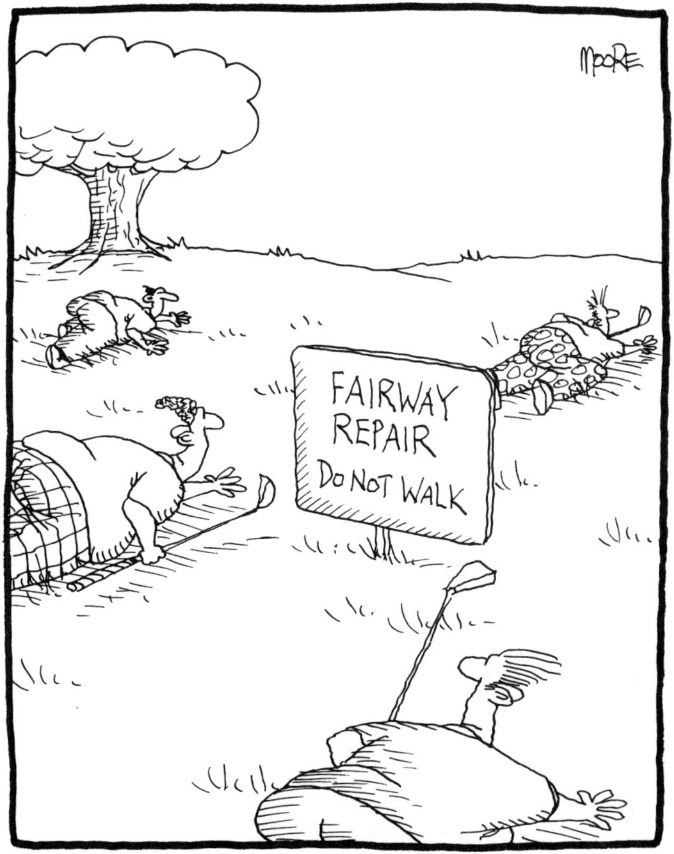
MOORE
FAIRWAY REPAIR
DO NOT WALK

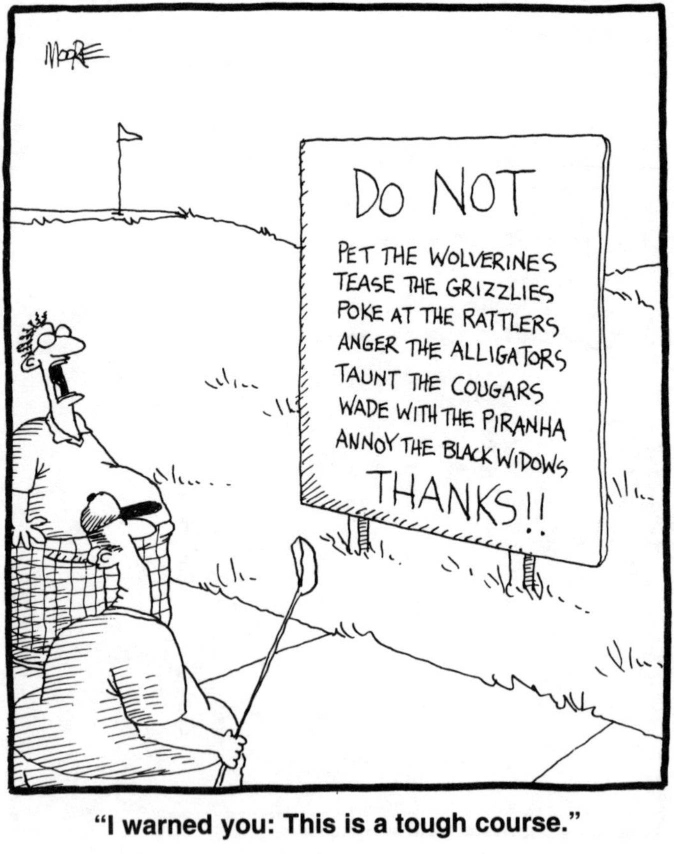
MOORE
DO NOT
PET THE WOLVERINES
TEASE THE GRIZZLIES
POKE AT THE RATTLERS
ANGER THE ALLIGATORS
TAUNT THE COUGARS
WADE WITH THE PIRANHA
ANNOY THE BLACK WIDOWS
THANKS!!

"I warned you: This is a tough course."

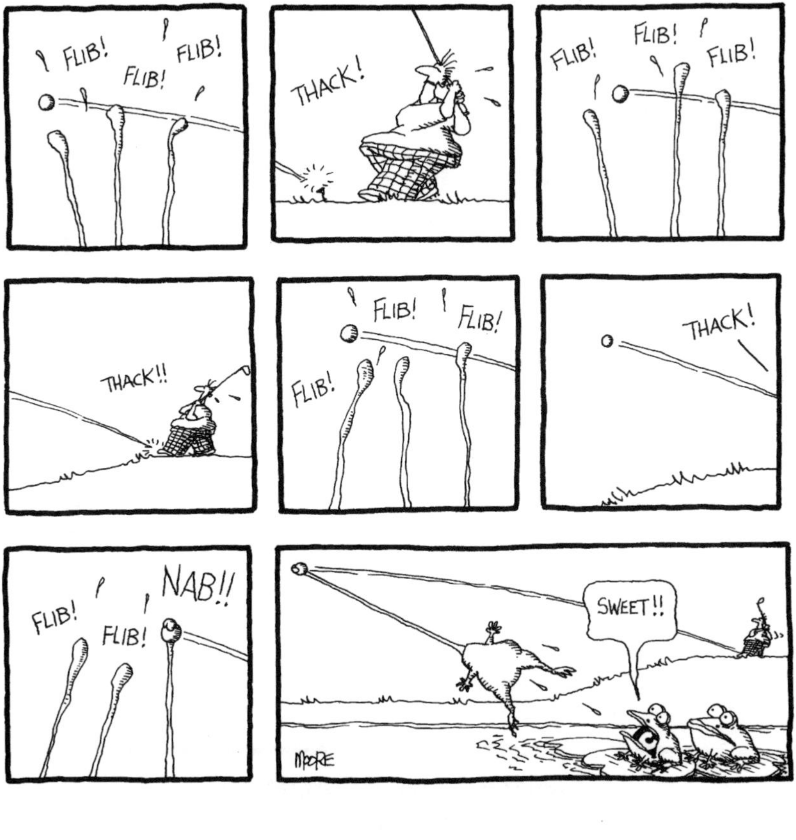
FLIB!
FLIB!
FLIB!
THACK!
FLIB!
FLIB!
FLIB!
THACK!!
FLIB!
FLIB!
FLIB!
THACK!
FLIB!
FLIB!
NAB!!
SWEET!!
MOORE

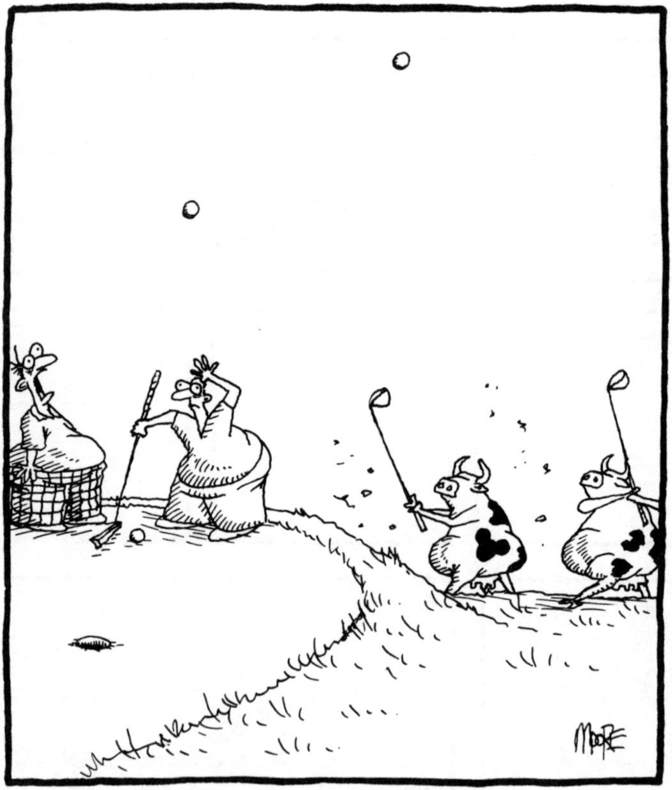
MOORE

"Watch out, Doug! Cow chips!"

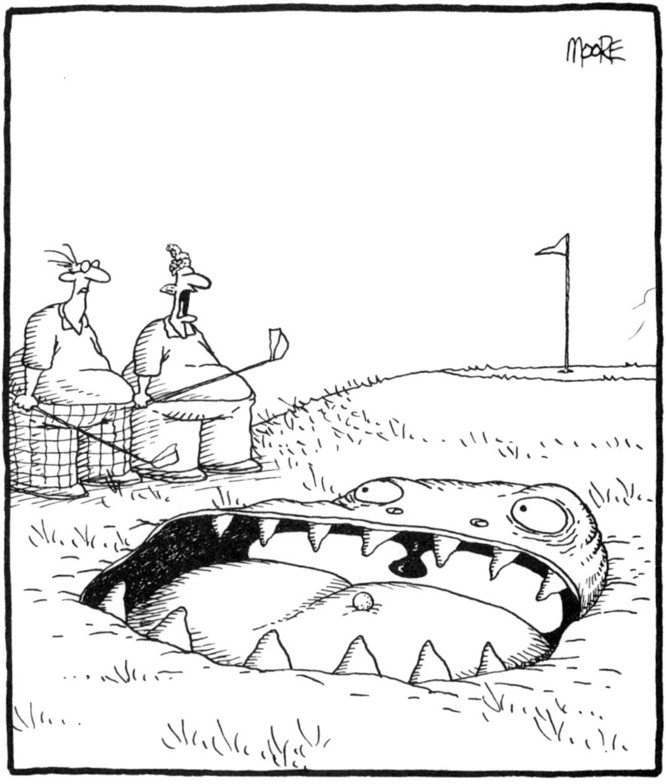
MOORE

"Bummer, Sid. Your ball landed smack in the middle of a death trap."

SPANKED IT!!
PLOOP
YEAAAH! I DID IT!!
A ONCE-IN-A-LIFETIME HOLE IN ONE!!
AND THANK GOODNESS YOU'RE HERE AS A WITNESS, ANDY!!
MOORE

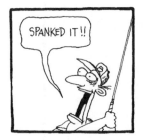

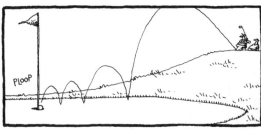

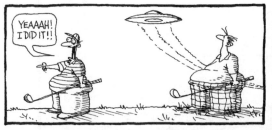

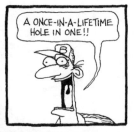

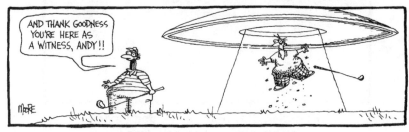

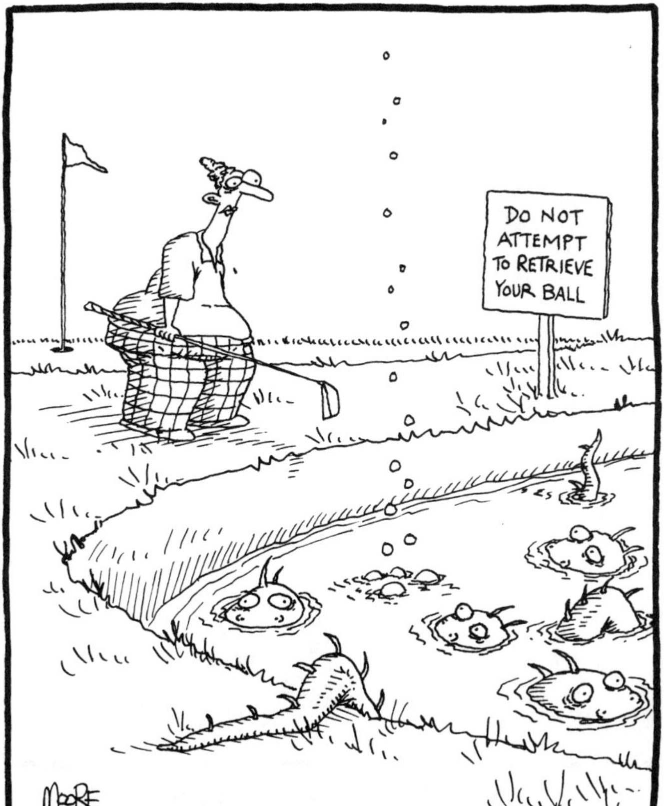
DO NOT
ATTEMPT
TO RETRIEVE
YOUR BALL
MOORE

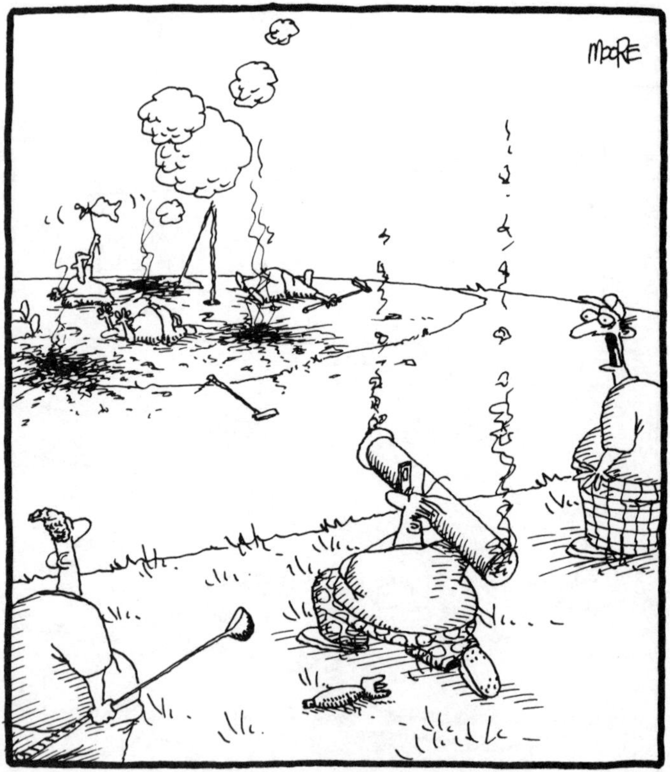
MOORE

"Cease fire! It looks like they've agreed to let us play through."

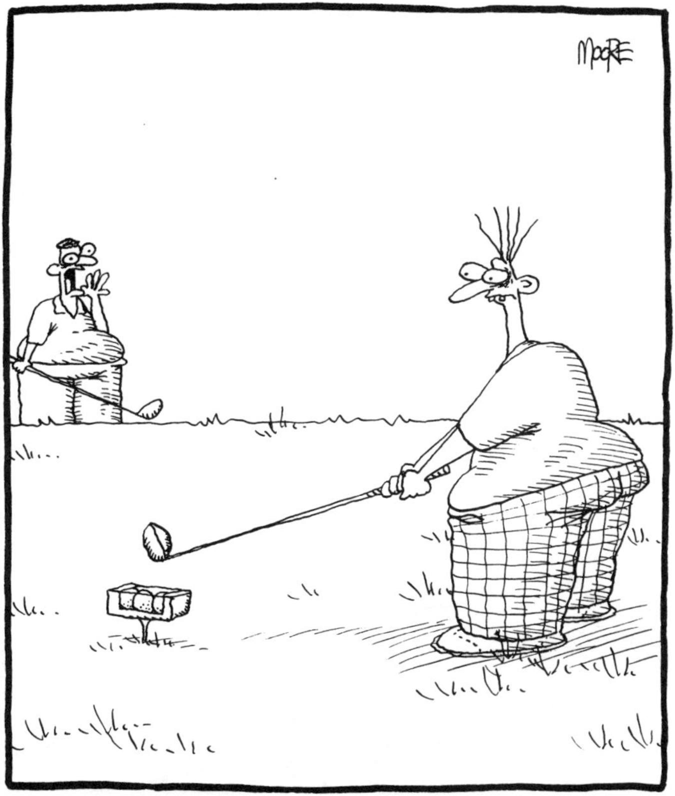
MOORE

"Leonard! First take your ball out of the box!!"

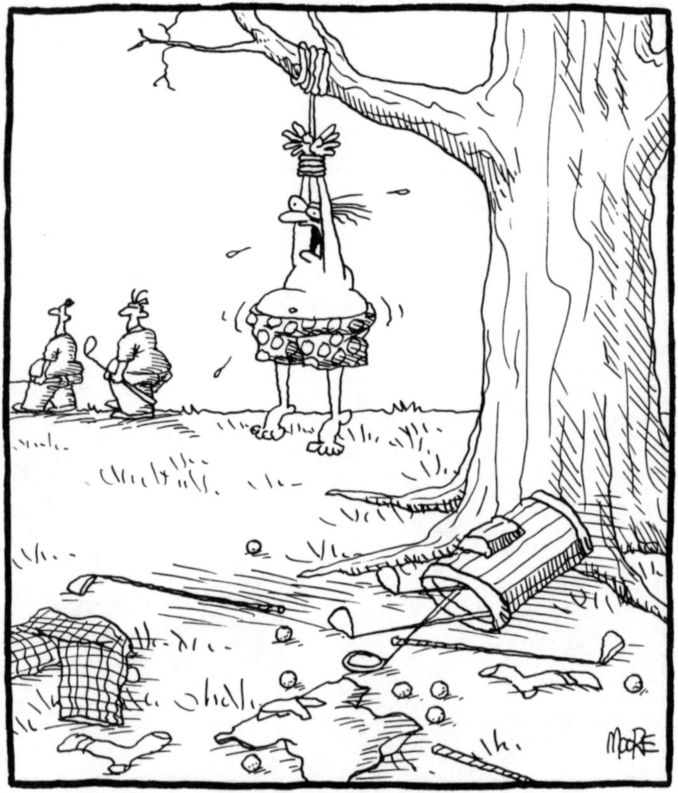
MOORE

“OK, OK! Come back! I promise to stop yelling ‘You da man!’”

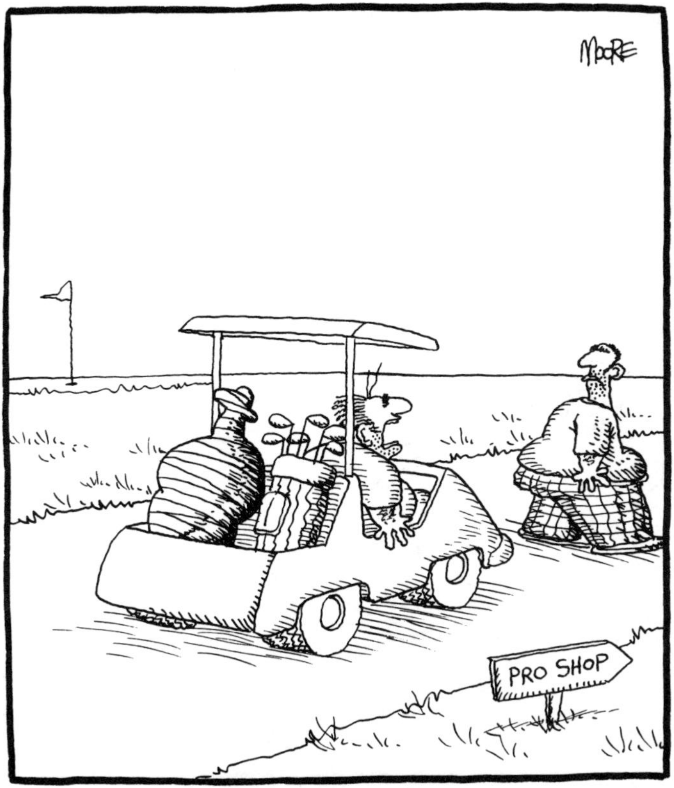
MOORE
PRO SHOP

"Grab some extra balls, a handful of tees, and a couple of shovels."

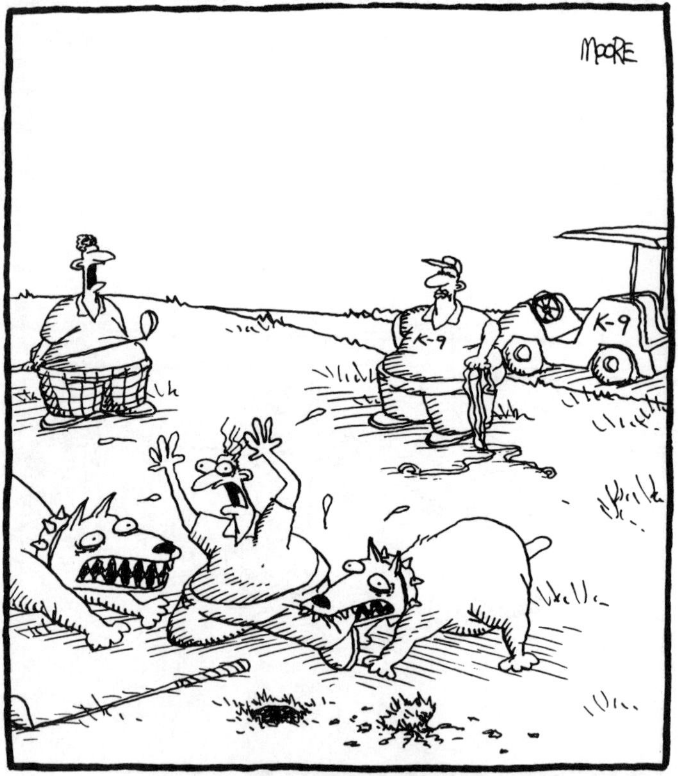
MOORE
K-9
K-9

"Don't be a fool, Dick! Do as he says!
Replace your divot!"

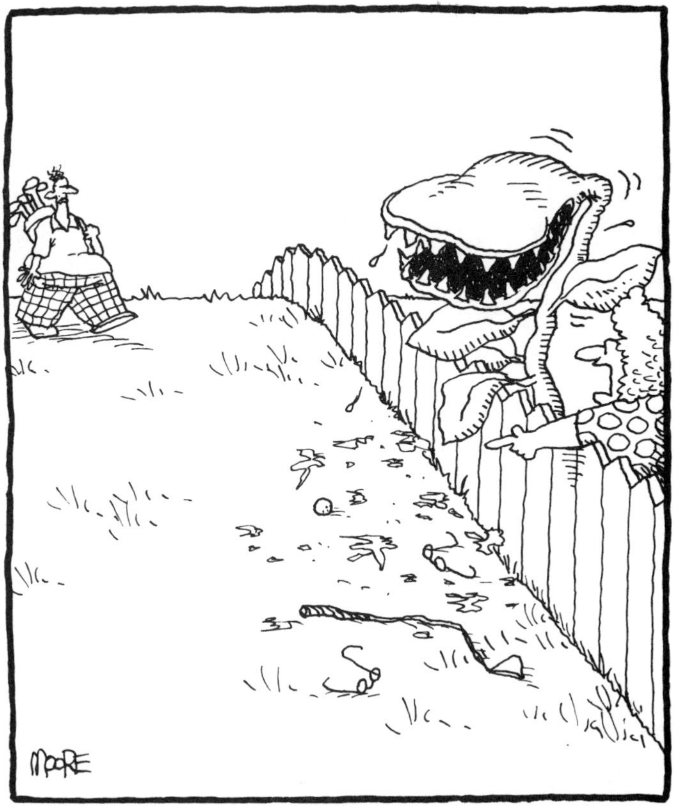
MOORE

"Mr. Golfer! Oh, Mr. Golfer! Here's your ball, Mr. Golfer!"

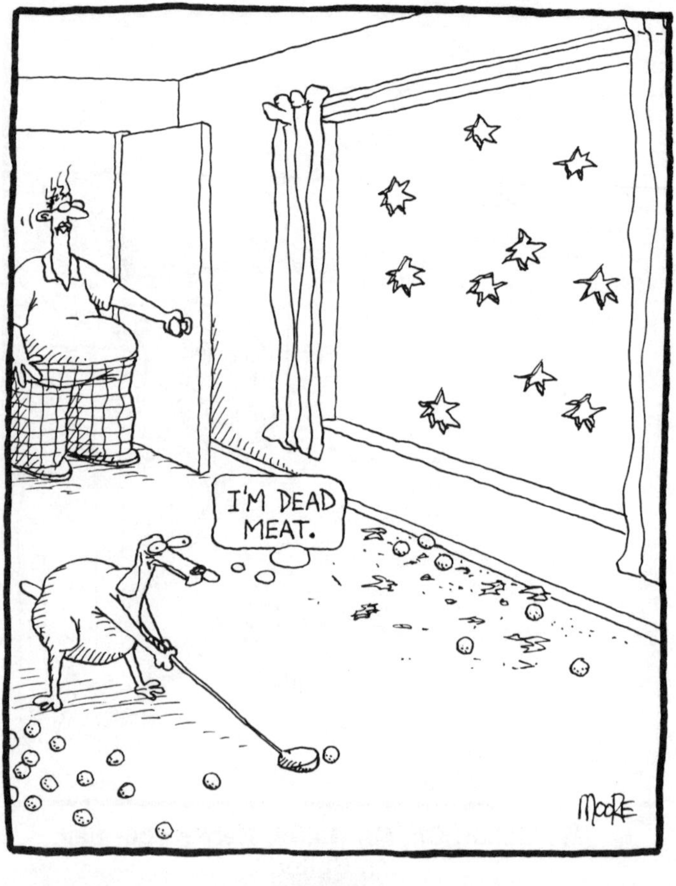
I'M DEAD MEAT.
MOORE

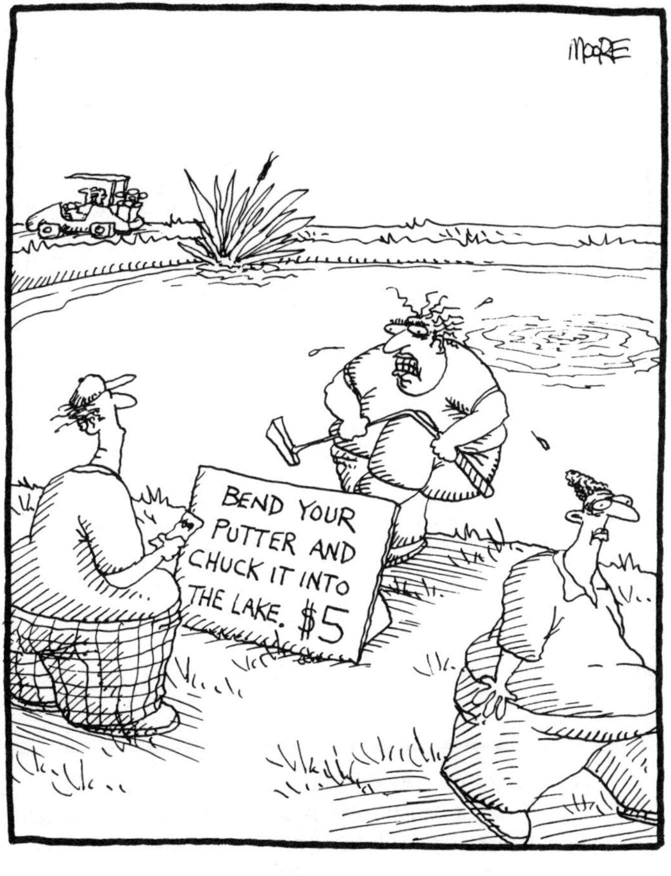
MOORE
BEND YOUR PUTTER AND CHUCK IT INTO THE LAKE. $5

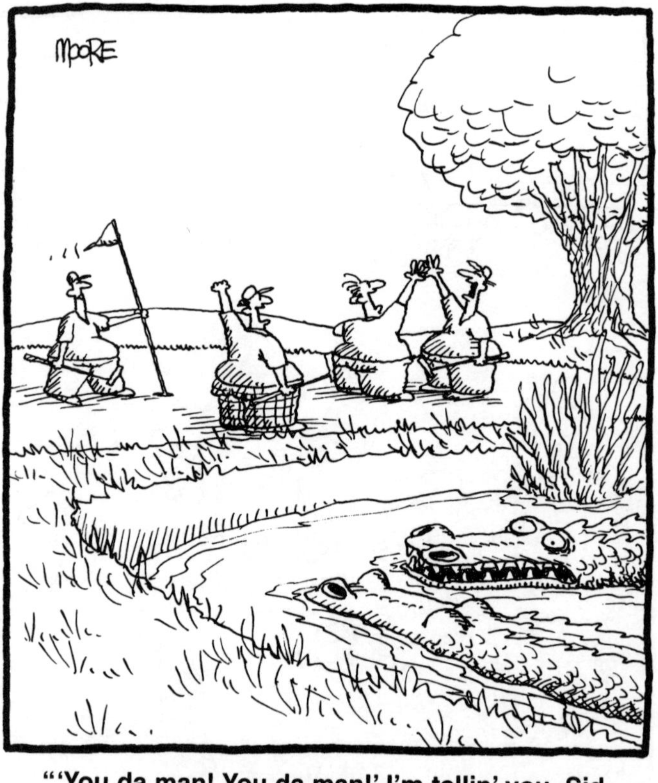
MOORE

"'You da man! You da man!' I'm tellin' you, Sid, if I hear 'You da man!' one more time, I'm gonna go freakin' prehistoric on someone."

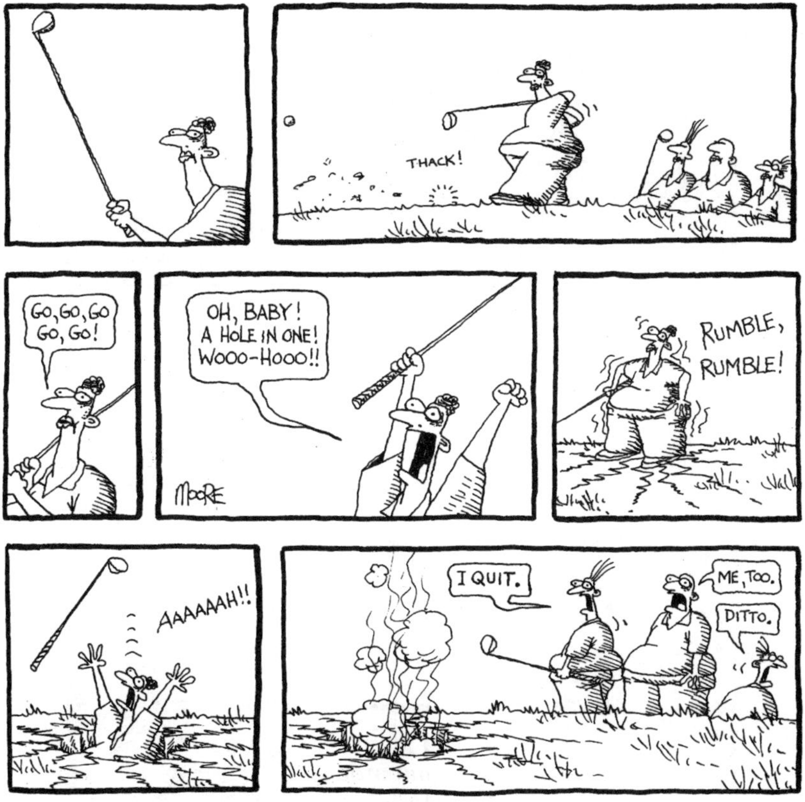
THACK!
GO, GO, GO
GO, GO!
OH, BABY!
A HOLE IN ONE!
WOOO-HOOO!!
MOORE
RUMBLE,
RUMBLE!
AAAAAAH!!
I QUIT.
ME, TOO.
DITTO.

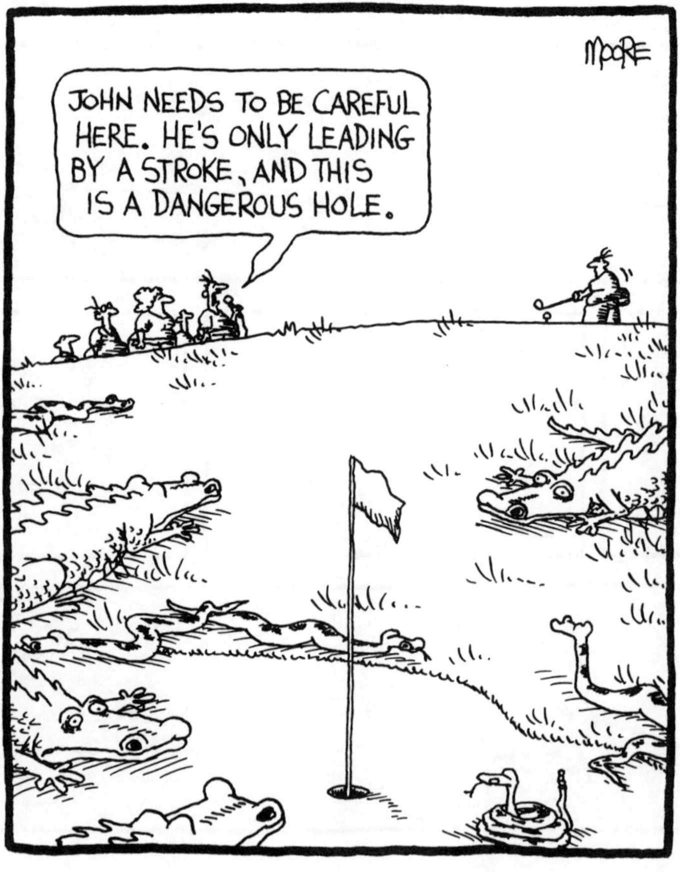
MOORE
JOHN NEEDS TO BE CAREFUL HERE. HE'S ONLY LEADING BY A STROKE, AND THIS IS A DANGEROUS HOLE.

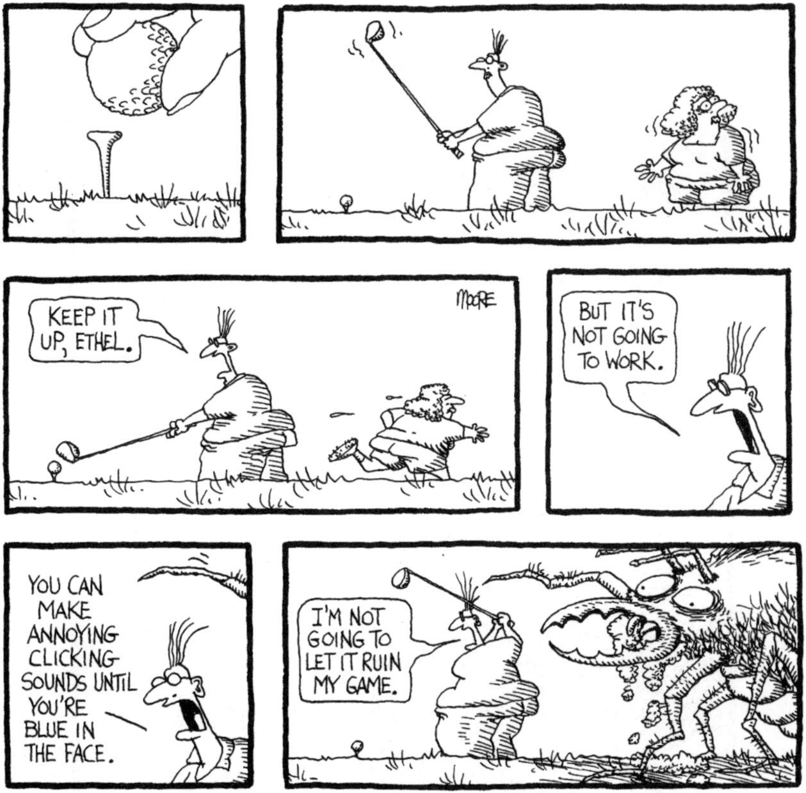
MOORE
KEEP IT UP, ETHEL.
BUT IT'S NOT GOING TO WORK.
YOU CAN MAKE ANNOYING CLICKING SOUNDS UNTIL YOU'RE BLUE IN THE FACE.
I'M NOT GOING TO LET IT RUIN MY GAME.

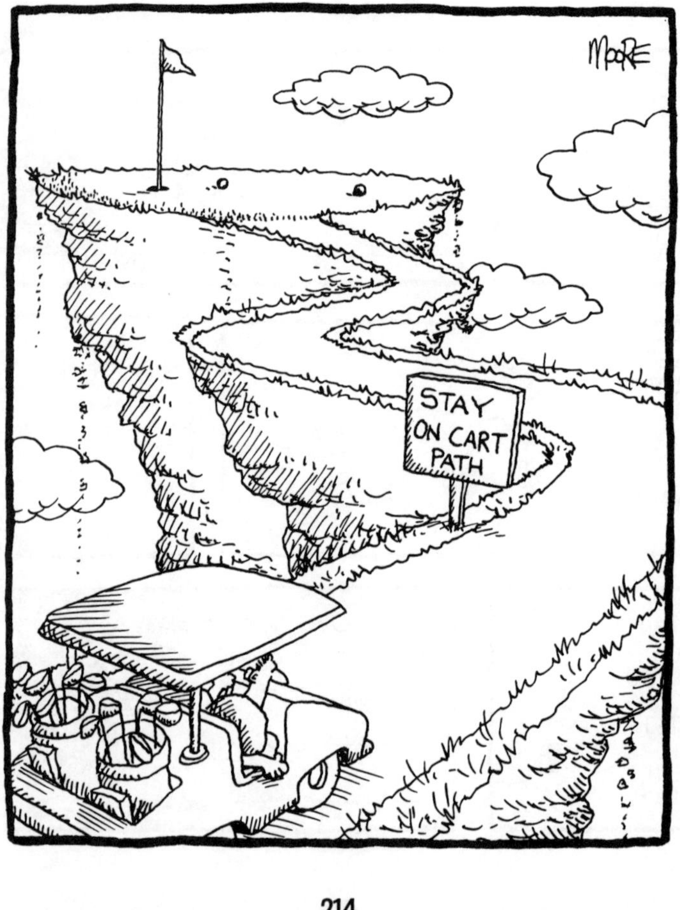
MOORE
STAY
ON CART
PATH

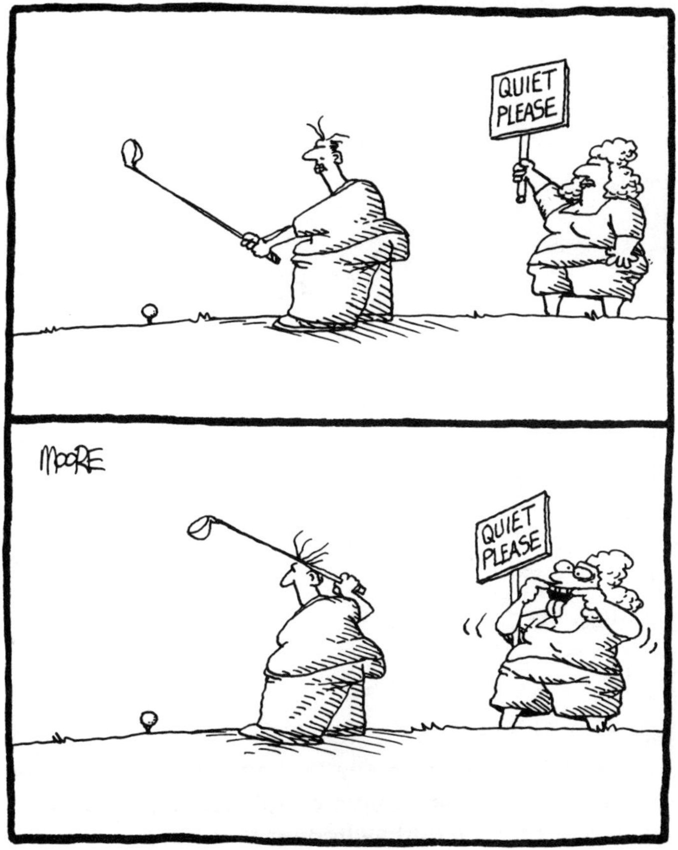
QUIET PLEASE
MOORE
QUIET PLEASE

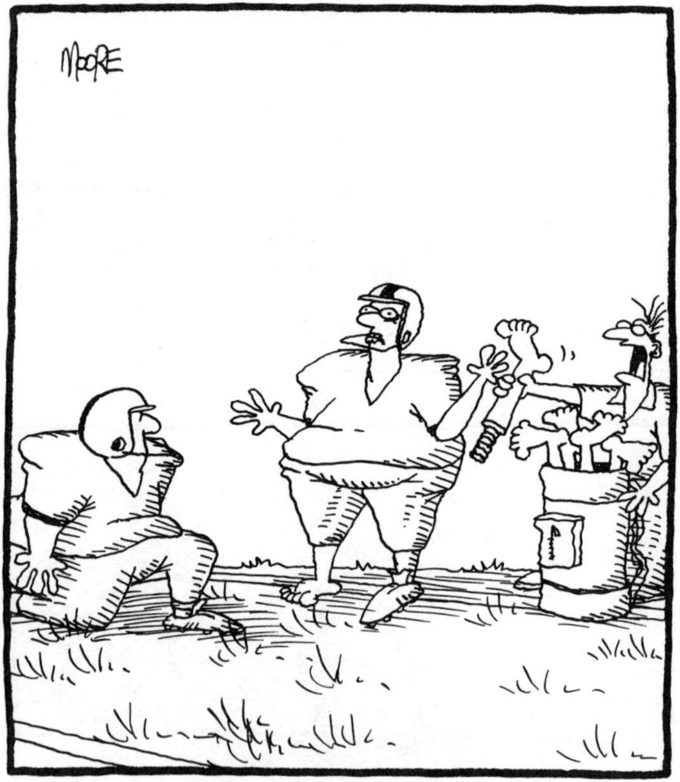
MOORE

"You're looking at a 30-yard kick against the wind. I recommend switching to a No. 7."

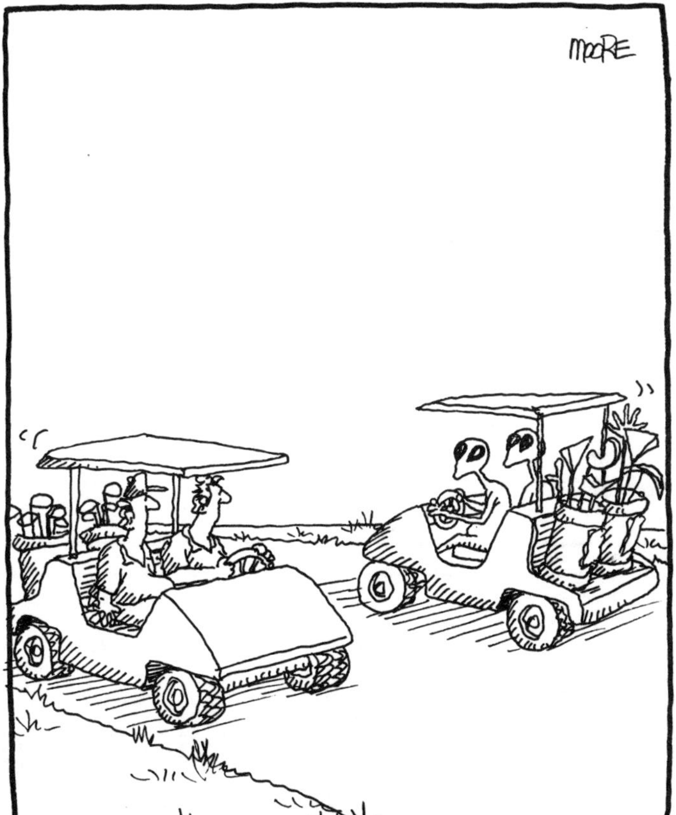
MOORE

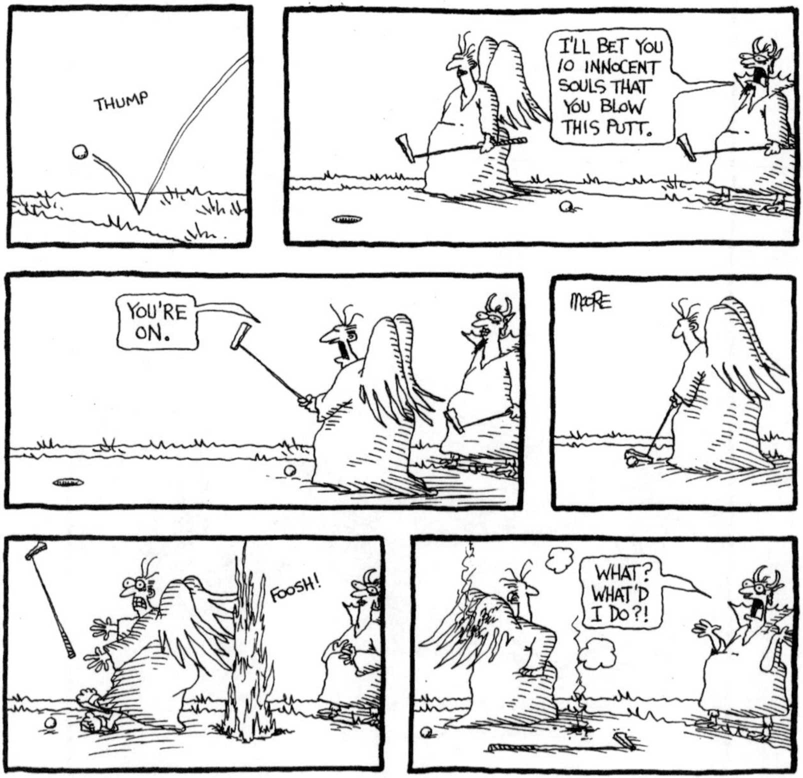
THUMP
I'LL BET YOU 10 INNOCENT SOULS THAT YOU BLOW THIS PUTT.
YOU'RE ON.
MOORE
FOOSH!
WHAT? WHAT'D I DO?!

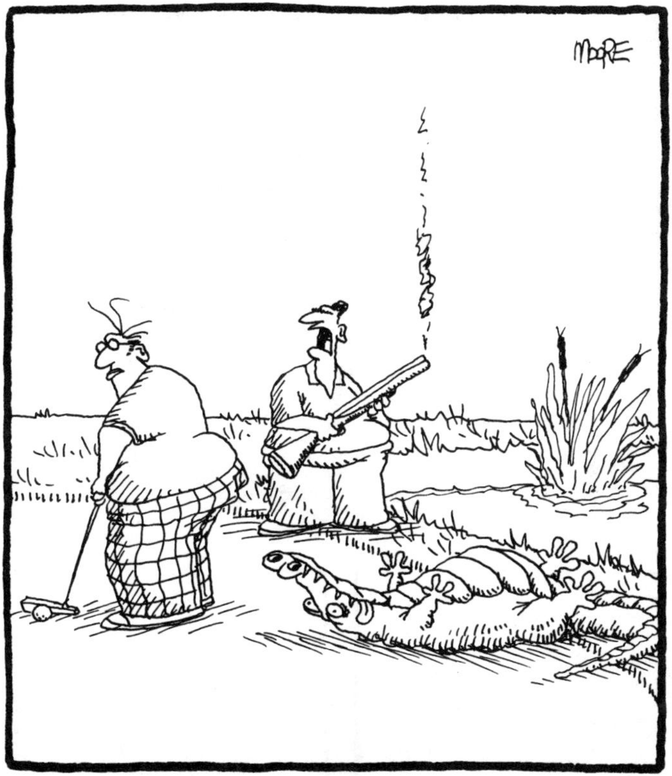
MOORE

"Where was I?... Oh, yeah. Knees bent. Elbows out.
Total concentration."

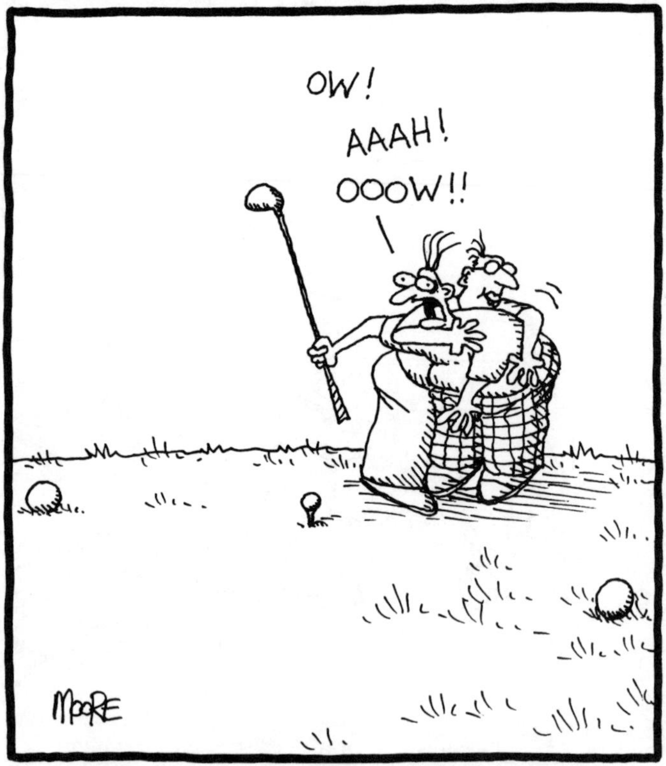
OW!
AAAH!
OOOW!!
MOORE

With a few quick spinal adjustments, the chiropractor straightened out Andy's tee shot.

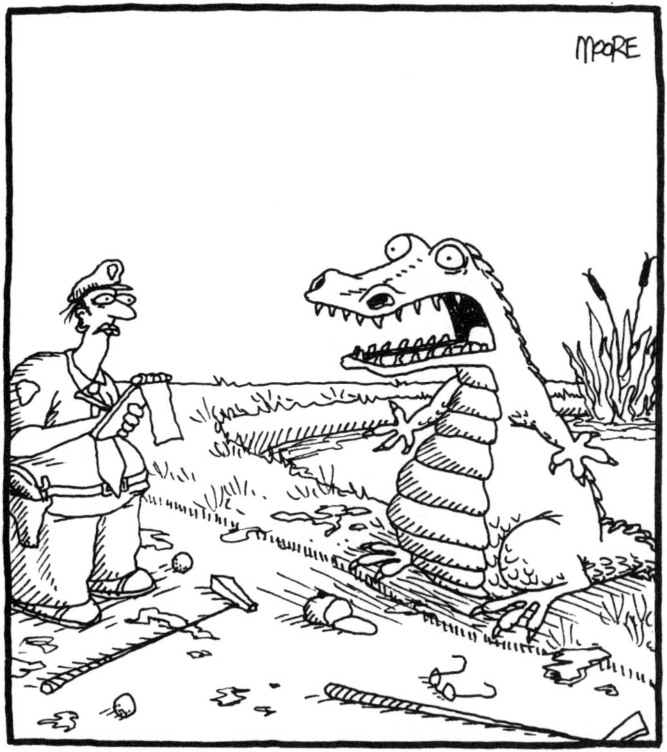
MOORE

"... Then this, um, spaceship swoops out of nowhere and—zap!—sucks both golfers right off the green. Swear on my mother's suitcase that's what happened. Can I go now?"

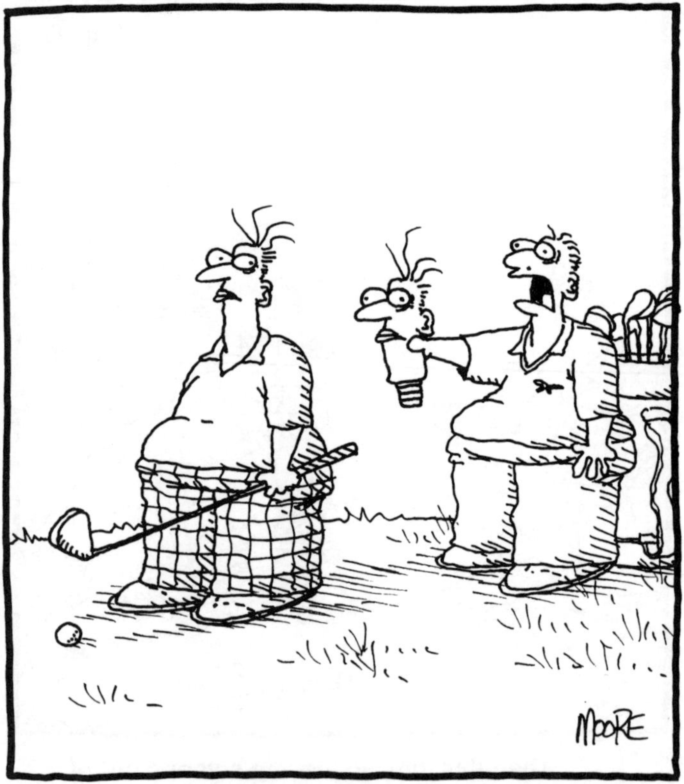
MOORE

"This is a tough shot. You'll need total concentration. . . . You'd better use your other head."

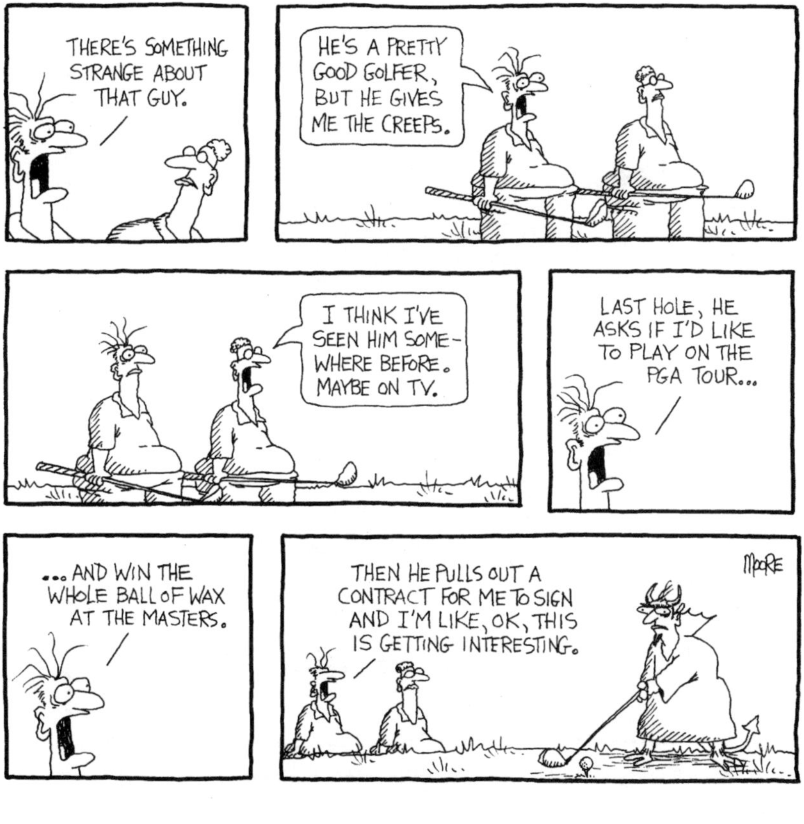
THERE'S SOMETHING STRANGE ABOUT THAT GUY.
HE'S A PRETTY GOOD GOLFER, BUT HE GIVES ME THE CREEPS.
I THINK I'VE SEEN HIM SOME-WHERE BEFORE. MAYBE ON TV.
LAST HOLE, HE ASKS IF I'D LIKE TO PLAY ON THE PGA TOUR...
...AND WIN THE WHOLE BALL OF WAX AT THE MASTERS.
MOORE
THEN HE PULLS OUT A CONTRACT FOR ME TO SIGN AND I'M LIKE, OK, THIS IS GETTING INTERESTING.

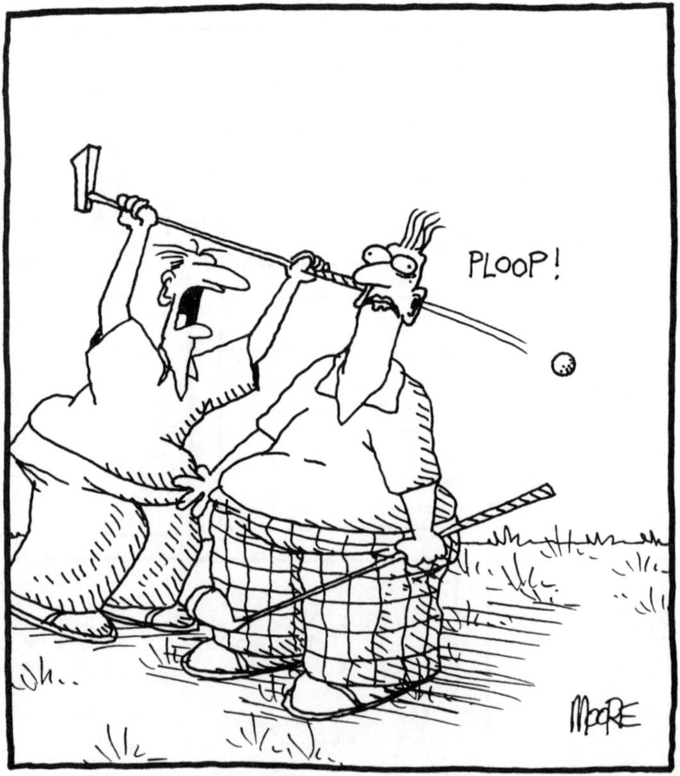
PLOOP!
Uh..
MOORE

"There's my ball. Easy . . . don't move. . . . Got it!"

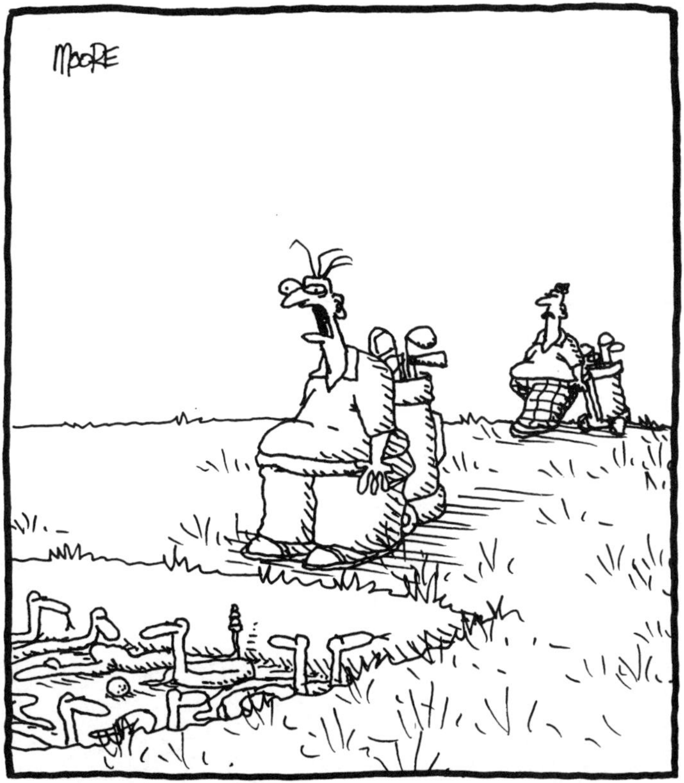
MOORE

"You'd better grab your snake wedge, Frank."

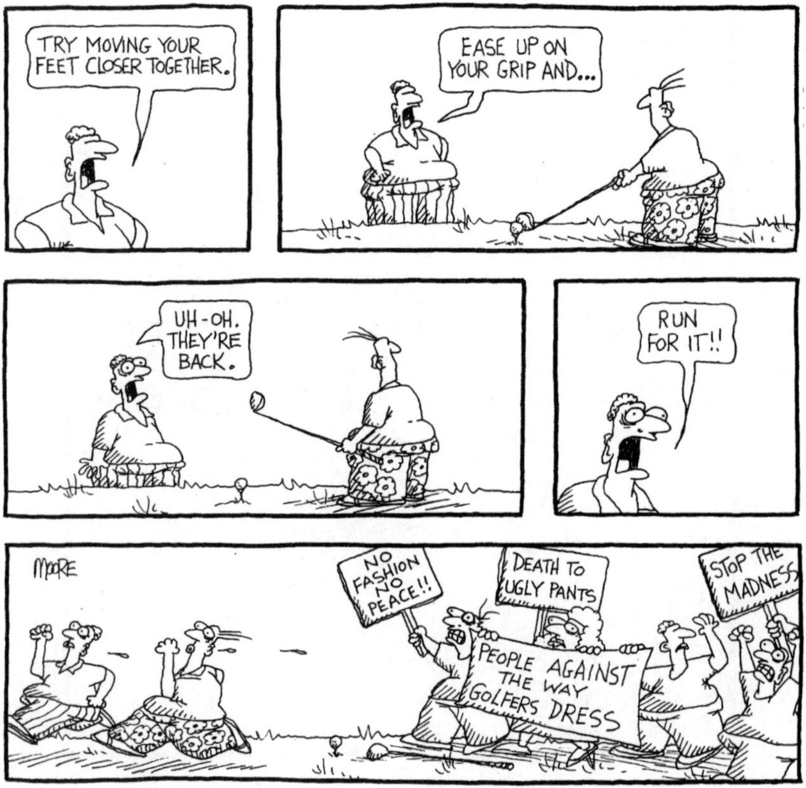
TRY MOVING YOUR FEET CLOSER TOGETHER.
EASE UP ON YOUR GRIP AND...
UH-OH. THEY'RE BACK.
RUN FOR IT!!
MOORE
NO FASHION NO PEACE!!
DEATH TO UGLY PANTS
STOP THE MADNESS
PEOPLE AGAINST THE WAY GOLFERS DRESS

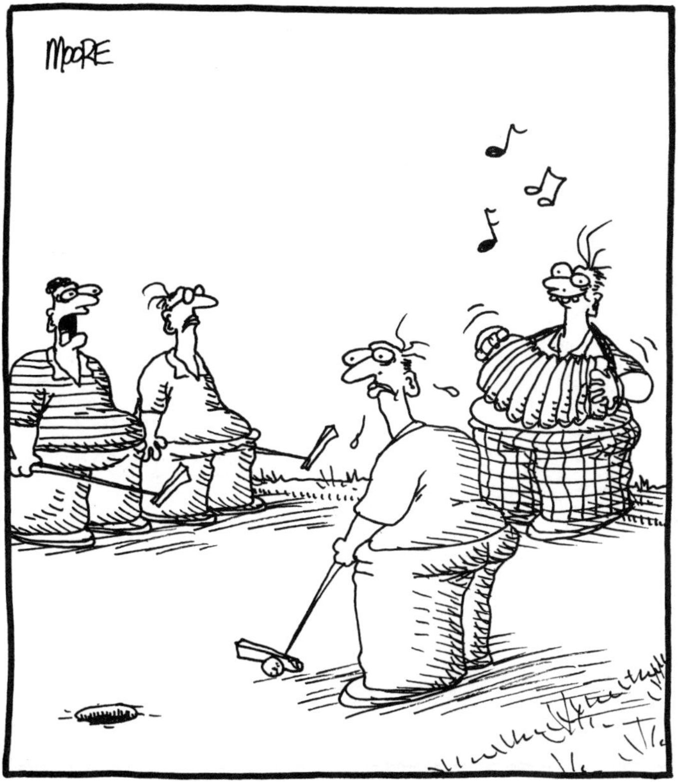
MOORE

"I *hate* playing with Morty."

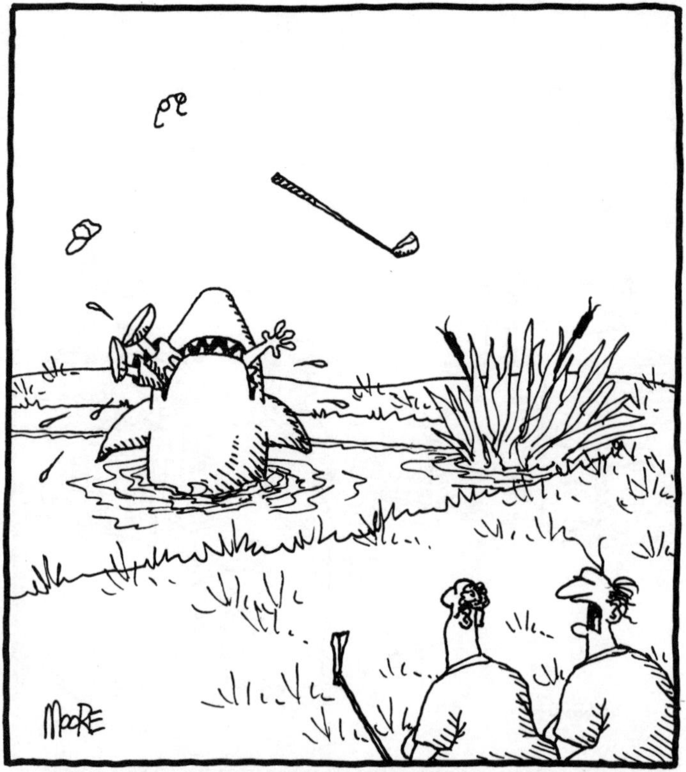
MOORE

"'Don't wade in there,' I said. 'Play another ball,' I said. 'Water hazards can be dangerous,' I said."

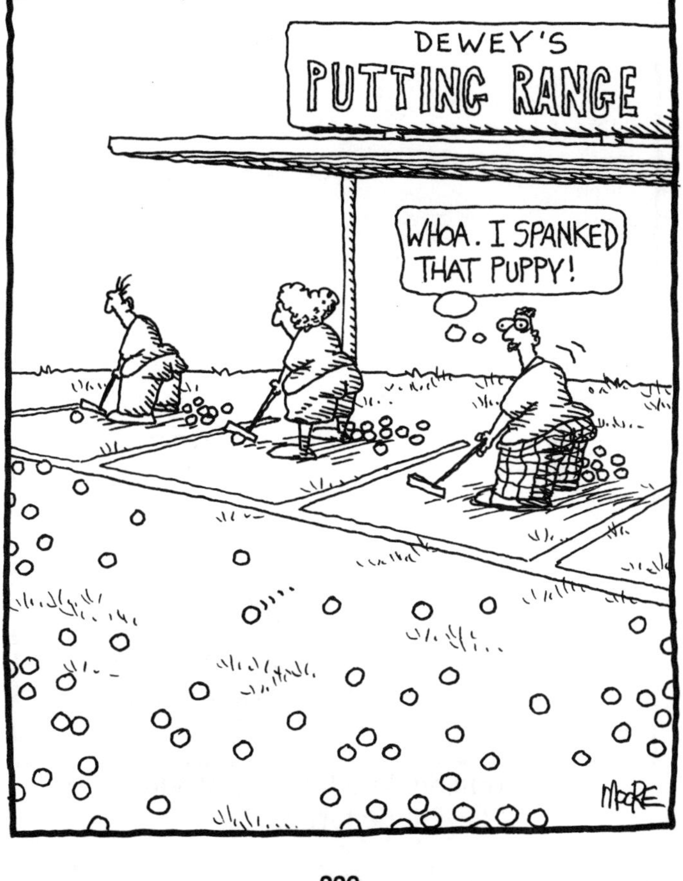
DEWEY'S
PUTTING RANGE
WHOA. I SPANKED THAT PUPPY!
MOORE

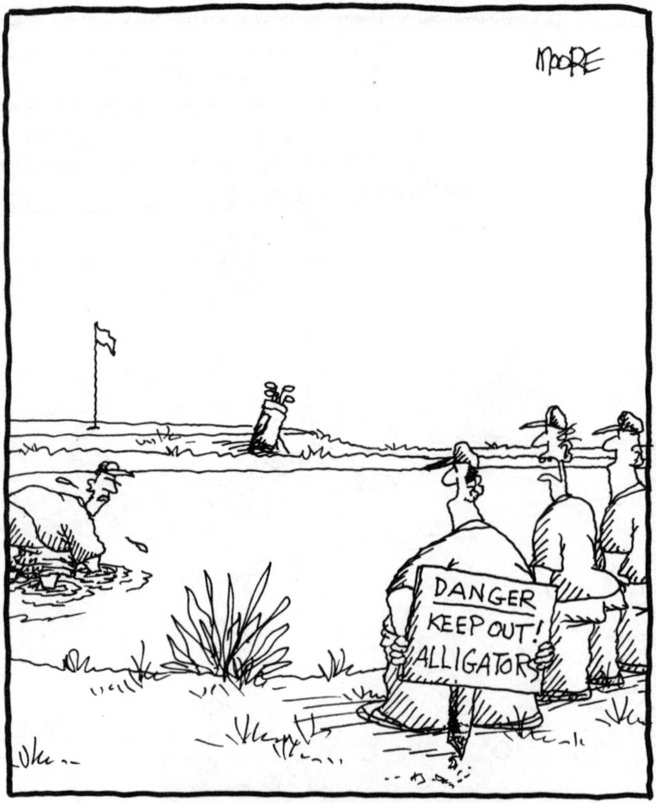
MOORE
DANGER
KEEP OUT!
ALLIGATORS

"Keep looking. You'll find it. Wade out a little farther."

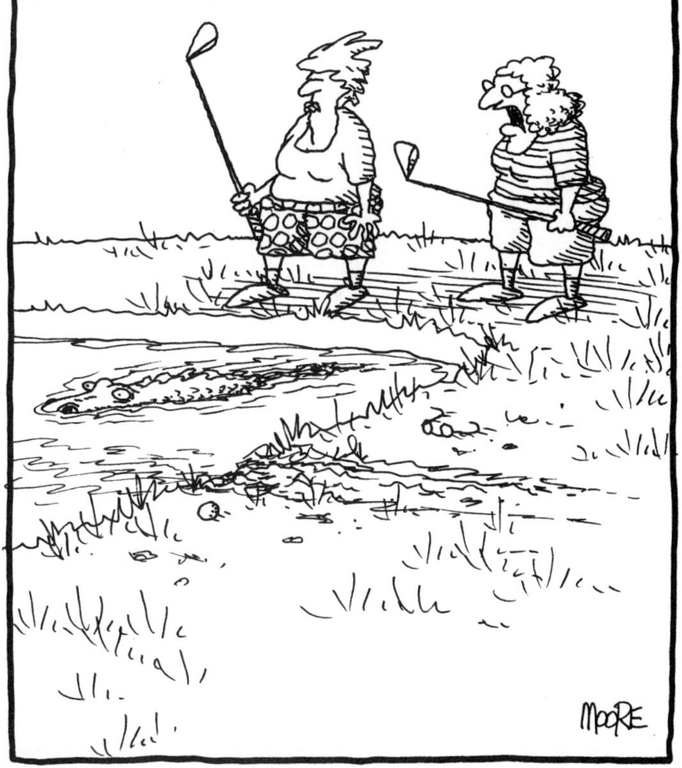
MOORE

"So then Vicky says, 'There's my ball right on the bank of the water hazard next to that log.'"

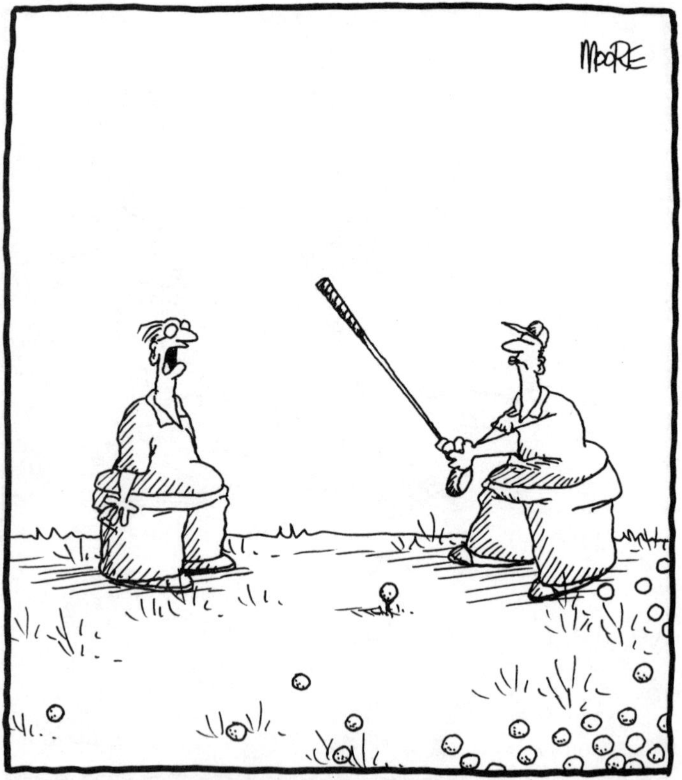
MOORE

"Hmmm . . . Maybe it's your backswing. Try slowing down your backswing."

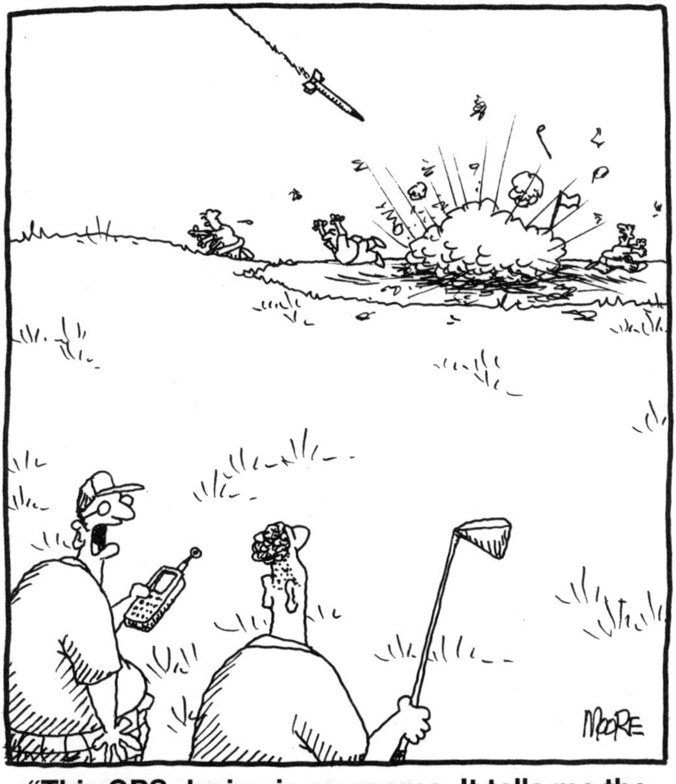
MOORE

"This GPS device is awesome. It tells me the exact distance to the pin while simultaneously launching a surgical air strike."

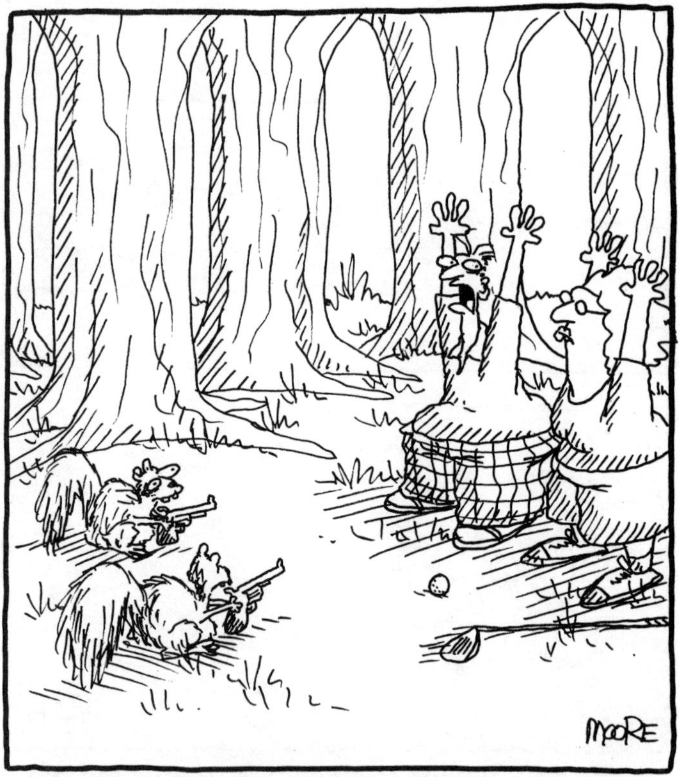
MOORE

"What'd I tell you, Alice? I said keep your ball out of the rough. . . . Well, live and learn."

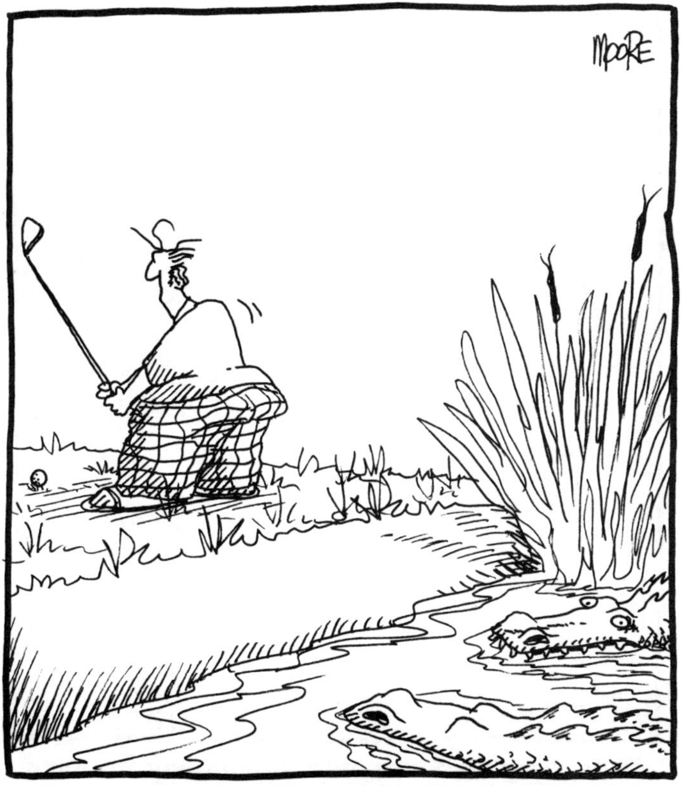
MOORE

"Here's the plan: You grab a leg, I grab a leg and—badda-boom, badda-bing—we both make a wish."

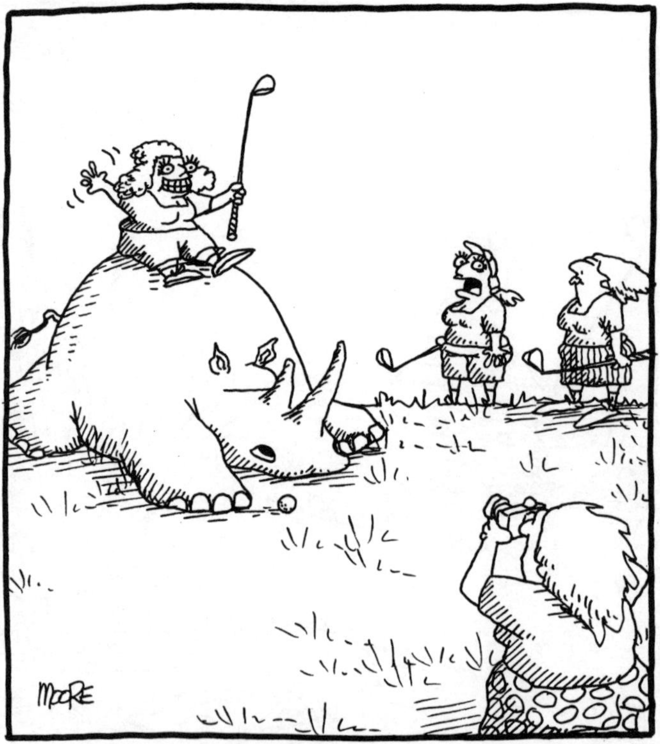
MOORE

"This thing wanders onto the fairway, so Alice nails it with a 5-iron from about 150 yards out and . . . hurry! Snap it. It's starting to come to."

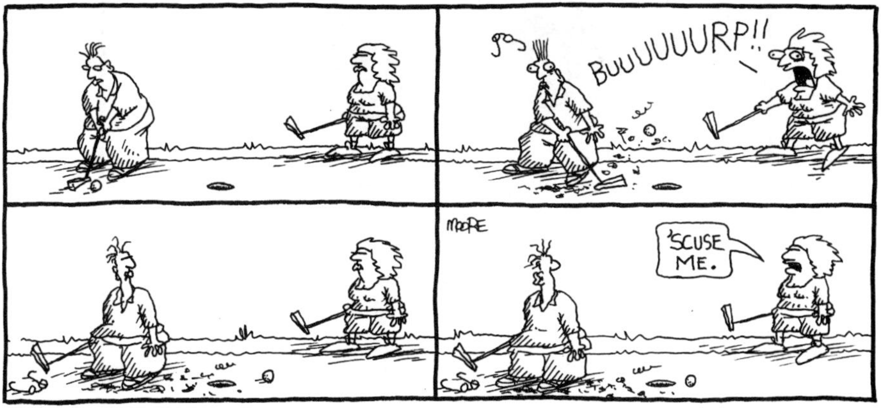
BUUUUUURP!!
MOORE
'SCUSE ME.

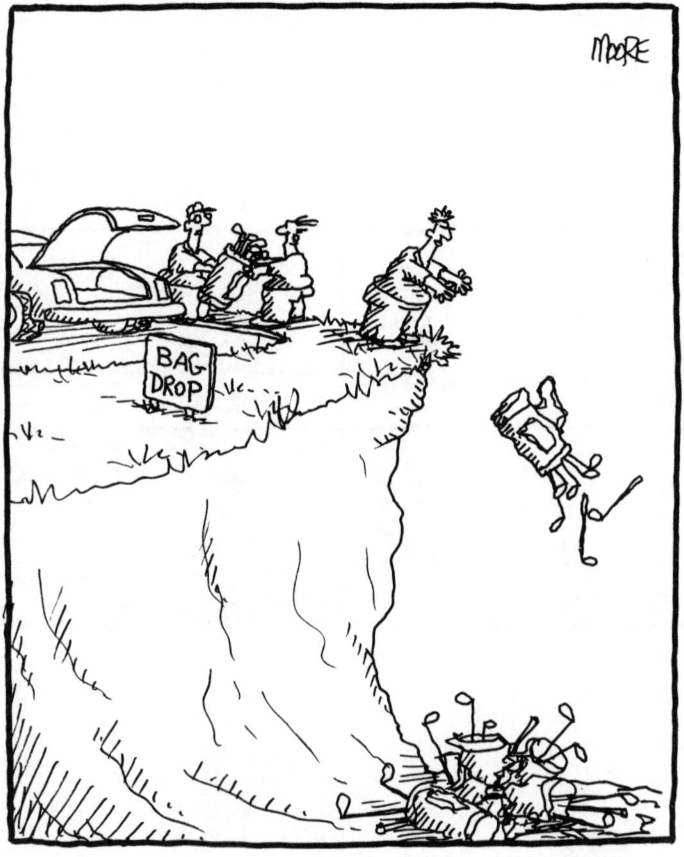
MOORE
BAG DROP

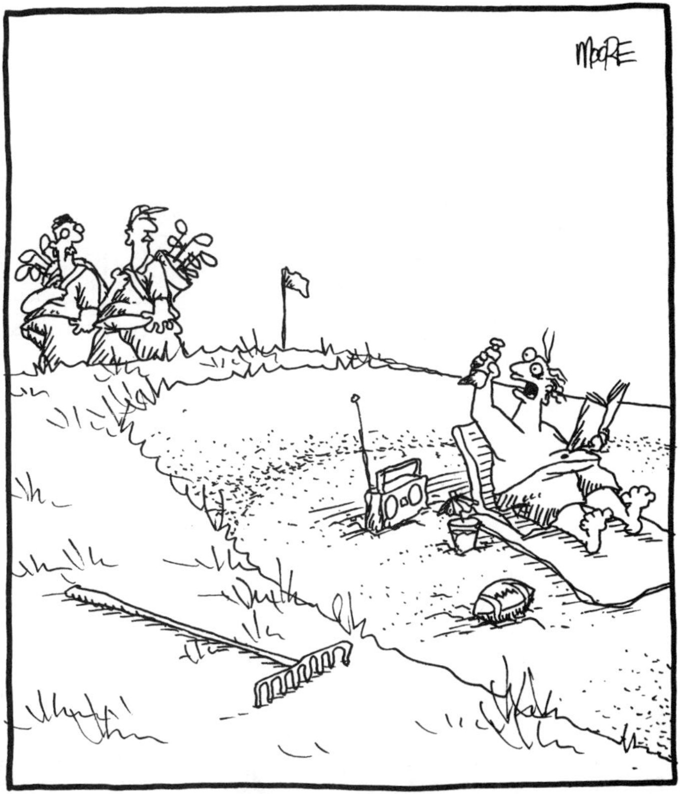
MOORE

"'Scuse me! Could one of you rub some lotion on my back?"

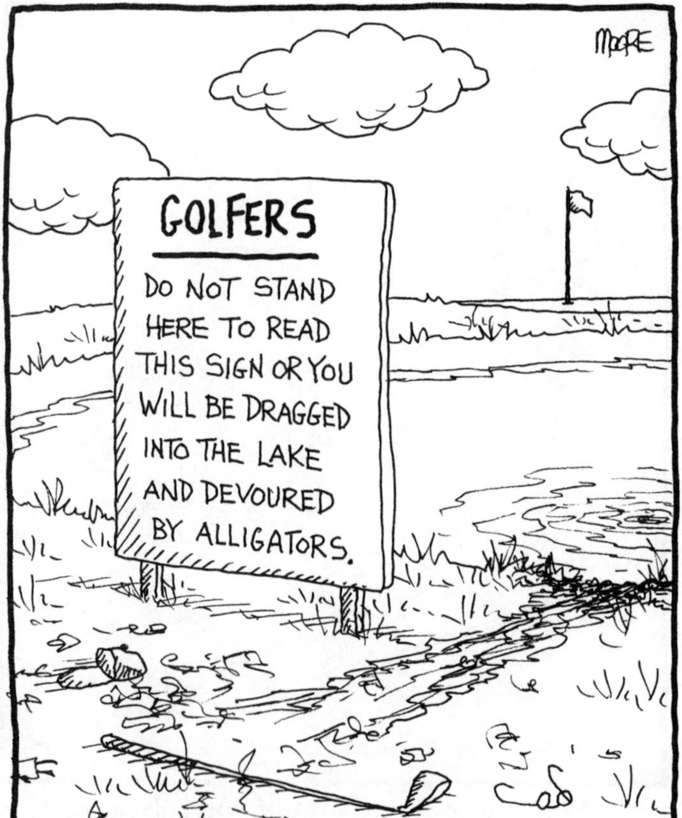
MOORE
GOLFERS
DO NOT STAND HERE TO READ THIS SIGN OR YOU WILL BE DRAGGED INTO THE LAKE AND DEVOURED BY ALLIGATORS.

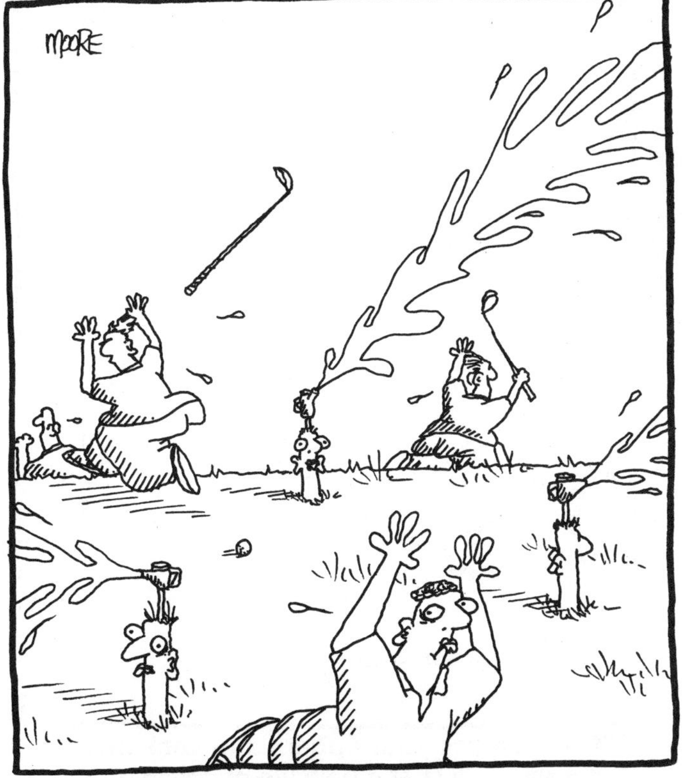
MOORE

Suddenly, sprinkler heads pop up in the fairway and soak the foursome.

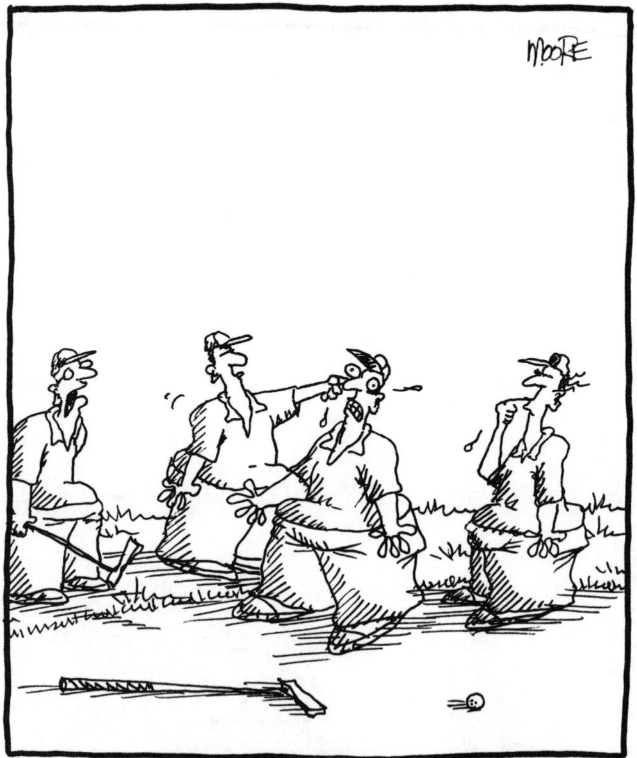
MOORE

"OK, now lick your fingers and stick them in his ears. . . . That's how we penalize golfers who make noises when someone's trying to putt."

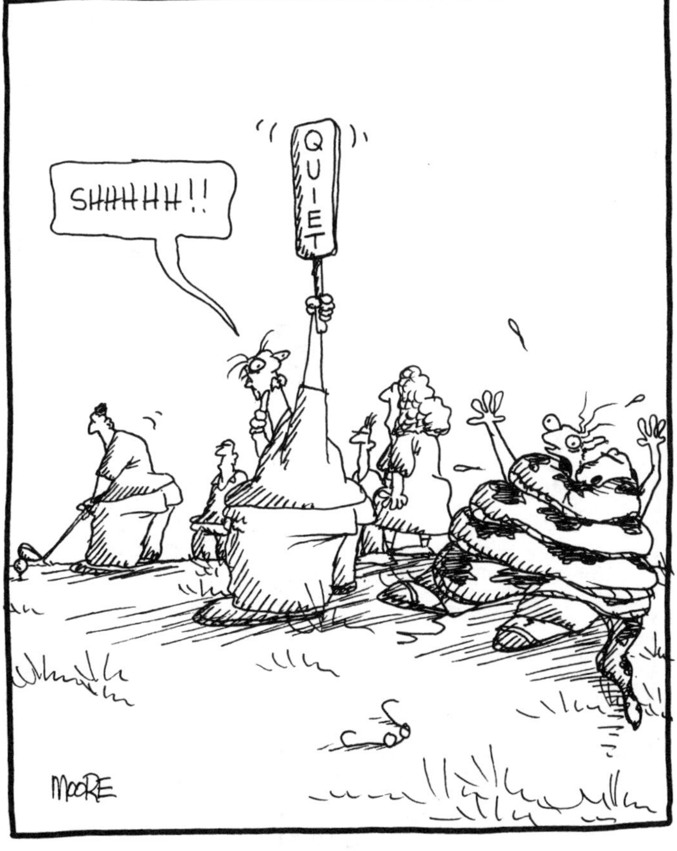
SHHHHH!!
QUIET
MOORE

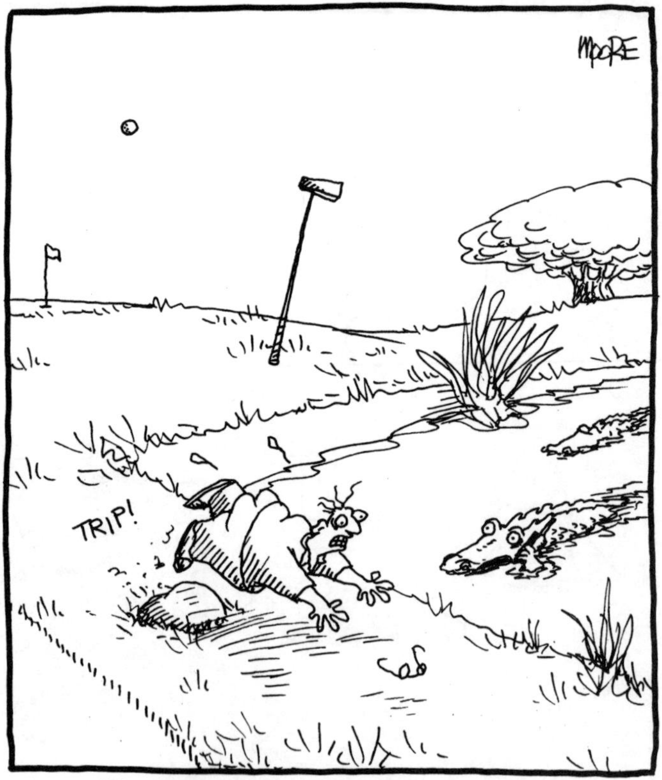
MOORE
TRIP!

**"Seventh green! Seventh green! . . .
Golfer down!"**

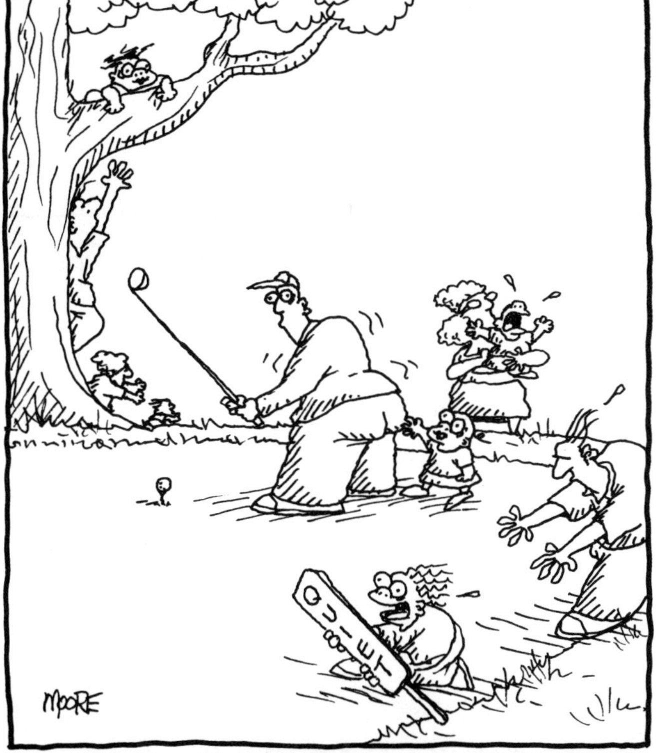
QUIET
MOORE

Immediately after the tournament, PGA officials pulled the plug on the "Bring Your 2-Year-Old, Get in Free" promotion.

PRESSURE'S ON, BOB. THAT'S A HUGE BUTT.
...PUTT! I MEANT A HUGE PUTT!!
MOORE

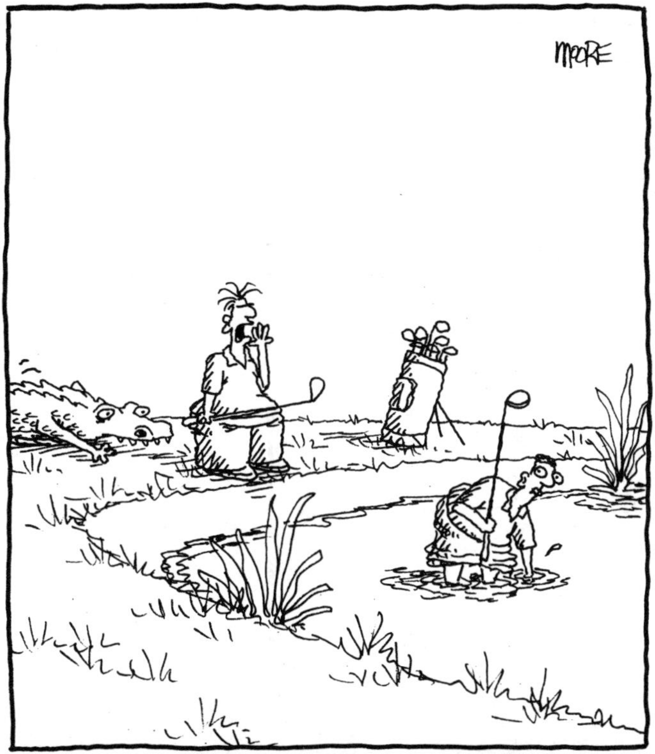
MOORE

"Look out, Bob! A gator! . . . Kidding! . . . No, wait! I see something big! . . . Just a log . . . Bob! For real this time! Coming right at you! . . . Ha! Gotcha again . . ."

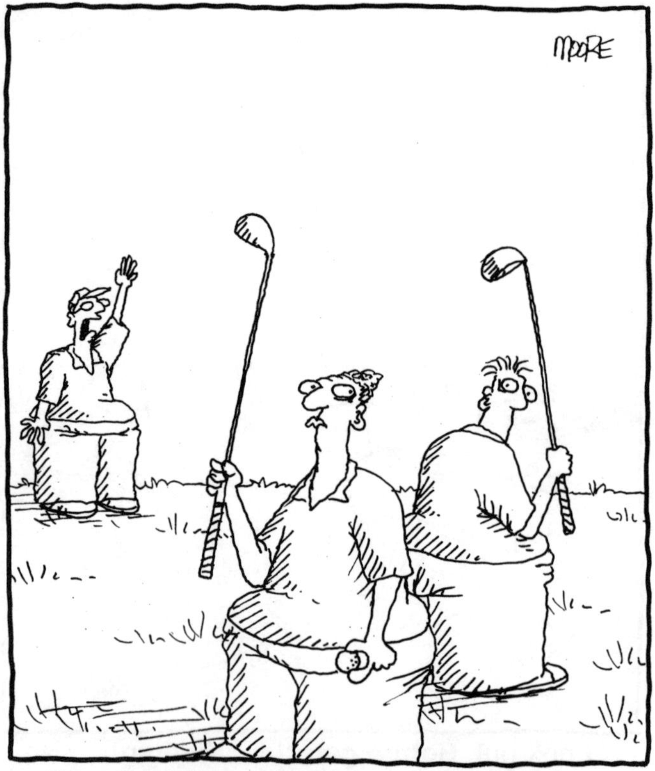
MOORE

"You both know the rules–walk 10 paces, turn, and tee off on each other."

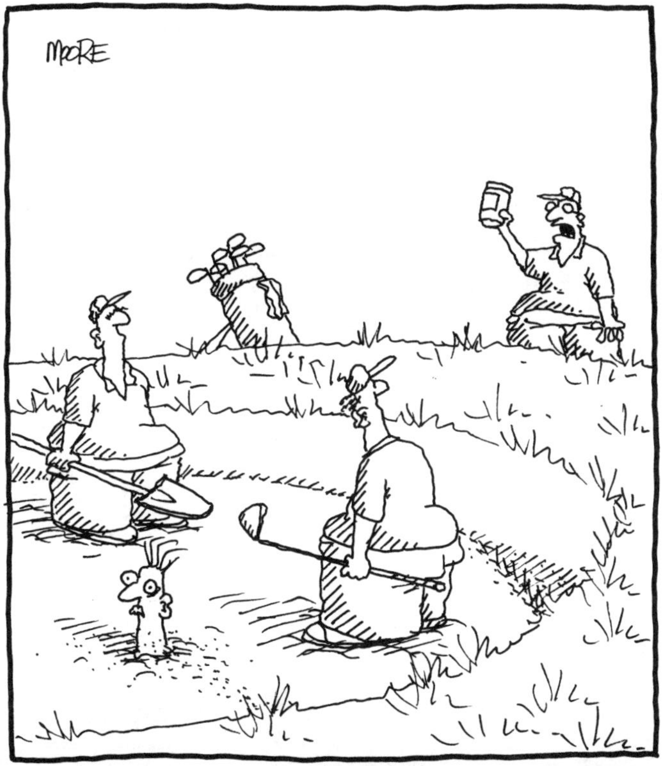
MOORE

"Excuse me! . . . I don't want to stick my nose where it doesn't belong, but you'll attract a lot more ants if you smear this jar of molasses all over your partner's head."

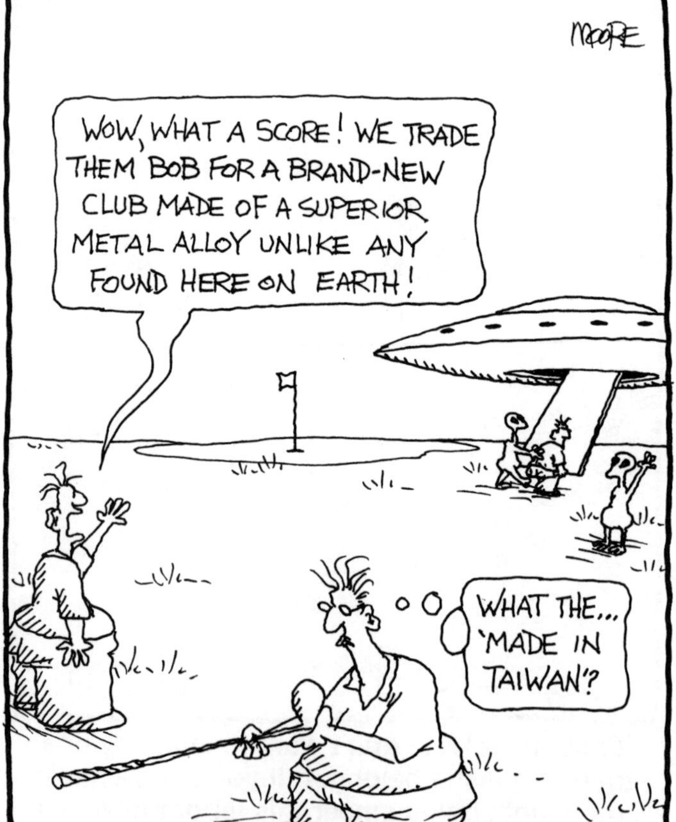
MOORE
WOW, WHAT A SCORE! WE TRADE THEM BOB FOR A BRAND-NEW CLUB MADE OF A SUPERIOR METAL ALLOY UNLIKE ANY FOUND HERE ON EARTH!
WHAT THE... 'MADE IN TAIWAN'?

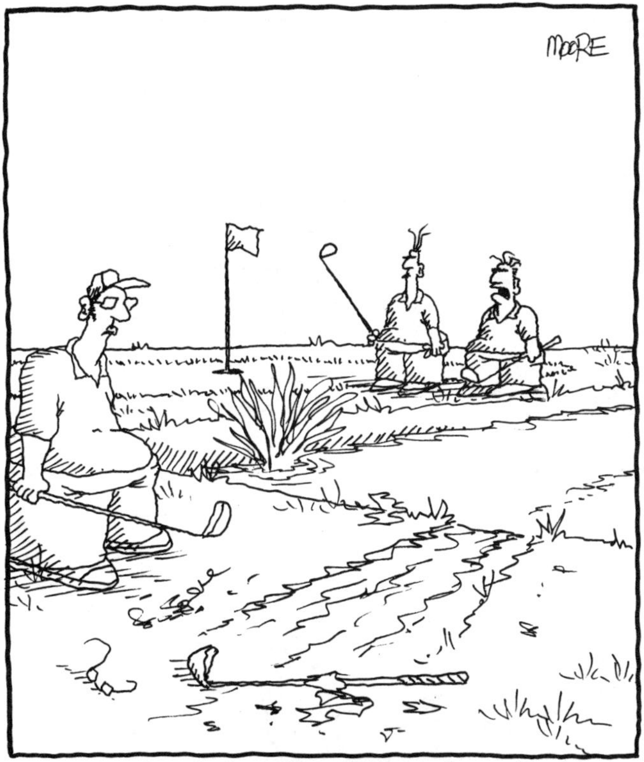
MOORE

"You're the tie-breaker, Dewey. I say it was a crocodile and Larry says it was a gator. . . . What do you think dragged Vince into the lake?"

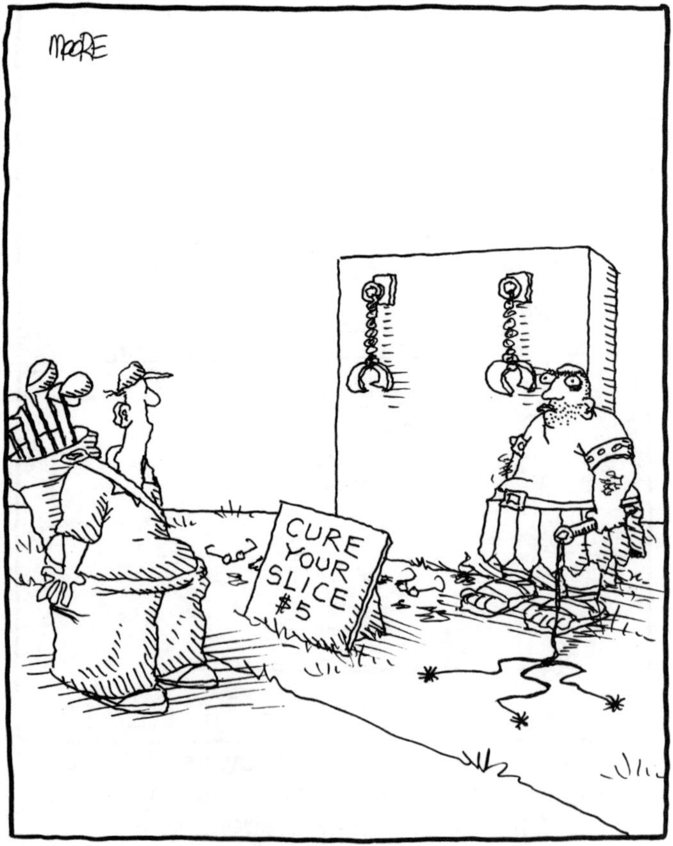
MOORE
CURE YOUR SLICE $5

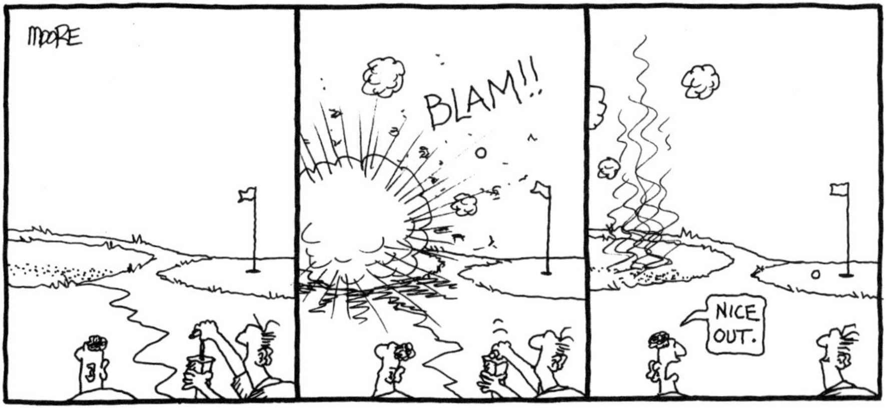
MOORE
BLAM!!
NICE OUT.

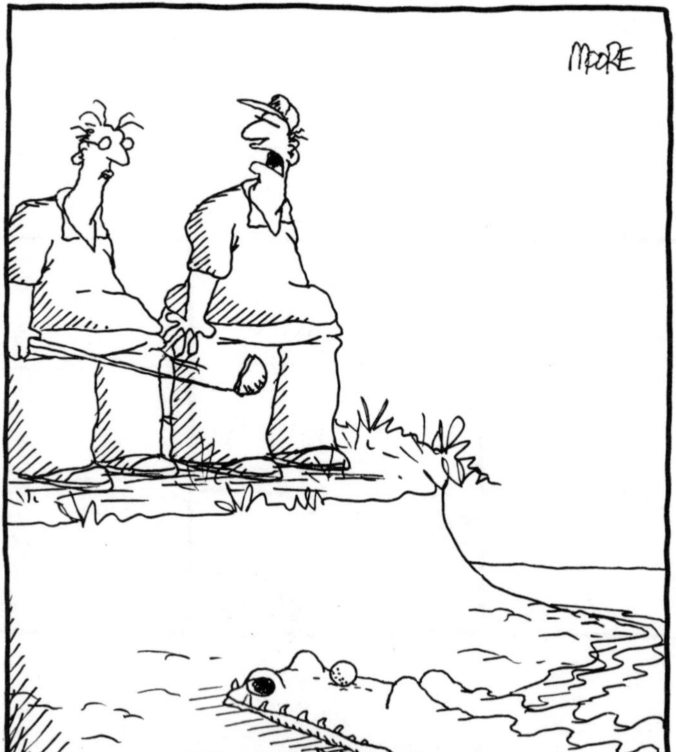
MOORE

"Hey, that's playable, Dewey. Go for it.
No guts, no glory."

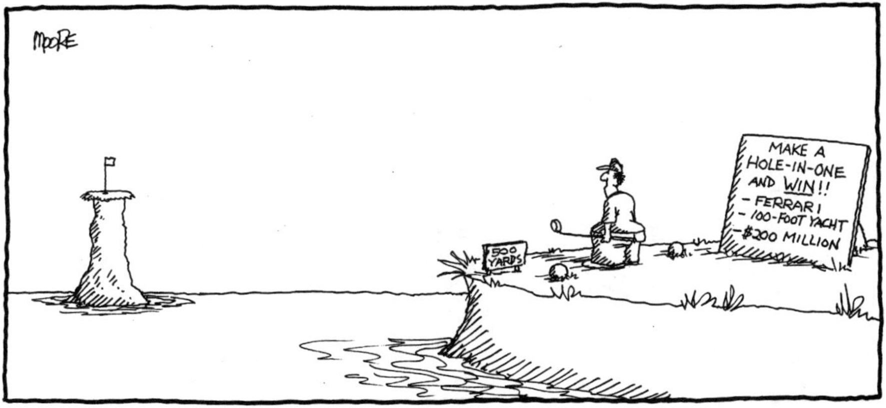
MOORE
500 YARDS
MAKE A HOLE-IN-ONE AND WIN!!
- FERRARI
- 100-FOOT YACHT
- $200 MILLION

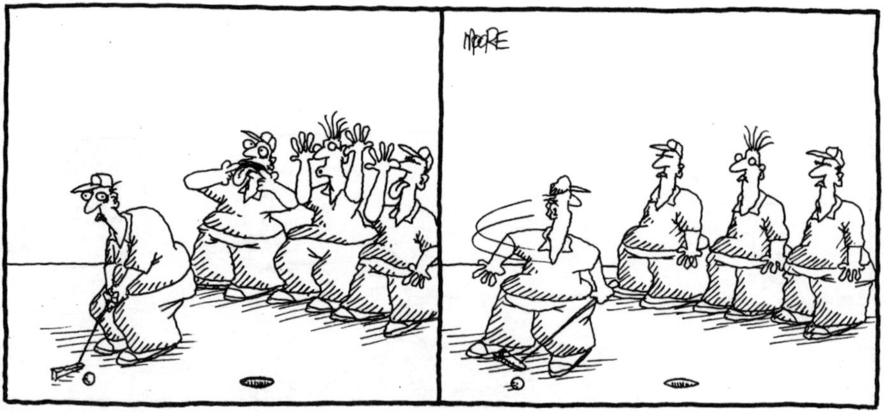
MOORE

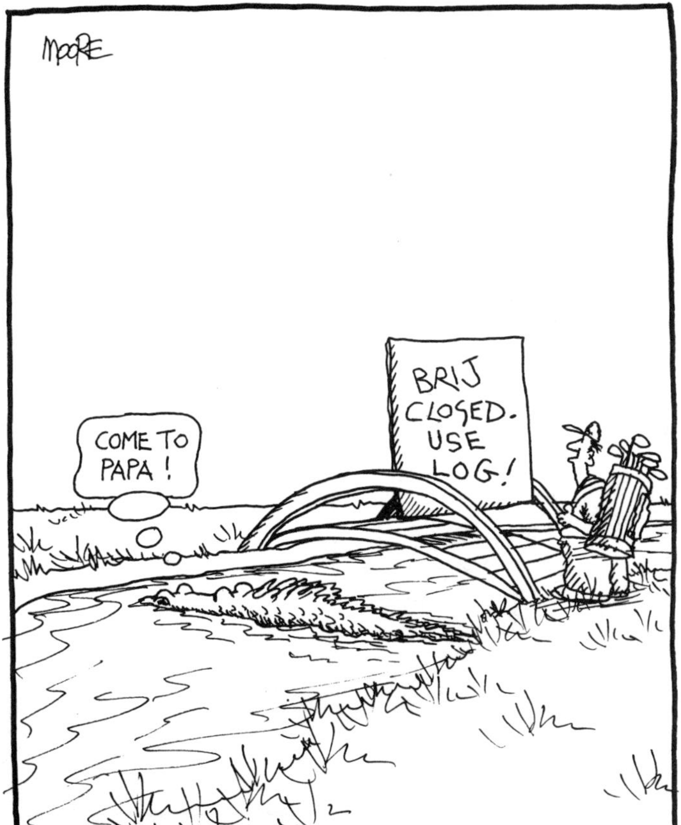
MOORE
COME TO PAPA !
BRIJ CLOSED. USE LOG!

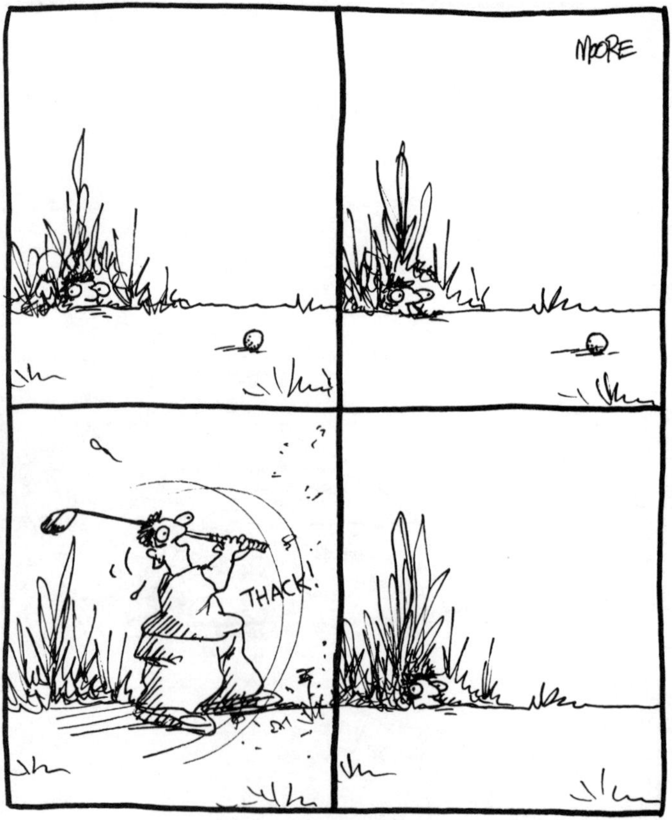
MOORE
THACK!

Guerrilla golf

HEY, I FOUND A GOLF CLUB!
MOORE
HEY, I FOUND A GOLF CLUB AND HAT!

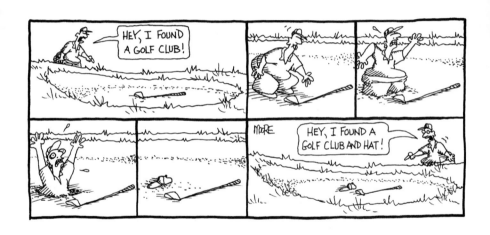

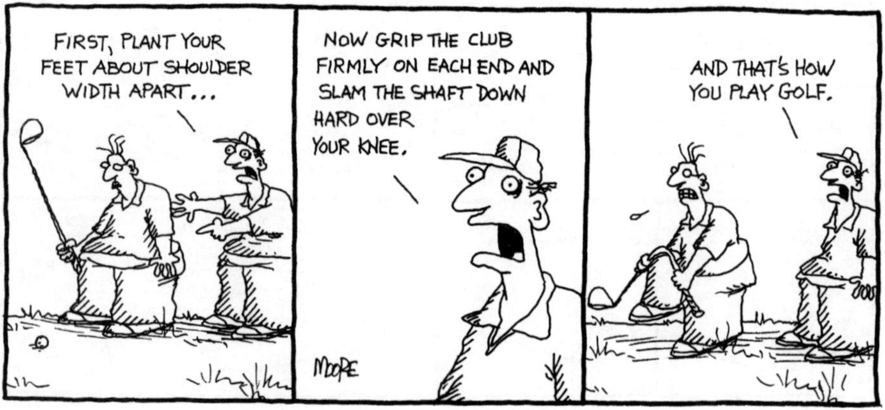
FIRST, PLANT YOUR FEET ABOUT SHOULDER WIDTH APART...
NOW GRIP THE CLUB FIRMLY ON EACH END AND SLAM THE SHAFT DOWN HARD OVER YOUR KNEE.
MOORE
AND THAT'S HOW YOU PLAY GOLF.

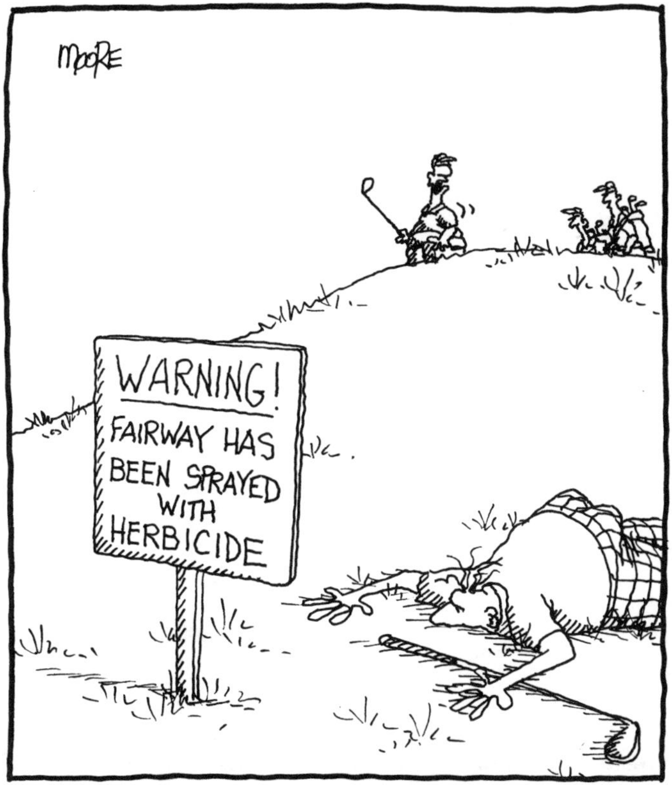
MOORE
WARNING!
FAIRWAY HAS BEEN SPRAYED WITH HERBICIDE

"Herb! Get up! . . . Hey, guys, come quick! Something's wrong with Herb!"

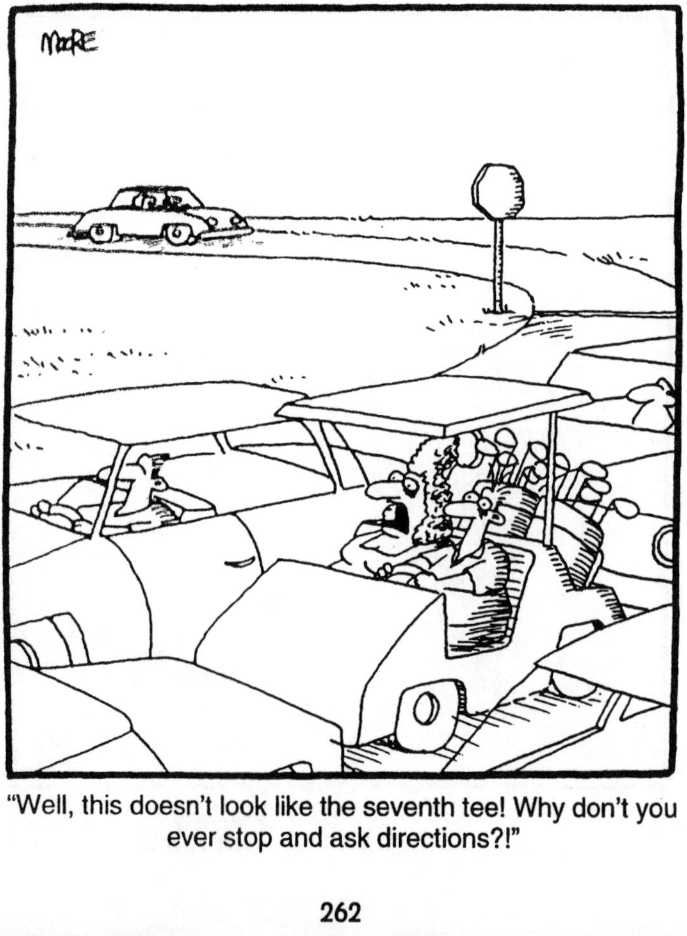
MOORE

"Well, this doesn't look like the seventh tee! Why don't you ever stop and ask directions?!"

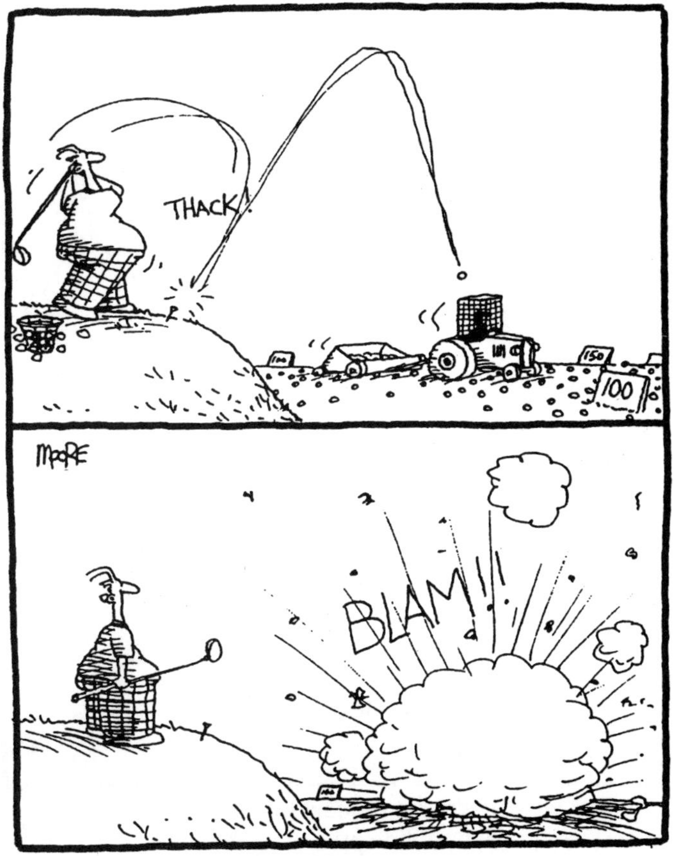
THACK!
100
150
100
MOORE
BLAM!!!

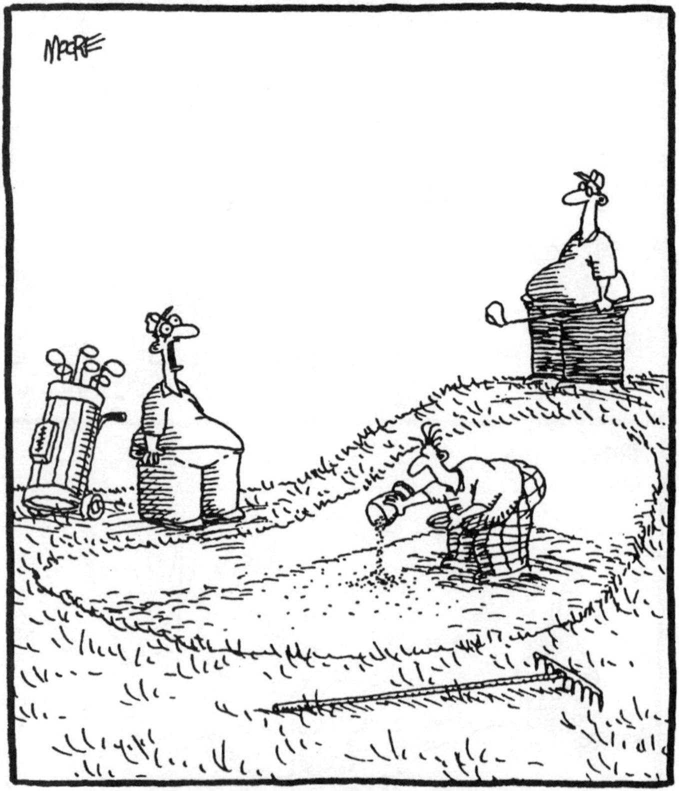
MOORE

"It was Bob's last request that we spread his ashes where he spent most of his time."

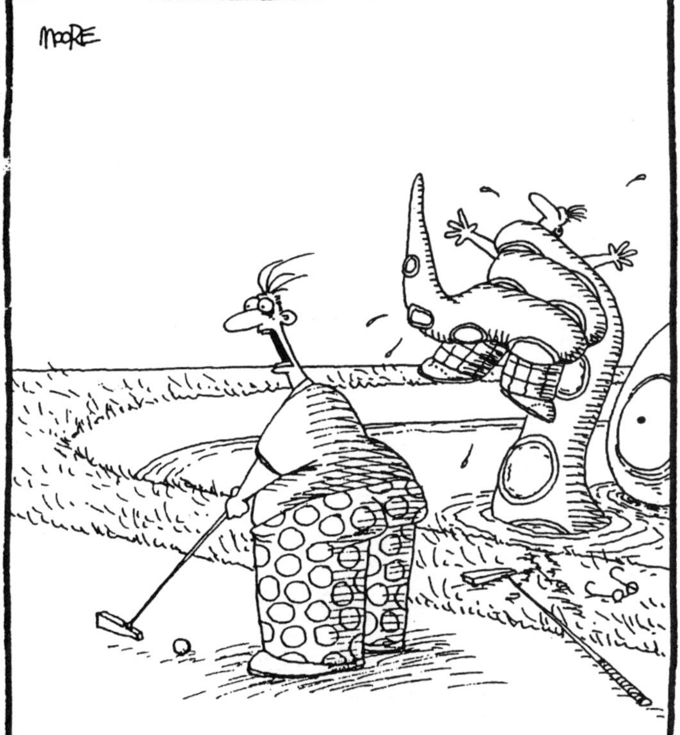
MOORE

"Is that the only way you can win, Paul? Is it? Making annoying gurgling sounds while I'm trying to putt?"

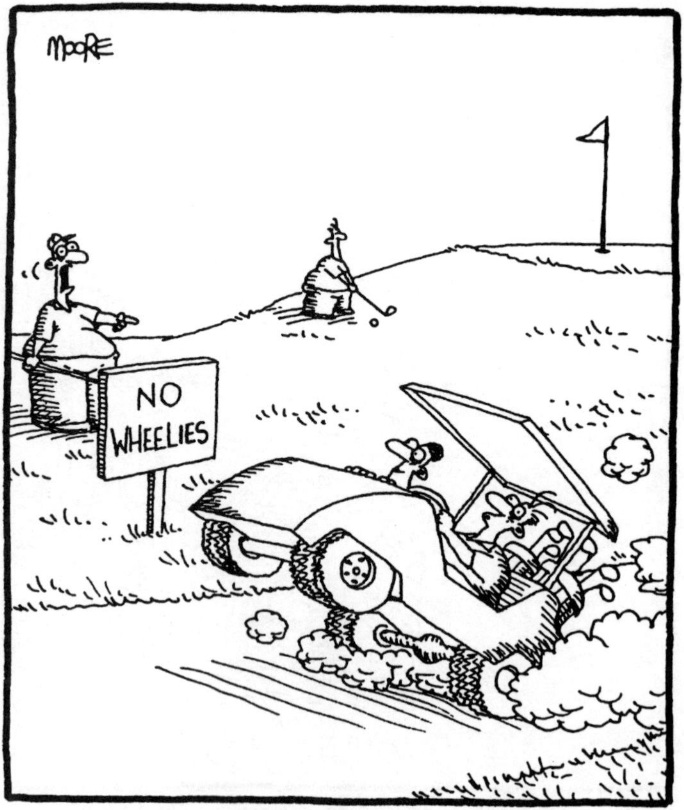
MOORE
NO WHEELIES

"Hey, hey, hey!!"

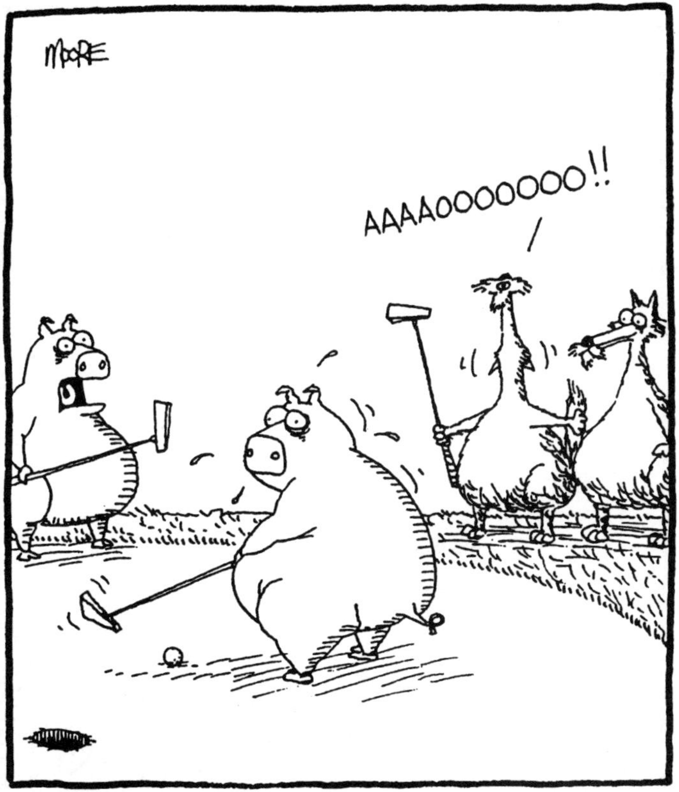
MOORE
AAAAOOOOOOO!!

"Ignore them, Bob. They're just trying to unnerve you."

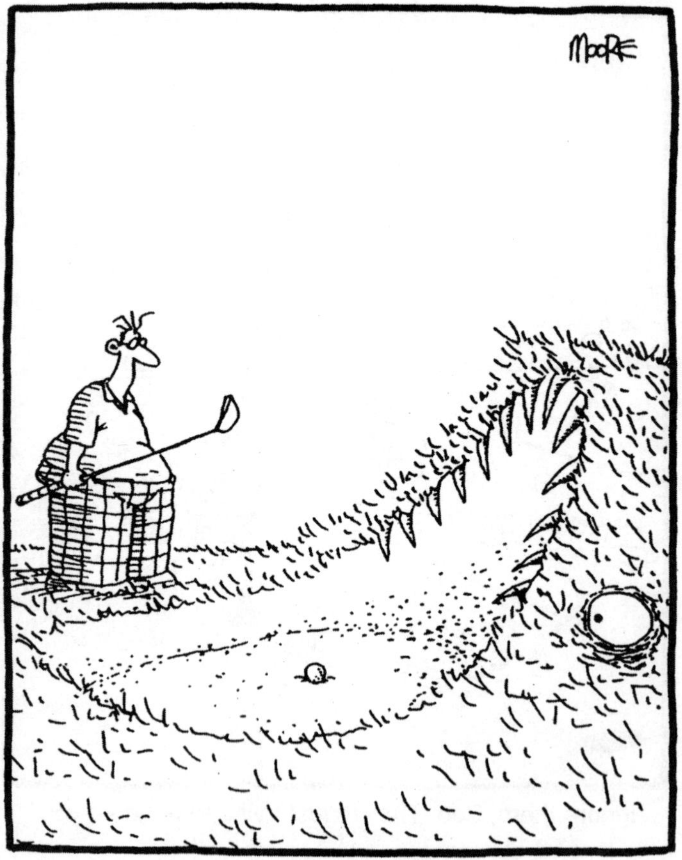
MOORE

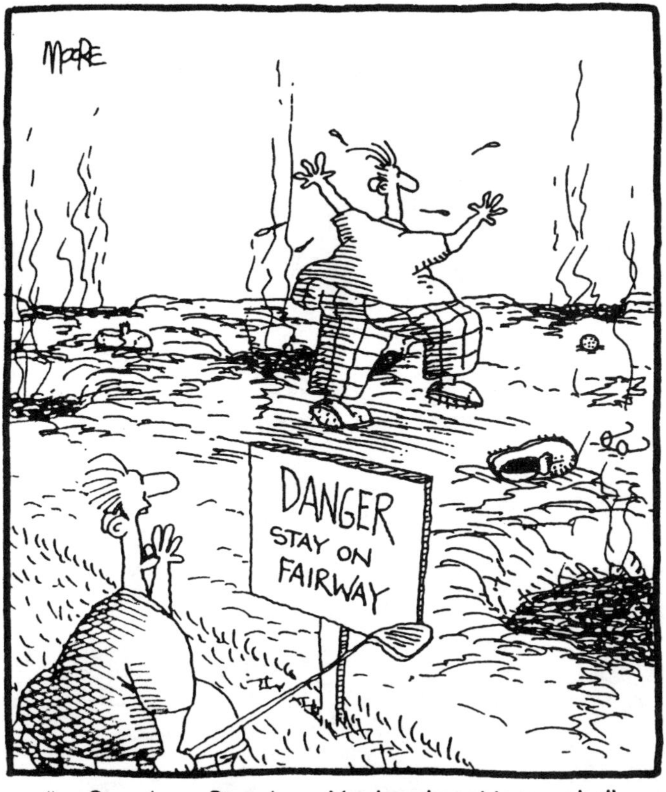
MOORE
DANGER
STAY ON
FAIRWAY

"... Steady ... Steady ... You're almost to your ball.
... *DON'T STEP THERE!!*"

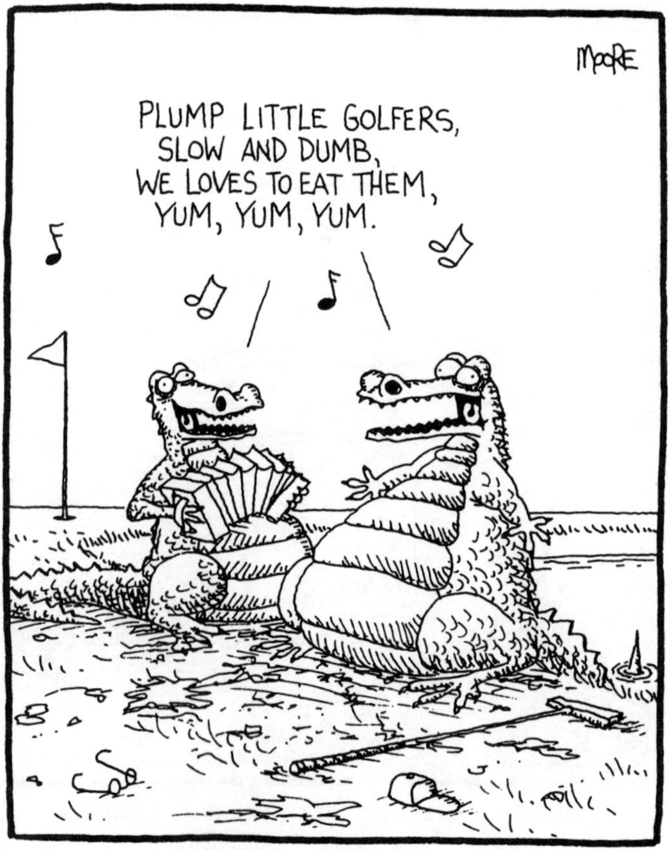
MOORE
PLUMP LITTLE GOLFERS,
SLOW AND DUMB,
WE LOVES TO EAT THEM,
YUM, YUM, YUM.

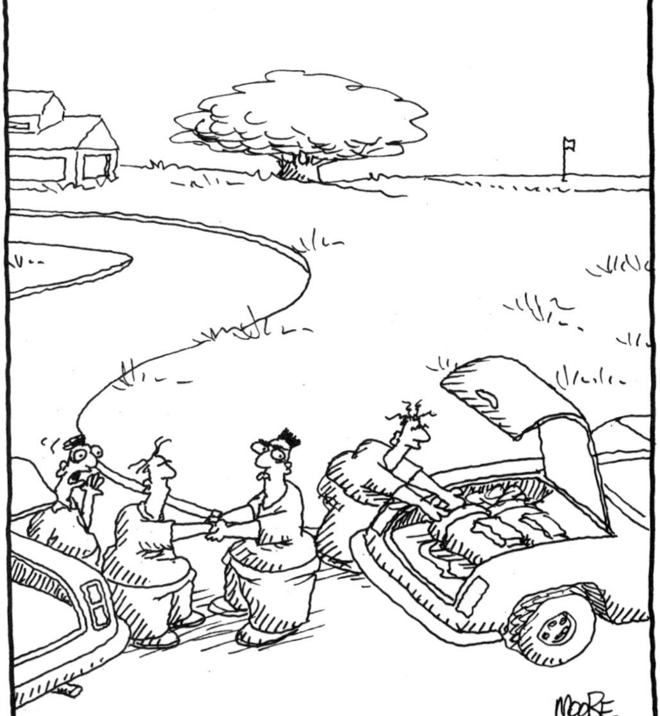
MOORE

"I don't know about this, Brad. I've heard of a bag drop, but I've never heard of a bag, wristwatch, cell phone, and billfold drop."

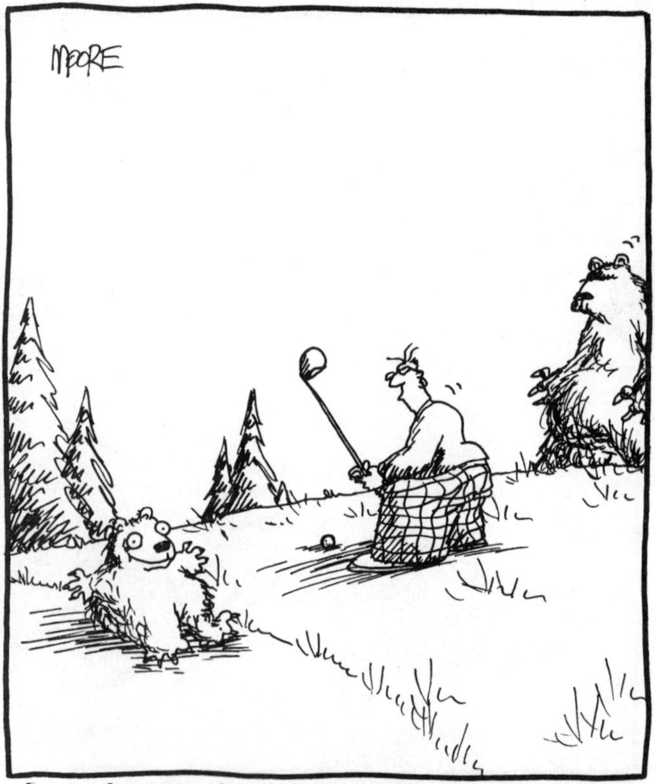
MOORE

Larry forgets the "always play another ball if your tee shot lands between a grizzly bear and her cub" rule.